The
New · Founde · Land

Farley Mowat

The
New·Founde·Land

M&S

Canadian Cataloguing in Publication Data

Mowat, Farley, 1921–
The New Founde Land

ISBN 0-7710-6689-9

1. Mowat, Farley, 1921–   . 2. Newfoundland –
Description and travel – 1951–1980.*
3. Newfoundland – Social life and customs.
I. Title.

FC2167.5.M6 1989   971.8'04   C89-094725-2
F1122.M6 1989

Printed and bound in Canada

McClelland & Stewart Inc.
The Canadian Publishers
481 University Avenue
Toronto, Ontario
M5G 2E9

BOOKS BY FARLEY MOWAT

People of the Deer (1952, revised edition 1975)
The Regiment (1955, new edition 1973)
Lost in the Barrens (1956)
The Dog Who Wouldn't Be (1957)
Grey Seas Under (1959)
The Desperate People (1959, revised edition 1975)
Owls in the Family (1961)
The Serpent's Coil (1961)
The Black Joke (1962)
Never Cry Wolf (1963, new edition 1973)
Westviking (1965)
The Curse of the Viking Grave (1966)
Canada North (illustrated edition 1967)
Canada North Now (revised paperback edition 1976)
This Rock Within the Sea (1968, reissued 1976)
The Boat Who Wouldn't Float (1969, illustrated edition 1974)
Sibir (1970, new edition 1973)
A Whale for the Killing (1972)
Wake of the Great Sealers (1973)
The Snow Walker (1975)
And No Birds Sang (1979)
The World of Farley Mowat, a selection from his works
(edited by Peter Davison)(1980)
Sea of Slaughter (1984)
My Discovery of America (1985)
Virunga (1987)

EDITED BY FARLEY MOWAT

Coppermine Journey (1958)

THE TOP OF THE WORLD TRILOGY
Ordeal by Ice (1960, revised edition 1973)
The Polar Passion (1967, revised edition 1973)
Tundra (1973)

Sources

*I have drawn extensively on some of my earlier writ-
ings in preparing this book, but have revised and
rewritten much of the original material. The original
sources are listed below.*

The Rock – *This Rock Within the Sea*, 1968
First Encounters – *Westviking*, 1965
The Outport Way – *This Rock Within the Sea*, 1968
Men, Seals and Ships – *Wake of the Great Sealers*,
1973
Other Lives – *Sea of Slaughter*, 1984
Deep-Water Men – *Grey Seas Under*, 1959
Come From Away – *The Boat Who Wouldn't Float*,
1969
Messers Cove – *A Whale for the Killing*, 1972

Contents

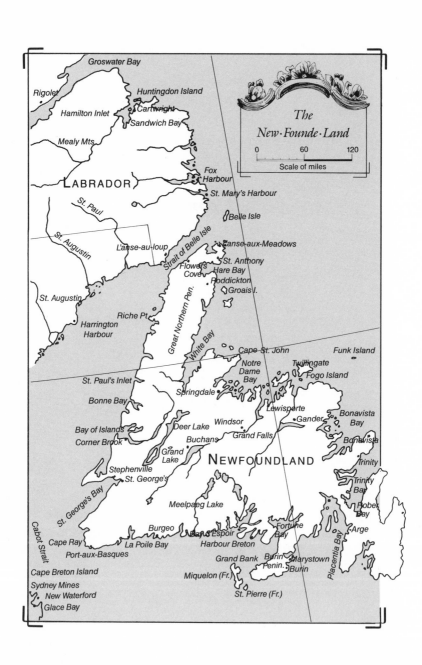

Groswater Bay

Rigolet

Huntingdon Island

Cartwright

Hamilton Inlet

Sandwich Bay

Mealy Mts.

LABRADOR

St. Paul

Fox Harbour

St. Mary's Harbour

St. Augustin

L'anse-au-loup

Belle Isle

L'anse-aux-Meadows

St. Anthony

Flowers Cove

Hare Bay

Roddickton

Groais I.

St. Augustin

Riche Pt.

Harrington Harbour

Great Northern Pen.

White Bay

Cape St. John

Funk Island

Notre Dame Bay

Twillingate

Fogo Island

St. Paul's Inlet

Springdale

Bonne Bay

Lewisporte

Bonavista Bay

Bay of Islands

Deer Lake

Windsor

Gander

Corner Brook

Buchans

Grand Falls

Bonavista

Grand Lake

NEWFOUNDLAND

Trinity

Stephenville

St. George's

Trinity Bay

St. George's Bay

Meelpaeg Lake

Rober Bay

Burgeo

Bay d'Espoir

Fortune Bay

Arge

Cape Ray

La Poile Bay

Harbour Breton

Burin

Placentia Bay

Cabot Strait

Port-aux-Basques

Grand Bank

Burin Penin.

Marystown

Cape Breton Island

Burin

Sydney Mines

Miquelon (Fr.)

New Waterford

St. Pierre (Fr.)

Glace Bay

The
New·Founde·Land

0   60   120

Scale of miles

Introduction

My discovery of Newfoundland began in the summer of 1953 when my father and I sailed his old Norwegian ketch, Scotch Bonnet, from Montreal to Halifax. After the long descent of the St. Lawrence River we gingerly felt our way across the broad waters of the Gulf and entered the Strait of Canso which separates Cape Breton Island from the mainland of Nova Scotia.

The intimidating presence of the great, grey sweep of the North Atlantic was now close at hand. Prudently we decided to put in to Port Hawkesbury, there to muster our courage for what loomed ahead.

We made fast alongside an old wooden wharf already partly occupied by a hundred-ton, two-masted schooner. Her hull still displayed the lovely lines of her heritage, but otherwise she was a sorry sight. Her spars had been cut down to mere stubs. Her gear was ancient and decrepit. Everything made of wood on and above her decks had bleached bone-white; and everything made of iron was rust-red. Her hull had once been black but now only vestiges of paint remained on her scuffed and weathered planking. She looked like something resurrected from a long sojourn in a watery grave.

We two fresh-water sailors had never seen anything like her before. As we scrambled up on the wharf for a closer look, the schooner's wheelhouse door was flung open and what might have been the Old Man of the Sea himself emerged onto the afterdeck, turned downwind, and casually relieved himself over the side. Short and heavy-set, he was clad in a ravelled, greyish sweater that hung almost to his knees. Not much was visible from there down except a pair of cracked rubber boots. A mat of grizzled hair framed a beard as grey and unkempt as his sweater.

Doing up his trouser buttons with one hand, he vigorously waved the other at Scotch Bonnet, *grinned benevolently at us and shouted:*

"I loikes de looks o' dat leetle bummer. Where would ye be bound?"

If my father felt indignant at hearing his vessel called a bummer, he did not show it. "Halifax," *he replied.* "Would you care to come aboard?"

So it was that we met Captain Josiah Coggins – Skipper Joss. He and his old schooner "belonged" to a fishing village called Belleoram in Fortune Bay on the south coast of Newfoundland. Skipper Joss talked a mile a minute as he sloshed back mug after mug of our rum, but it was difficult to make him out since he seemed to be speaking a medieval tongue and with an almost unintelligible accent. We did gather that "bummer" was not a derogatory term but a name given to any small, two-masted Newfoundland sailing vessel. We also learned that his schooner was called Annie and Mabel – "arter me Woman and me Maid" – *and that she was en route from Prince Edward Island to Fortune Bay with a cargo of potatoes.*

When our rum bottle had been drained – a procedure that seemed to take no time at all – Skipper Joss returned the compliment and invited us to come aboard his vessel, "for a noggin and a scoff." *The noggin consisted of about four fingers of "white stuff" – potato alcohol – poured into a battered tin cup, to which Skipper Joss added a spoonful of molasses before topping the mixture up with boiling water. Two mugs of this seemed to sharpen my understanding so that I had small further difficulty comprehending what the skipper said.*

The Annie and Mabel *(the* Ai *and* Emm, *he called her) had been built in Bay Despair some forty years earlier and, with Skipper Joss at her helm, had spent the next twenty years "banking" – dory fishing on the Grand Banks. Then the skipper took her "foreign" – carrying salt fish to European ports.*

"Den de Jarmin War* troo all dat into a casket. Everytin' went adrift arter dat," *he told us sadly.* "Vessels under sail was all

---

*World War II

condemned and done up, and sailin' men alongside o' dey. But the Ai and Emm and me been spliced fer forty year. Us went up togither, and I don't doubt us'll go down togither on the end of it. Us keeps each other goin' jist out of orneriness. Can't carry canvas now 'cause I got nary crew. Dey's only young Simeon, me maid's last-born, to turn a hand on deck, and a brace of dem old bullgines down below fer to drive her."

The "last-born," a taciturn youth of perhaps fourteen years, was filling the dank and dingy aftercabin in which we sat with strange aromas from a black iron pot simmering on an ancient, coal-fired galley stove. The pot contained the scoff, which consisted (as best I could ascertain) of pork fat, salt beef, onions, turnips and boiled ship's biscuits.

"Sim biles up enough o' dat ole stuff to last we a week," Skipper Joss told us proudly as he ladled vast helpings into our bowls. "Gits more strengt' into it the longer it sets."

It was certainly solid fare. As we made our way back to our own vessel I was especially careful to avoid falling off the wharf. I would have sunk like a stone.

My father mulled over our visit to the Annie and Mabel for a long time as we lay in our bunks listening to the skirl of wind making up.

"God damn it, Farley, he doesn't have a single chart. He's got no radio, no radar, no Loran. And he doesn't even have a compass! He traded it in Charlottetown for a couple of gallons of potato alcohol! Now, how the hell can he find his way about?"

The gale that blew up that night lasted for two days, and was followed by fog so thick it was palpable. Nothing dared move through the invisible Straits of Canso except thundering, grey-beard combers rolling in across Chedabucto Bay from the open ocean. Snugged down in Scotch Bonnet's cabin, we were thanking our lucky stars that we were in such safe shelter when a rattle of staccato explosions brought us up on deck all-standing, as the saying goes.

We could not see to the end of the wharf where the Annie and Mabel lay, but the explosions were coming from that direction. We felt our way towards her through the murk and arrived at the pier-head just in time to see Simeon's wraith-like form hauling in the old schooner's bow lines. The awful noise was coming from her two ancient engines, both of which had long ago worn out their mufflers. Skipper Joss was standing in the open wheel-house door, a ghostly presence enmeshed in tendrils of fog.

My father waved his arms through the soup surrounding us, in the direction of the harbour entrance where gigantic, unseen seas were roaring against the rocks.

"Great God!" he bellowed over the racket of the engines. "You surely aren't going out in this?"

"Oh yiss, bye," came the cheerful reply. "Dey's fifty barrel o' Island spuds down in me hold and I can hear 'em sproutin'. Aside o' dat, I promised the Woman us'd be tied up alongside by Satiday night, plenty toime to walk her off to church come Sunday marnin'."

"But Belleoram must be two hundred miles from here!" my father cried, outraged. "How the devil are you going to find Newfoundland in this muck, let alone Belleoram?"

The Annie and Mabel was slowly drawing away. As she slipped into the wall of fog and vanished from our sight we caught Josiah Coggins' faint reply.

"No fear, me sons. I knows right where she's to."

When we were back in Scotch Bonnet's little cabin again I made a vow:

"Someday I'm going to try living in a place where they make men like that!"

Skipper Joss was not the only Newfoundlander I met during that voyage. On several occasions Scotch Bonnet found herself lying near ocean-going tugs belonging to Foundation Maritime, a deep-sea salvage, rescue and towing company. Many of the men serving in these vessels turned out to be Newfoundlanders, and they could not seem to do enough for us, whether in the way of assistance in repairing our engine, or of providing information about the inscrutable world of waters through which we were timidly making our way. They also enthralled me with some of the most marvellous sea stories I had ever heard.

By the time our voyage came to its end I had become so enamoured of the tugboat men that I devoted the next two years to writing a book about them and their exploits. This necessitated several visits to Newfoundland, which greatly strengthened the fascination I felt for the "Rock" and for its people. In the late 1950s I went a step farther and acquired (or was acquired by) a little Newfoundland bummer of my own. Then, in 1961, I finally redeemed my vow when my wife and I settled in Burgeo, a remote outport on Newfoundland's Sou'west Coast.

From this firm base I investigated the Rock and its surrounding waters. I went to sea aboard coastal steamers and packet freighters; with inshore fishermen in their small boats; with the offshore men in big draggers and seiners.

I went "to the ice" both in the Gulf of St. Lawrence, and at "The Front," off the northeast coast of the island, with some of the last of the sealers. In between times I sailed my little schooner into a hundred hidden nooks and crannies of the island's coasts.

I also explored the vast interior, hoping to recapture something of the lives of the vanished Beothuk Indians; and, by air, sea and land, I visited scores of outport villages. Best of all, I lived for several years in close propinquity with the people of Burgeo, and came to understand them at least a little, and to admire them immensely.

In those times Newfoundlanders were but little understood and even less admired beyond the confines of their own island so I decided I should do something about that. At first I nurtured the grandiose design of writing a full-scale history of the Rock. To that end I went to England to poke into the islanders' beginnings. I spent long days sequestered in the sepulchral Reading Room of the British Museum Library, but there, as elsewhere, I found only dusty memories of life gone by. I am a slow learner, but it eventually dawned on me that I did not want to write about the boneyards of the past. What I really wanted to do was celebrate life as it was still being lived on the great island. I began writing about that, if in a somewhat disorganized and piecemeal fashion.

The years slipped by to 1988 and I had not yet delivered myself of a magnum opus about the Rock and its people. One day I was bemoaning my failure to Newfoundlander and fellow writer, Harold Horwood. He brought me up short.

"Farley," he snapped in his waspish way. "Don't be so bloody dense! You've already written your 'Great Book' about us, but you've been flinging the pieces of it about like so much confetti. All you need to do is gather the bits together. Why don't you just get on with it?"

My publisher, Adrienne Clarkson, agreed with Harold. Moreover, as she pointed out, 1989 would mark the 40th anniversary of Newfoundland becoming part of Canada.

"If you want to celebrate the island with a book, what better time to do it? Of course you could postpone it to the 50th anniversary . . . but that's ten years down the road and you mightn't make it."

What follows, then, is my celebration of a place . . . a people . . . and a way of life . . . which I have dearly loved.

FM
Cape Breton Island
1989

I

The Rock

Newfoundland is of the sea. A mighty granite stopper thrust into the bell-mouth of the Gulf of St. Lawrence, it turns its back upon the American continent, barricading itself behind the three-hundred-mile-long rampart which forms its western coast. Its other coasts all face the open ocean, and are so slashed and convoluted with bays, inlets, runs and fiords that they present more than five thousand miles of shoreline to the sweep of the Atlantic. Everywhere the hidden reefs and rocks (called, with dreadful explicitness, "sunkers") wait to rip the bellies of unwary vessels. Nevertheless, these coasts are a seaman's world, for the harbours and havens they offer are numberless.

Until a few generations ago the coasts of the island were all that really mattered. The high, rolling plateaux of the interior, darkly wooded to the north but bone-bare to the south, remained an almost unknown hinterland. Newfoundland was a true sea province then, perhaps akin to that other, lost, sea province called Atlantis; but, instead of sinking into the green depths, Newfoundland seemed to have been blown adrift to fetch up against our shores, there to remain in unwilling exile, always straining back towards the east. The great island is the most easterly land in North America, jutting so far out into the Atlantic that its capital, St. John's, lies six hundred miles to the east of Halifax and almost twelve hundred miles east of New York.

Thousands of years ago Newfoundland was over-mastered by a tyranny of ice. Insensate yet implacable, the glacial presence crept out of the arctic, flowing from the northwest towards the southeast across the spine of the Labrador peninsula; arming itself with the jagged shards of mountains it had crushed in its inexorable passage. Bridging the narrow Straits of Belle Isle, the invader engulfed the island. Great, tearing, granite teeth embedded in the ice stripped the living flesh of soil and vegetation from the face of Newfoundland and gashed gigantic furrows into the underlying rock. The mountains of the interior were ground down to form a vast plateau, a realm of utter desolation. When the ice reached the southern coast (which in those times presented a mountain wall to the sea) it slashed a series of immensely deep wounds in the fronting cliffs; wounds that eventually became mighty fiords.

Having vanquished the island, the ice moved on to engage the sea in a titanic struggle. It thrust outward from the southern and eastern shores, forcing the waters back until its snout extended three hundred miles to seaward. This was no superficial conquest: the glacier was a solid entity whose base rested upon the ocean floor hundreds of fathoms down while its ice valleys and ice mountains lay glittering beneath an arctic sky.

Many thousands of years intervened before the ice age approached its end. Then the sun burned with renewed passion and the congealed surface of the northern seas softened and reliquefied. Illimitable ocean began to eat into the cold invader. The glacier, at bay, could not retreat as the sea had done; it could only stand and die. In death it delivered itself of billions of tons of soil and pulverized rock stolen from the land. This debris sank to the sea floor, where it remains as the vast area of shoal banks, including the Grand Banks, which fringe the southern and eastern coasts of the island.

So the ice rotted from the sea and left the sea unmarred. But when it melted from the land it left the island scarified, denuded, a polished and eroded skull. Life crept back upon that bared bone with infinite slowness for, although the glacier itself was gone, the shadow and the influence of the vanished ice remained. Out of the polar seas flowed, and flows still, an arctic river called the Labrador Current. Sweeping down out of Baffin Bay and Hudson Strait, it chills the shores of Labrador and Newfoundland and, for several months of every year, wraps much of the island in the frigid embrace of the drifting arctic pack.

The polar pack and the polar current chill the lands they touch; but life on the coasts of Newfoundland must also endure other inimical influences. One of these is the fog that in spring and summer can shut off the light of the sun for days on end. Then *there is the wind. Raging unchecked out of the cyclonic cauldron of the Caribbean come some of the world's most majestic and consuming storms. The island lies full across their track; and from September through to May the furious winds seldom rest. The tortured air clamours against the sea cliffs, driving the salt storm-wrack far inland as the winds scythe on towards the stony barrens of the interior.*

Newfoundland's coasts are not a world hospitable to men who must make their living from the land. Even the native Beothuk Indians eschewed the shores except during a few weeks in summer when they descended from the wooded highlands to make a hurried harvest of sea birds, eggs and shellfish.

Yet the very elements which repelled these inland dwellers held a hidden promise for men of another culture. The glacial ice had created the offshore banks, which became the greatest fish pastures in the world. The cold Labrador Current paralyzed the coasts it touched, but produced on the banks ideal conditions for an unbelievably fecund proliferation of living things.

After the passing of the glacier, life exploded in the offshore waters. Minute plankton animals and plants formed a veritable soup through which untold numbers of fish of innumerable species swam, fattened and spawned. At the surface, horizon-filling flocks of sea fowl fed on small fry and, with their guano, began the slow process of restoring life to denuded islands and bleak sea cliffs. Millions of pelagic seals came drifting south each winter to whelp on the pack ice. Pods of great whales in numbers that may never have been equalled in the world's seas lazed along the sweep of high and rocky coasts. Hordes of walrus invaded the bays and the shallow, sandy lagoons. Otters appeared along the tide water. Salmon began to enter the regenerating rivers. Lobsters, mussels, winkles and crabs returned to the shore rocks. And wavering jungles of kelp began to lift above the inshore reefs. So it went until the entire infinitely varied world of life within the sea was re-established around the island mass which itself had hardly begun to be reclaimed by living things.

Life within and on the sea was the key to life upon the coasts, the key with which to open the rock-ribbed island casket; but it could only be grasped by men who were truly of the sea.

The first such, sailing from European shores, saw from afar a looming wall of rock thrusting hundreds of feet out of the sea foam: a forbidding granite wall which, at first sight, must have appeared totally inhospitable to mariners and ships.

With trepidation they ventured closer, the lead swinging steadily and the helmsman ready at a moment's notice to put about for the safety of open water. They found a bold coast – "bold water," seamen call it – offering a deep passage almost to the shoreline. And as they came under the loom of the sea cliffs they saw that the apparently unbroken wall had many doors. Every few miles there was an opening, sometimes as narrow as a knife wound, sometimes wide enough to admit a dozen ships sailing abreast.

At the head of most of the great bays on the northeastern shores and of the mighty fiords of the west and southern coasts, rivers rushed to the sea, sometimes through forests so dense that it seemed only the caribou – and the Beothuk Indians – could penetrate them. Shelter for ships there was in plenty in those vast indentations but the land about offered little hospitality to European venturers into a new world. The key to settlement and survival remained in the sea's keeping, and the homes of the newcomers had, perforce, to be close to the unquiet waters of the western ocean.

Perhaps no other ocean emanates such a disturbing feeling of sentience. It is not just a realm of water, it is a presence – one of incalculable moods. It is seldom still. Even in its rare moments of brooding calm, a long and rhythmic swell rolls under the surface so that it ripples like the hide of a monster. It is at times such as these that men of the sea distrust it most. They view the quiet interludes with foreboding; "weather breeders" they call such days, and they prepare for what they know will follow: a passionless and almost inconceivable violence of wind and water.

For Newfoundlanders living by and upon it, the sea is the ultimate reality. They accept it as their master, for they know they will never master it. The sea is there. It is their destiny. It gives them life, and sometimes it gives them death. They do not inveigh against its imponderable strength, nor do they stand in braggart's opposition to its powers.

"Ah, me son," a dragger man once told me, "we don't be takin' nothin' from the sea. We has to sneak up on what we wants – and wiggle it away."

II

First Encounters

The earliest recorded European venture to Newfoundland dates to the late summer of 985 when an Icelandic trader named Bjarni Herjolfsson set sail for Erik the Red's newly established settlement in Greenland. Bjarni was blown off course and eventually reached the east coast of Newfoundland. He did not go ashore, but made his way north along the Labrador coast, crossed the mouth of Davis Strait, and so eventually reached his intended destination.

Ten years later Erik's son, Leif, who had grown up on tales of Bjarni's unintended journey to the west, decided to seek out that unknown land. Making a direct crossing from the southern tip of Greenland, he too reached Newfoundland's eastern coast. He explored it to the north and west, overwintering near the foot of Trinity Bay. Returning to Greenland the following spring he brought back with him a cargo of local produce, including hardwood and softwood timbers, which were of inestimable value in treeless Greenland. Leif made his fortune on this single voyage, and Vinland, as his discovery came to be called, became a legend in his own time.

Over the years other Greenlanders tried to emulate Leif's exploit, but none succeeded until, just after the turn of the millennium, a major Icelandic/Greenlandic venture was mounted, both to rediscover Vinland's wealth and, if possible, to establish a settlement there.

This expedition was the subject of several laconic sagas. Some have endured into our times and I have used these to reconstruct the story of what transpired and, especially, of the first encounters between Europeans and the natives of Newfoundland. The aboriginals consisted of two quite different peoples: an early Eskimoan culture living on and by the sea along the western and northwestern coasts; and the Beothuks (the original "Red Indi-

ans") who inhabited the southern, eastern and interior regions. Both peoples have since vanished out of time, and the only surviving descriptions of the Eskimoan culture are those preserved in the old Norse sagas.

The Saga Tale (c. 1003-4)

There was a man named Thorfinn Karlsefni who lived in the north of Iceland. He was a man of fine family and was very wealthy. Karlsefni was a successful sea-going trader. One summer he outfitted his ship with the intention of going to Greenland. Snorri Thorbrandsson accompanied him, and there were forty other people aboard the ship with him.

At the same time Bjarni Grimolfsson and Thorhall Gamlisson also outfitted a ship carrying forty people, with the intention of making a [trading] voyage to Greenland. When they were ready, Karlsefni and the others put to sea with their two ships in consort. It has not been recorded how long their voyage took them but it is said that both ships arrived at Eriksfiord, in Greenland, in the autumn.

Erik the Red and other inhabitants rode down to the ships and a good trade was soon established. Erik was asked by both skippers to take such of their wares as he wished as gifts, and he responded with great generosity by inviting both crews to take up winter quarters with him at his home, called Brattalid. The merchants accepted the invitation with thanks . . .

Some time later Karlsefni approached Erik on the subject of his marrying [Erik's widowed daughter-in-law] Gudrid, for he assumed Erik would have the right to bestow her hand in marriage, and Gudrid seemed to him a beautiful and accomplished woman.

The result was that Gudrid was betrothed to Karlsefni; a banquet was arranged; and the wedding was duly celebrated. And all of this happened at Brattalid during the course of that winter.

At this time there began to be much talk about the prospects of exploring Vinland the Good. It was said that the country possessed many fine qualities. The result of the matter was that Karlsefni and Snorri outfitted their ship, intending to go in search of that country in the summer. Bjarni Grimolfsson and Thorhall

Gamlisson also joined the expedition with their ship and all who had accompanied them to Greenland.

There was a man named Thorvald [Eriksson]. He also joined the expedition, together with Thorhall the Hunter [and many other Greenlanders, in a third ship].

The same summer that Karlsefni went out to Greenland there had come another ship to Greenland. It was skippered by two brothers who were Icelanders. They too stayed the winter in Greenland [but not at Brattalid].

Now it is to be told that Freydis [a bastard daughter of Erik] made a journey to visit these brothers. She asked them to take her and her people to Vinland in their ship, and to go halves with her of all the profit they might make there. They agreed to this.

Then Freydis went to visit her brother Leif and asked him to give her the houses he had built in Vinland. But he answered her saying he might let her use the houses but would not give them to her.

Now they all sailed out to sea, having agreed that they should keep together if possible . . . All told there were one hundred and sixty people.

After leaving Greenland, the flotilla of four ships crossed Davis Strait to Baffin Island, coasted south to Hudson Strait, and continued south along the coast of Labrador. This was not the route Leif Eriksson had followed and it is clear that Leif was uncooperative towards this new enterprise to the point where he had refused to reveal the exact whereabouts of Vinland. Consequently Karlsefni was looking for a needle in a haystack, even though he did possess a general description of the region as preserved in the saga tales.

Leaving the Labrador coast near Battle Harbour, the questing ships sailed out into the Strait of Belle Isle. They anchored temporarily in the lee of Belle Isle itself while men rowed ashore and scaled the cliffs to the high tableland above.

They were rewarded by a stupendous view. From the top of this great rock they could look westward down the throat of the strait as far as L'Anse Amour on the bald northern shore – a distance of nearly sixty miles. They could see much less of the southern shore for it is generally low, but their impression was of a very deep bay narrowing away into the blue distance. They named it Straumfiord – Fiord of the Strong Currents.

The description of the approaches to Leif's Vinland, even as preserved into our day in the saga accounts, comes remarkably close to fitting the mouth of Belle Isle Strait; and hopeful that they had now reached the portals of Vinland, the seekers crossed the remainder of the strait and began searching its southern shore for Leif's harbour and his winter houses.

They were doomed to disappointment. Cruising the labyrinthine, rock-strewn bays and inlets at the tip of Newfoundland's Great Northern Peninsula, they found no sign that any European had ever been on these low coasts before them. And they found nothing to answer to the saga description of Vinland, or of the magnificent mixed forests which had made Leif wealthy.

Summer was already nearing its end and now dissention broke out between would-be settlers and those who were only interested in exploiting the removable resources of these new lands. The former were worried about the survival of their accompanying livestock and were clamouring to get the animals ashore. The latter, believing that the riches of Vinland lay nearby, were intent on persevering in the search. Perhaps because his Greenland wife, Gudrid, was by then some six months pregnant, Karlsefni elected to make a pause.

He sought a temporary base from which further explorations could be launched while the colonists remained behind to see to the welfare of the stock, and he found such a place at the foot of a small inlet which today is called Epaves Bay. Here the ships turned landward and on a day in the late summer of the first decade of the eleventh century, men, women, children and cattle began making their way ashore to establish the first known European lodgment in the New World.

The Saga Tale (c. 1004-1005)

Now they explored the country thereabouts. There were mountains in the vicinity and the land was fair to look upon. They did nothing but explore the country. There was tall grass thereabouts.

They spent the winter there but they had a hard winter and one for which they had not prepared. The fishing fell off and they grew short of food. Although their livestock fared well, there was little food left [for the people]. They called on God to send them food, but did not get a response as quickly as they needed it.

Then Thorhall the Hunter disappeared. They searched for him for three days and on the fourth day Karlsefni and Bjarni Grimolfsson found him on a clifftop.

He was lying there with eyes, mouth and nostrils gaping, and was scratching himself and muttering something. They asked him why he had come to this place and he told them not to be concerned by what he did, for he was old enough to look after himself.

Then they asked him to go home with them, and this he did.

Soon afterward a whale washed ashore and they got it and flensed it, but no one could tell what kind of whale it was. Karlsefni had much knowledge of whales, but he did not recognize this one. When the cooks had prepared it the people ate of it and they were all sickened by it.

Then Thorhall the Hunter approached them and said: "Did not Red Beard [Thor] prove more helpful than your Christ? This [whale] is my reward for the verses I dedicated to Thor the Trustworthy. Seldom has he failed me."

When the people heard this none of them would eat, and they threw [the meat] into the sea and invoked God's mercy.

The weather then improved so they could row out to go fishing and they no longer lacked the necessities of life. In the spring they went out into Straumfiord and obtained provisions from both regions; hunting on the mainland, and gathering eggs and going deep-sea fishing.

Since summer was almost spent when they went ashore, all hands ought to have buckled down to the task of making ready for the winter. But many of them saw Epaves Bay only as a temporary halting place where the animals could be fed back to health and the people could refresh themselves after the long, crowded and uncomfortable voyage while exploring parties were sent out in the ships' boats along the nearby coasts to find Leif's Vinland.

Thoroughly, but fruitlessly, a flotilla of half a dozen ships' boats explored the coasts of the Great Northern peninsula for some distance to the south and west beyond Cape Norman; and to Hare Bay, or beyond, to the south and east.

As the boats returned to Epaves Bay, and their skippers reported finding no signs of Leif's haven, hope of locating Vinland that season finally died. By then it was too late to think of seeking another site at which to spend the winter.

Epaves Bay was not such a bad place, at least by Greenland standards. A natural shore meadows at the foot of the bay provided sufficient pasture for the cattle. This was (and remains) fine berry country; there was no shortage of firewood lying in windrows above the high-tide mark already dry and ready for use; the shore fishery was excellent, and harbour seals, whales and ducks abounded.

The people were not much concerned about the long-term food supply at first. Their most pressing task was to build sod-and-timber houses and to put the ships into winter quarters. With one hundred and sixty people to house, and four big ships to haul out and secure, there would have been little time for worrying about what lay ahead.

The climate in Karlsefni's time was milder, but the arctic pack ice would have been a menacing presence during the midwinter months, denying the strait to the lightly built Norse boats. Consequently there were long periods when the settlers could not go fishing.

As the winter winds blew and food grew scarce in the crude sod shanties—booths, they called them—many people must have wished they had given up the search for Vinland earlier and used the extra time to make dry fish or to go whaling. They were not actually starving or they would have turned to the almost-last resort and begun butchering their cattle, which were foraging for themselves on the shore pastures, kept largely snow-free by the strong winds.

Nevertheless, the people were hungry enough to call on their gods for help. The Christians in the party prayed to White Christ; whereupon an intractable Greenland pagan, Thorhall the Hunter, decided to call on Thor. The way to solicit his aid was to go to some lonely place and alternately argue, bribe, threaten and cajole him – and the most efficacious cajolement was a poem of praise in his honour recited to the wind and sky.

The clerics who were responsible for transcribing and preserving the sagas must have been distressed by what ensued, for Thorhall was answered, and the Christians were not. Shortly after Thorhall made his plea a whale blundered into the bay or was found dead among the ice.

Great fires were promptly lit and everyone gathered around while the cooks filled the pots with meat and hung strips of blubber beside the coals. The gorging which followed may have resulted in stomach aches, but it is questionable whether the meat actually poisoned those who ate it. This could be the interjection of some righteous cleric at a later date.

With the approach of spring, the shortage of food was relieved. As the weather improved and the pack ice disappeared, the boats were again able to venture into the open waters of the strait which thronged with fish, with enormous herds of migrating seals and endless pods of whales of all kinds and sizes.

During this hard winter Gudrid gave birth to a son. He was named Snorri, in honour of Snorri Thorbrandsson, who was not only Thorfinn Karlsefni's closest comrade but also the elder wise man of the expedition.

Snorri Thorfinnsson, who lived to become a famous man in his own right in Iceland, may have been the first child of European parents born in North America, for whatever that may be worth.

The people were no longer suffering from hunger now, but there was a good deal of bickering and contention among them as to what they should do next. Apart from the absence of wild grapes (which seem to have had the same magical significance to early voyagers as spices had for later ones), there were no hardwood forests here and few fur-bearing land animals. The Greenland colonists, who were inured to hardship and a tough existence, were the least discontented, but the Icelanders were primarily traders whose chief interest in the western lands lay in gathering a valuable lading of local products. For them Straumfiord was a major disappointment. Moreover, Karlsefni was convinced that Vinland *could* still be found, and that the expedition ought to carry on searching for it. Most of the Icelanders and some of the Greenlanders, including the woman Freydis, agreed with him.

There was, however, no agreement as to which way to search. The Icelanders were united in the conviction that Vinland ought to be sought for to the southwest of Straumfiord, and that the entire expedition should set sail in that direction. The Greenlanders, on the other hand, felt it would be wiser for the majority of the people, together with the cattle and the precious ships, to remain at Straumfiord camp while long-distance boat expeditions were sent out to seek for Vinland to the north and west.

This divergence of opinions led to three separate exploring expeditions being mounted during the second season in the New World.

The Saga Tale (c. 1005)

Now they took counsel together concerning their expedition, and came to an agreement. Thorhall the Hunter wished to go northward [along the Labrador coast] to seek Vinland, while Karlsefni wished to proceed southward off the coast, believing that the farther to the southward, the better the country would be.

Thorhall had only nine men in his party.

One day while Thorhall was watering his boat he took a drink and then recited this poem:

> Famous Leaders told me I would have
> The best of drink when I came hither,
> Therefore I cannot blame the land.
> But see, you Helmeted Champions,
> How instead of drinking wine
> I must raise this pail [of water]
> Which I had to stoop to fill at the spring.

Then Thorhall and his men put to sea and Karlsefni accompanied them out beyond the island. Before they hoisted sail Thorhall recited another poem:

Let us go to that quarter
Discovered by our countrymen.*
We will explore well
Beyond the keel place and the sweeping sands,
Travelling on the sea
While these Great Warrior Chiefs
Who think so highly of this land
Remain behind and gorge upon
Whale meat on this so marvellous strand.

Then they sailed away to the northward but they encountered
westerly gales and were [eventually] driven ashore in Ireland,
where they were savagely treated and thrown into slavery. And
there Thorhall was killed, according to what traders have related.

Thorvald Eriksson gave orders to have an afterboat made ready
for a voyage to the western part of the country, intending to make
use of the summer exploring in that direction.

To [those who went on this voyage] that land [the north shore
of the Gulf of St. Lawrence] seemed good. It was well wooded
and it was not far from the woods to the sea, and there were white
sands. There were many islands and shoals.

They found no dwellings of men or beasts but in one of the
western islands they found a storage shed of wood, but no other
work of man. They came back to the [Straumfiord] booths at
harvest time.

Now it is to be told that Karlsefni cruised southward off the
[west] coast [of Newfoundland] with Snorri and Bjarni and their
people.

They journeyed a long time until they came at last to a river
which flowed down from the land into a lake and thence into the
sea. There were such great sandbars at the mouth of the estuary
that it could only be entered at the height of flood tide. Karlsefni
and his people sailed into the estuary and called it there, Hop.

They found wild wheat fields on the low-lying land, and wherever there was woodland they found [grape] vines. Every brook

---

*Meaning Leif's Vinland

was full of fish. They dug trenches on the tidal flats and when the tide fell there were flatfish in the trenches. There was a great number of wild animals of all kinds in the woods.

They remained there two weeks enjoying themselves and not keeping any watch. They had their livestock with them.

Now one morning when they looked about they saw nine skin boats, and staves were being brandished from these boats and they were being whirled in the same direction that the sun moves, and they made a noise like flails.

Then Karlsefni asked: "What can this mean?"

Snorri Thorbrandsson answered him: "It may be that this is a peace signal, so let us display a white shield."

This they did, whereupon the strangers rowed towards them and came ashore and the Norse marvelled at them. They were swarthy people and queer looking, and the hair of their heads was ugly. They had remarkable eyes and broad cheeks. They stayed for some time, staring curiously at the people they saw before them, then they rowed away to the southward around the point.

Karlsefni and his men had pitched their booths above the lake, some of their houses being at the lake and some farther away near the main part of the land. They remained there all that winter. No snow came and their livestock found their own food by grazing.

The cattle went up on the land there, but it soon happened that the males became unruly and caused much trouble. They had a bull with them.

They profited by all the products of the land thereabouts; both grapes, deer and fish and all good things.

While the balance of the Greenlanders remained at Straumfiord waiting for the boat expeditions to complete their search for Vinland to the west and north, the Icelandic contingent, together with Freydis and her group of Greenlanders, packed themselves aboard three ships and departed.

The vessels first stood west across the mouth of Pistolet Bay until Cape Norman came abeam. Course was then altered to follow the bleak, unbroken western shore of the Great Northern Peninsula towards the south.

They sailed south past Port au Choix but did not land. Had they done so they would have discovered that they were not alone in this new world. One of the largest Eskimoan sites so far discovered by archaeologists lies on the Port au Choix headland. The ground in and around the many house ruins is so heavily carpeted with seal bones that in places they form a layer a foot thick, and most of the bones are from young seals.

When the harp seals in their untold thousands are whelping on the ice in the Gulf of St. Lawrence, prevailing westerly winds often set the pack tight against this section of the coast, and from an out-thrust peninsula like Port au Choix it is no trick for men to go off on foot and make a great slaughter of the young seals as they lie helpless on the pans. The Eskimos evidently concentrated at Port au Choix around March of each year; made a big kill of young seals, and then subsisted on stored meat and blubber until early summer when they scattered to various rivers southward along the coast to engage in salmon fishing.

From Port au Choix the Norse ships sailed past a flat coastal plain only recently (in geological time) emerged from the sea, extending inland to the foot of the long Range Mountains which rise to heights of 2,000 feet. Covered by spruce bogs and muskeg, the intervening plain is a depressing place. Even if there had been any cove along its coast to shelter their vessels, it is unlikely that the Norse would have bothered to land.

As they sailed on along this dreary coast the people would have observed that the mountain wall was drawing closer and closer to the sea until, by the time they were abeam of Cow Head, the coastal plain had shrunk to a mere five miles in breadth.

The twin crescentic indentations of Shallow Bay and Cow Head Cove are not true harbours, being fully open to the west, but their broad sandy beaches must have seemed very welcoming after the long voyage down a rock-girt shore. The ships nosed up to the beach and people jumped ashore to climb the nearest elevation and spy out the land.

From the top of Cow Head they beheld a broad body of water a few miles to the south and running right back into the mountains. Where it entered the sea there was a great estuary or lagoon – a *hop*, in old Norse – broadly fringed with grassy meadows. Most exciting of all, the bar between it and the open ocean was pierced by a channel. They had found the esturine/lake complex which we know today as St. Paul's Inlet, and which very closely resembled the hop described by those who had been to Vinland with Leif Eriksson.

Shortly thereafter the ships approached the opening. As they felt their way cautiously through the narrow channel into the lagoon, the penned cattle on the decks smelled the fresh grass and raised their voices in a lugubrious chorus of desire. Three score men and women crowded into the bows or ranged along the bulwarks staring intently shoreward for a first glimpse of Leif's booths. Anchors were dropped; the afterboats launched; and men pulled for the shore. During the next three or four days the immediate neighbourhood was thoroughly explored . . . but no sign of booths or, indeed, of any recognizably human habitation was found. At last it was borne in upon the Norse that this was not Leif's Vinland.

Vinland or no, the voyagers concluded that they had found an excellent potential place for a settlement. The rough pasture immediately available around the shores of the lagoon could have supported twenty times the number of animals they had brought with them. There was sufficient hay on the flat, sandy meadows to fill any number of barns. Strand wheat and wild peas flourished near the beaches. The estuary and the lake behind it teemed with birds and with a big resident population of seals and walrus. Shellfish of half a dozen species abounded, and lobsters were as abundant as sea lice. The short river which breached the rocky dyke separating the estuary from the lake proper was full of salmon. In the shallow waters of the estuary flatfish drifted over the gravel, and it was no trick to spear them. Later, using an ancient trick (it is still in use in parts of Newfoundland), men dug trenches near the half-tide mark into which they dumped offal. When the tide rose over the pits, flatfish came in to feed, and when the tide fell again the Norse were able to fork them out of the trenches with ease.

Some of the people rowed through the gut separating the estuary from the main lake to find a magnificent sheet of water running eastward for six miles and penetrating deeply into the mountain ramparts whose lower slopes supported a dense coniferous forest. Berries of several species and even wild grapes were abundant. While exploring the shores of the big lake the Norse noted the crisscross patterns of innumerable caribou trails deeply impressed into the surface of the bogs and muskegs, and they may even have seen some of the animals; although, at this season, the major part of the herds would have been high up in the mountain plateau country.

The saga states that no snow fell here, and that all winter long the livestock found their own food by grazing. When I visited St. Paul's I mentioned this description to a local farmer. It did not surprise him. He told me that during several winters within his memory there had been so little snow that the ground never did become covered. He also told me that, except during very severe winters, most of the livestock was left out to forage.

I searched the coast of the estuary, and concluded that the most likely site for the Norse camp was on the south shore, midway between a grassy point and the gut leading into the lake proper. This site fulfils all the requirements of the saga.

The two weeks which, according to the saga, the Norse spent "enjoying themselves" passed quickly, for there was a great deal to see and do. Having anchored the ships in the lagoon under the lee of the land, the people pitched tents or built temporary booths ashore. The cattle were turned loose on the grassy meadows with someone to keep an eye on them in case they strayed too far across the great bog pasture.

No other watch was kept. There seemed to be no need, but on a morning during the third week at Hop some early riser went to the door of his booth and glanced casually out over the estuary. He was startled to see a flotilla of small boats – probably kayaks – approaching slowly across the shoal waters. His shout of alarm wakened the camp and brought the men pouring out, hastily buckling on their gear. It would have been a moment pregnant with grim possibilities, for those were superstitious times, and trolls and other weird beings still infested the wildernesses of Iceland and Greenland.

How the approaching natives must have stared at the great Norse ships lying at anchor, and at the alien mob upon the beach. But Eskimos have historically been inclined to expect the best from strangers. Slowly they edged their boats towards shore and, when they felt secure enough, they made a landing.

The Norse were acute enough to greet these fur-clad, dark-skinned, almond-eyed strangers without hostility. After all, the visitors were the inhabitants of the country and Karlsefni's people would have had no way of knowing how great their numbers were, or how much of a threat they might pose. Regardless of their prowess as fighting men, the Norse were a very long way from home and friends, and it behove them to walk softly.

So good relations between the two peoples were established at this first meeting and when they parted it was in friendly style. The Norse had tried to lay the basis for future trading by giving small gifts to the natives and by indicating that they would like furs in return. What the Eskimos hoped for we cannot know.

This first contact with the Skraelings (savages, in old Norse) was fraught with many possibilities, both good and bad. These became major topics of conversation during the months which followed, but the appearance of the Skraelings did not discourage the Norse from their earlier conviction that St. Paul's was a fitting place to establish at least a semi-permanent settlement. With this in view they began erecting wooden houses.

The events of the balance of that summer and of the ensuing winter have vanished from the record, but we can be sure the people did not repeat the mistakes of Straumfiord. Hay would have been gathered; strand wheat cut and threshed; grapes and berries picked and dried; sea fish and salmon caught, dried, salted and smoked; firewood stocked beside the houses; ships hauled and covered; and corrals built for the livestock. With the advent of autumn, hunters would have gone into the country to meet the migrating caribou while other men harpooned seals and walrus in the estuary to lay in a supply of fat and oil. During the winter, groups of men went lumbering in the valleys of the Long Range Mountains, dragging roughly squared softwood logs (there were no large hardwoods in this region) out onto the ice of the inlet, from whence they could be floated down to the ships come spring.

The Saga Tale (c. 1006)

When spring arrived they discovered, early one morning, a great number of skin boats rowing from the south around the headlands. These were so numerous it looked as if charcoal had been scattered on the surface of the estuary.

From every boat, staves were being waved. Thereupon Karlsefni and his people displayed white shields and, when the two parties came together, they began to barter with each other. The Skraelings particularly desired weapons in exchange for pelts, but Karlsefni forbade the sale of weapons.

Karlsefni considered the matter and then he ordered the women to carry milk outdoors to the Skraelings. As soon as they [tasted] the milk they wanted it alone. So this was the way the trading went – they carried off their bargains in their stomachs.

Some of the cattle were near at hand, and the bull ran out of the woods and began to roar and bellow. This terrified the Skraelings and they ran. [Some of them] turned towards Karlsefni's house and tried to enter it, but Karlsefni defended the door against them. Then the Skraelings raced to their boats and rowed away, leaving behind them their packs and goods.

Now it is to be told that Karlsefni had a strong stockade of posts erected around their houses, and put everything in readiness.

"We had better take counsel," said Karlsefni, "for I think they may call on us for a third time, with many men, and not in peace. We shall follow this plan. Ten men will go out on the point and show themselves there, but another part of our company shall go into the woods and cut a path along which our cattle can be driven. When our company attacks from out of the woods we shall have our bull go ahead of us . . . " Everything was done which Karlsefni had proposed.

For three weeks nothing more was seen of them, but at the end of this time a great multitude of Skraelings was discovered coming from the south like a river of boats . . . Thereupon Karlsefni and his men took red shields and displayed them. The Skraelings sprang from their boats, and they met and fought together.

There was a fierce shower of missiles, for the Skraelings had slings. Karlsefni and Snorri observed the Skraelings lifting up on poles large, ball-shaped objects nearly the size of a sheep's belly and bluish-black in colour. They hurled these inland over Karlsefni's followers and they made a frightening noise when they fell.

This so terrified Karlsefni and all his men that they could only think of flight and of making an escape up along the edge of the river . . .

Freydis came out of doors and seeing that Karlsefni and the men were fleeing, she cried: "Why are you running from wretches like these? I would have thought such gallant men as you would have slaughtered them like cattle. If I only had a weapon I think I would put up a better fight than any of you!"

But they paid no attention to what she said and so Freydis tried to join them in their flight but she could not keep up, for she was pregnant. Nevertheless she followed them to the woods, with the Skraelings close behind her. Now she saw a dead man in front of her. This was Thorbrand, Snorri's son, and his skull had been pierced by a flat stone.

His naked sword lay beside him and Freydis picked it up and prepared to defend herself. The Skraelings came closer, whereupon she let fall her shift and slapped her breasts with the naked sword. Seeing this the Skraelings were frightened and ran down to their boats and rowed away.

Karlsefni and his companions joined her and praised her courage. Two of Karlsefni's men and four Skraelings had been killed. Karlsefni's party had been defeated by superior numbers.

The flotilla of skin-covered boats which entered St. Paul's Bay that spring morning so many years ago probably carried a group of northward-bound seal hunters, some of whom may have been members of the small party which had visited Hop the previous summer while on their way south.

Trading seems to have begun as soon as the native party landed, and the description of how Karlsefni's people handled it demonstrates that there has been little change in business ethics since those days. The vignette of the shrewd Norsemen manoeuvring the Eskimos into exchanging their furs for a few gulps of milk bridges the abyss of the centuries. It is noteworthy that Karlsefni forbade the selling of weapons. The Norse had no wish to see the natives armed with Scandinavian fighting gear, which the settlers believed was invincible. It seems never to have occurred to them that the Skraelings might not only be their equals but their superiors in weaponry.

While the Norse were busily engaged in driving their bargains, some of the Skraelings were tentatively investigating their surroundings. We can imagine them staring with fascination at the buildings, the ships and all the strange things which had appeared so mysteriously upon the shores of St. Paul's Inlet.

Then something happened which was to be of paramount importance to Norse attempts to establish colonies in North America.

The settlers' bull was an intractable and ill-natured beast. He chose this moment to appear out of the scrub woods which bordered the bog pasture. Evidently he did not approve of the fur-clad natives he saw before him. He bellowed, pawed the ground and charged.

The Eskimos were tense anyway in the presence of the Norsemen with their great swords and axes, their long beards, their strange clothing, and their great stature. The sight and sound of this huge, unknown creature thundering down on them triggered a panic flight. Those natives nearest the boats fled towards them. Some few who had ventured farther away from the shore, in among the Norse buildings, bolted for the shelter of the houses in a frantic attempt to escape the bellowing behemoth.

Karlsefni, so the saga tells us, "defended" the door of his house against the Skraelings, and we can be sure he did not use gentle methods. It is clear from the settlers' subsequent behaviour that Skraeling blood was shed.

After the hurried departure of the Eskimos (northward to the sealing grounds, for they had to pursue their livelihood even if the country *was* afflicted with blood-thirsty foreign devils), the Norse picked up the abandoned packs of furs and perhaps congratulated themselves on a profitable day's work. Nevertheless, they now expected trouble.

Stockades were built around the houses. A council of war was called at which Karlsefni, Snorri and the other leaders worked out a complicated plan to ambush any approaching Skraelings on the low sandy point at the entrance to the estuary. Ten men were to be posted there with orders to act as bait. The balance of the Norse warriors was to lurk in concealment in the scrub spruce fringing the southern end of the sandy point. Paths were to be cut so that these men could rush to their positions unseen as soon as Skraelings were reported in the offing. Still other paths were cleared to the seaward edge of the woods, along which the horned cattle could be driven onto the beach in advance of the attacking Norse.

The sagas say that nothing happened for three weeks, at the end of which time the guard came pounding into camp with the news that a group of Skraeling boats was approaching. Now the Norse put their "strike-first" plan into action.

This second party of natives appearing from the south was probably unaware of what had happened to the earlier party. As the Eskimos cleared Broom Point and struck across the shallow bight towards the mouth of the estuary, they saw some of the strangers, about whom they had probably heard during the winter, appear on the sandy point waving their arms in what was intended to look like an invitation to land.

The kayakers turned towards these men. But as soon as the boats grounded and the Skraelings jumped out to haul the light vessels up on the beach, the Norse attacked.

The Skraelings were not helpless for their sealing weapons were within easy reach. The sagas tell us that these included missiles, slings and something which looked like a sheep's belly that came hurtling through the air and frightened the Scandinavians out of their wits.

Eskimoan people of that time made the most beautiful stone points in a wide variety of shapes and sizes which were used to tip arrows and several kinds of spears and harpoons. They also had throwing boards which enabled a man to fling a spear two or three times the effective distance he could achieve by hand

and arm alone; slings, similar to the one with which David slew Goliath; and bows and arrows. These were all hunting weapons, but they could be used equally effectively against human beings. As for the mysterious ball-shaped objects, these were undoubtedly bladder floats attached to sealing spears; harmless in themselves but, being an unknown quantity to the Norse, capable of engendering an unreasoning fear.

The Norse seldom used missiles in battle. They considered such things unmanly. They preferred close combat weapons suitable for stabbing, hacking or bludgeoning. Against a people who refused close combat, but kept their distance and pelted one with sling stones, flung spears and arrows, the Norse armament was virtually useless. So it happened that, shortly after the beginning of the battle and before they had been able to cut down more than a few of the Skraelings, the Norse were forced into ignominious flight.

The rout was so complete that the warriors did not even attempt to defend their stockaded houses or their women and children. Most of these noncombatants joined in the wild flight. If the Skraelings had vigorously pursued the fleeing foreigners they would have had no difficulty in catching and slaughtering many of them. That they did not choose to do so is confirmed by the saga, which states that the Norse lost only two people during the battle.

The encounter with Freydis is of special interest. Being in an advanced state of pregnancy, she could not keep up with the other fugitives. The stinging rebuke which she flung at the backs of the fleeing men, and the way they single-mindedly ignored her and continued their panic-stricken flight, illustrates with merciless clarity the abject terror which gripped the Norse warriors when their intended victims displayed such unexpected fighting prowess.

Freydis snatched up Thorbrand's sword. The business of dropping her shift, exposing her bosom and then proceeding to slap her breasts with it (some sources have it that she whetted the sword on her breasts) would have given anyone pause. The story is really too good to spoil, yet it probably did not happen as described in the sagas.

There is no other record in Scandinavian history of a woman attempting to intimidate armed attackers by exposing her naked breasts. On the other hand, there are well-authenticated accounts of Beothuk women in early historic times baring their breasts when they were in danger from early Newfoundland settlers, whose hobby it was to hunt the Indians for the pleasure of the chase. The Beothuks had a strong taboo against killing women, and assumed that other people shared this taboo. Thus the act of baring the breast was intended to ensure that an attacker would recognize his potential victim as a female, and so would not harm her. As a way of warding off death or injury from white men, the gesture was seldom if ever helpful. In two recorded instances the white men calmly raised their guns and shot the women dead.

The gesture of baring the breasts was doubtless known to, and used by *both* the Beothuks *and* the Eskimos, who had lived in close propinquity for centuries. The Norse probably observed its use during the first skirmish with the Skraelings; and Freydis made use of it herself when she thought she was in danger.

The final stages of the "battle," including the Freydis incident, make it clear that, far from being aggressors, the Eskimos were the victims of a surprise attack, and were concerned only with defending themselves until they could make their escape. They neither looted nor attempted to destroy the buildings or the ships, nor did they massacre noncombatants – all of which they could have done had they come to Hop bent on aggression. Instead, having routed their attackers, the natives retreated to their boats, anxious only to escape as rapidly as possible.

The Saga Tale (c. 1006)

It now seemed clear to Karlsefni and his people that although this was an attractive country their lives would be filled with constant fear and turmoil because of the inhabitants, and so they immediately prepared to leave . . .

They sailed to the northward along the coast and found five Skraelings dressed in skin-doublets asleep near the sea. There were wooden containers beside them which contained animal marrow mixed with blood. Karlsefni and his people decided that [these people] must have been outlawed from their own country, and so they put them to death.

Later they found a cape upon which there was a great number of reindeer and this cape looked like one expanse of manure because so many reindeer had used it during the winter.

Then they arrived again at Straumfiord, where they found a great abundance of everything they needed.

Some men report that Bjarni Grimolfsson and Freydis remained behind here [at Straumfiord] with a hundred people, and went no farther, while Karlsefni and Snorri proceeded to the southward with forty men, returning again that same summer after tarrying at a hop there for barely two months.

[Meanwhile] Thorvald [Eriksson] went eastward in his ship and then to the northward [down the Labrador coast in search of Thorhall the Hunter] and then bore to the westward into the mouth of the fiord which lay there, keeping the land on the port side. The country thereabouts was forest land as far as they could see, with scarcely an open space anywhere.

When they had journeyed a considerable distance they came to a wooded headland which jutted out. They made their ship fast to the land and put out their gangplank to the land. Then Thorvald and his followers went ashore.

"This is a fine place," said Thorvald. "I would not mind living here."

After that they returned aboard the ship and on the sands within the headland they saw three hummocks, and when they approached them they saw these were three skin boats, with three men under each of them.

They divided their party and captured them all except for one who escaped in his boat. Then they killed the eight they had captured.

[Afterwards] they came to a river which flowed down from east to west. They sailed into the mouth of this river and lay to along the southern bank. Then they went out on the nearby cape and looked about them. Some distance up the fiord they saw some hillocks, and they supposed that these were human habitations.

They were extremely weary and could no longer keep awake, and so they went to sleep.

Then a call from up above woke them up.

"Wake up, Thorvald, and all the company if you want to save your lives. Get to the ship with all the men and sail off from the land as fast as possible!"

Now innumerable skin boats appeared from within the fiord and came towards them.

"Hang the shields over the sides of the ship and we shall defend ourselves as best we can," cried Thorvald, "but do not carry the fight to them."

They did as he instructed, and the Skraelings shot at them for a while and then fled away as fast as they could go.

Thorvald asked if any of his men was wounded, and they replied that none of them was.

"I have a wound under my arm," he said. "An arrow flew in between the shield and the ship's side." He pulled out the arrow and exclaimed: "Even though there is a lot of fat around my guts this arrow will be the death of me. It seems we have found a good land, but are not likely to get much profit from it. Now I advise you to get ready and go back [to Straumfiord] as soon as you can. But first you shall carry me to that headland which I thought was such a good place to inhabit. It seems I spoke the truth when I said I might dwell there for a while. You shall bury me there, and set up a cross at my head and at my feet and forever after call that place Krossaness."

Thorvald died and his men did all he had told them to do, and then they went away and rejoined their comrades [at Straumfiord]. They told the people there all that had happened, and they dwelt there that winter.

The shock sustained by Karlsefni's people as a result of their defeat at Hop was tremendous. Their intransigent pride was humbled, and their belief in their own invincibility badly shaken. They also lost two men, one of whom, Thorbrand Snorrisson, was the son of one of their leaders.

Their hurried decision to abandon Hop was an admission of the extent of their loss of confidence. That they were also vengeful is evident from the way they behaved during their flight northward when they surprised five of the now-feared and hated Skraelings. These they slaughtered out of hand. The excuse given, that they were believed to be outlaws under sentence of banishment, and therefore (as in Scandinavian countries) outside the laws of humanity, is pitifully weak. This was a revenge killing pure and simple. Perhaps it made the Norse warriors feel a little better.

When they passed the Port au Choix peninsula they may well have seen considerable activity at the large sealing settlement there; but if so they steered well out to sea, giving the peninsula a good wide berth. There is no evidence that the Norse ever again – even in Greenland – dared make an assault upon an alert and numerous band of Eskimos.

So Karlsefni's contingent arrived back at Straumfiord. The return of the Icelandic ships must have been reassuring to those who had remained behind. There was still no sign of Thorhall the Hunter, and the forty or so Greenlanders at Straumfiord had put in a gloomy and apprehensive winter while the conviction grew that some catastrophe had overtaken not only Thorhall, but Karlsefni's expedition too, leaving those at Straumfiord to face an unknown fate alone.

After exchanging experiences the leaders called a council to decide which course they ought to follow next. Thorvald Eriksson, leader of the Greenlanders, decided to make a ship voyage north along the Labrador coast in search of Thorhall the Hunter; but the rest of the people were divided.

Some would-be settlers were in favour of making one more attempt to find a suitable, and safe, site for a colony. Others were prepared to remain in the Straumfiord area which, although it had its drawbacks, was better than anything Greenland had to offer, and seemed to be free of Skraelings.

The trader-skippers were still hopeful of acquiring more cargo before turning for home, especially some of the invaluable hardwoods which Leif had found. With this in mind, Karlsefni concluded it would be worthwhile to make one last search for Vinland in the only direction which had not yet been explored – southward down the *east* coast of the Great Northern Peninsula.

So Karlsefni and Snorri accompanied by a party of forty Icelanders prepared to voyage south in one ship, while the rest of the Icelanders remained at Straumfiord with those Greenlanders who chose not to accompany Thorvald Eriksson on his search for Thorhall.

Thorvald's route course lay north from Straumfiord to the mouth of Grosswater Bay, where he turned east into the inland sea we now call Hamilton Inlet.

Once past the mid-channel guardian rock of Eskimo Island, Thorvald coasted westward until he reached Reed Point, a massive headland rising to 700 feet and separated from the mainland by a broad and grassy isthmus. He was so much taken with this spot that he seems to have considered settling there. But first he wished to complete his search for Thorhall.

As the Greenlanders continued along the stretch of coast below Reed Point, her people were quick to spot three skin boats upturned upon the shore, with their owners asleep beneath them. Having heard first-hand of the experiences of the Icelanders at Hop, the Greenlanders knew what to do. Only one native woke in time to escape death. He managed to launch one of the boats, and paddled frantically off to warn his fellows farther down the lake of the menace which had come upon them.

The Norse returned victoriously to their ship and sailed on past the sandy beach where the bloody bodies of eight Skraelings lay sprawled. When they rounded the low point separating the south end of the sandy beach from what is now called English River, they were delighted to see a calm and protected stretch of estuary with sand banks on either side. Carefully they felt their way into the river mouth and moored under the southern bank.

Southwest of the mouth of English River is a prominent hill. Some of the Norse climbed it to assure themselves that there were no natives in the immediate vicinity. From its crest they saw a number of "hillocks" several miles distant in the direction of Long Point, and they identified these as human habitations, presumably Skraeling.

Such a sight should have sent them hurrying back to their ship intent to remove themselves from the vicinity as rapidly as possible. But they seem to have been so overblown with confidence after their easy victory that they pitched their shelters on the shore, made themselves comfortable and calmly went to sleep.

A sentry on the hill saw a flotilla of Skraeling boats appear on the southeastern horizon at dawn the next day and shouted the alarm which roused the camp.

Doubtless repenting of their foolhardy decision to spend the night in such dangerous proximity, the Greenlanders rushed to their ship, cast off the shore lines and manned the oars. There was no wind, otherwise they could have hoisted sail and made their escape before the Skraelings reached them. As things stood they realized that they could never row the big vessel fast enough to get away from the swift kayaks and so, at Thorvald's orders, they prepared to defend themselves where the ship lay drifting.

On this occasion the Skraelings, alerted by the man who had escaped the slaughter, were definitely hostile. In their light, speedy and easily manoeuvred boats they surrounded the ship and, coming in as close as they dared, let fly with slings and bows.

Sheltered behind oaken bulwarks and further protected by rows of shields hung over the ship's sides, the Norse were well protected. They could have been seriously threatened only by a boarding party; and the natives, who probably hoped only to drive the murdering strangers away, made no attempt to board. After firing stones and arrows at the ship with no apparent results, the Skraelings withdrew.

They had done better than they knew. When the crew took stock of the results of the attack, they found that Thorvald Eriksson had been mortally wounded.

He seems to have died well, which was in the Viking tradition. Being great givers of death, the Norse could accept it without demur. He was buried, according to his wishes, on Krossaness, the headland which had caught his fancy. Then, giving up the search for Thorhall the Hunter, his shipmates turned back for

Straumfiord. They now believed they knew what had happened to Thorhall. His disappearance would have been laid at the door of the Skraelings.

The tale that Thorvald's men had to tell when they reached Straumfiord increased the people's dread of the Skraelings until they wondered fearfully if there was any safety to be had in all this land.

The Saga Tale (c. 1006)

Bjarni Grimolfsson and Freydis remained behind at Straumfiord with a hundred people and went no farther, while Karlsefni and Snorri proceeded to the southward with forty men, returning again that same summer after tarrying at a hop there for barely two months . . .

They travelled a long distance until they came to a well-forested land. There they sailed into the mouth of a river . . .

It happened one morning that Karlsefni and his companions saw something in an open space in the woods above them. It seemed to gleam at them and they shouted at it. It moved and they saw it was an Einfoetingr [One-Footer] and he came down to where their ship was lying . . . Afterward he ran away to the northward with Karlsefni's men pursuing him and catching glimpses of him from time to time. The last they saw of him he was running up a stream valley.

Then they turned back and one of the men recited this verse:

> We men pursued, this is the truth,
> A One-Footer who came to the shore,
> But the strange man fled,
> Running swiftly over the hills.
> This we tell you, Karlsefni.

[Later] they [again] became aware of natives. A great troop of them came out from the woods. Neither side could understand the other's language.

Their packs contained grey furs and sable. They were especially desirous of procuring red cloth. They also wanted to buy swords and spears but Karlsefni and Snorri forbade this.

In exchange for perfect pelts the natives would accept a span length of red cloth which they would bind around their heads.

So the trading continued for a while until Karlsefni and his people began to grow short of cloth, whereupon they divided [what they had left] into such narrow pieces that it was not more than a finger's breadth in width; but still the natives continued to give just as much or more in exchange for it.

Gudrid remained seated inside the door of a booth beside the cradle of her son Snorri. A shadow fell through the doorway, and then a woman entered who wore a narrow black kirtle. She was rather short in stature and she had chestnut-coloured hair and a band around her head. Her eyes were pale and so large that no one had ever seen such large eyes in any human skull.

She came up to where Gudrid sat and Gudrid asked: "What is your name? My name is Gudrid. What is your name?"

"My name is Gudrid," [parroted] the woman.

Then housewife Gudrid stretched out her hand indicating that the woman should sit down beside her, but at that moment Gudrid heard a loud noise whereat the woman vanished. [The noise was caused by] the killing of a native by one of Karlsefni's house slaves at this same time, because he seemed about to take [one of] their weapons.

One of the natives had picked up an axe. He looked at it for a while and struck at a tree with it and one after another the others tested it. It seemed to be a real treasure because it cut so well. But then one of their number seized it and struck at a stone with it and the axe broke. It seemed to him to be of little use since it would not cut stone, and so he threw it away.

Now there was a battle and many of the native host were slain. One man in the host was tall and fair and Karlsefni thought he might be the leader.

Then the natives ran away into the woods, each man for himself, and so ended their encounter . . .

It was probably late in June when Karlsefni's ship rounded Cape Bauld and turned her bows southward, along the east coast of the Great Northern Peninsula.

From Quirpon Island to Canada Bay, Karlsefni and Snorri would have seen little to interest them in this bald and forbidding coast. Beyond Canada Bay the spine of the peninsula lifts higher and higher as the Long Range Mountains grow in stature. The coastal cliffs become more and more formidable, in places plunging hundreds of feet into the sea below. The Norse sailed along this unprepossessing coast as quickly as they could, heartened by the fact that they saw no sign of Skraelings.

Up to the time they passed Great Harbour Deep they were sailing along an open seaboard with nothing to the east of them except a few islands and the wide Western Ocean. But not long after passing Great Harbour Deep the lookout caught the loom of land to the east. At first this loom might have been mistaken for another offshore island, but as it grew into a continuous line of highlands the Norse realized that they were again sailing into the mouth of a great fiord. This discovery led to renewed hopes that they had at last found the fiord which ran southward to terminate at Leif's Vinland.

Did Vinland and its hop lie waiting close ahead? Excitement mounted as the Icelanders ran down the last few miles into Hampden Bay, and saw the foot of the fiord before them.

Their hopes reached a climax when the ship brought up on the edge of a sand and gravel tidal flat which extended out from the river mouth, and when the lookout at the masthead called down the news that he could see a bar and a small lagoon behind it. A boat party rowed through the gap in the bar and found a tiny estuary only a few hundred yards in diameter.

This was indeed a hop, although a minute one. It bore no comparison to the fabulous harbour ascribed to Leif's Vinland, nor even to the hop Karlsefni had discovered on the west coast of the peninsula. Vinland had again eluded the Norse.

Nevertheless, there were compensations. The steep-walled valley of the Hampden still supports some of the finest mixed forest in Newfoundland. Ever since the early years of the colonial period, it has been famous for its timber, and today remains a lumbering region. In the past it was not unusual for birch logs two and even three feet in diameter to be floated down the river on the spring floods, and for many generations there was a busy shipyard at the village of Hampden. Every kind of timber, both hard and soft, needed for ship construction was available here. In Karlsefni's day the virgin forests at the foot of the bay must have been all that he had ever hoped to find. Here the Norse set up camp.

Anyone camped at the foot of Hampden Bay during the early summer months at the turn of the first millennium would inevitably have made contact with the Beothuk Indians. These people used to leave their wintering grounds in the interior in June and follow the river routes to the coasts. The Icelanders may already have been established at the mouth of the Hampden before the first of the Beothuks who wintered in the area around Grand Lake and Sandy Lake completed their annual journey down the Hampden River in their birch-bark canoes. These Indians were heading for summer camps at Sops Arm and other inlets along both the east and west coasts of White Bay, where scores of Beothuk sites have since been found.

The Indians must have discovered the presence of strangers at the river mouth long before the Norse knew they were about. The sounds of axes in the forest; the cries of men busy lumbering; the discovery of stumps and other signs of the felling of big trees—all these would have served to alert the Beothuks, who would have run their canoes ashore while some of their number went forward to reconnoitre. One man perhaps climbed the steep western side of the valley and worked his way north along the crest as far as Mount Haggerty or Mount Corbett, from whose slopes he could obtain a clear view of the bay shore and the river mouth.

The sight of the ship, Norse booths and strange men moving about would have amazed the Indian, but perhaps it did not frighten him unduly. Isolated as they had been for countless centuries except for contact with the Eskimos on the coasts, the Beothuks showed no hostility towards or fear of early Europeans in colonial times. On the contrary, they were so trusting that Gaspar Cortereal, in 1501, had no difficulty in luring fifty or sixty of them aboard his ship, preparatory to carrying them off to Spain as slaves.

The Beothuk scout either deliberately exposed himself to the sight of the strangers, or some particularly sharp-eyed Icelander happened to spot him, perhaps because of the reflection of sunlight on the numerous polished bone pendants the Beothuks wore around their necks and across their chests. In any event, the Norse shouted at him, and the man interpreted this as an invitation to come down. The saga says that he limped, or hopped, down to where the ship lay, and from this we gather that he was lame, although still able to get along well enough.

The appearance of a lone stranger tempted the Norse into another act of folly. They tried to seize him. But, crippled or not, he outdistanced or outmanoeuvred the Icelanders and vanished up a stream valley to the north. His winded pursuers returned to the camp, where they made their excuses to Karlsefni.

Several days may have elapsed before the Beothuks made up their minds what to do. Since the Norse were camped astride the route to the Indian summer camps, some kind of meeting could hardly be avoided.

Meanwhile the Icelanders, doubtless nurturing bitter memories of their encounters with the Skraelings, were making haste to complete their lumbering. Some of their number may have been told off to build defensive works around the booths, but every man would have gone about fully armed and alert to the possibility of a surprise attack.

Then the day came when the Norse beheld a company of Beothuks coming out of the woods towards them. The atmosphere would have been explosive as the Indians, their bodies glistening with a mixture of oil and red ochre from which their European name was derived, slowly advanced across the open ground.

Consistent with their behaviour in later times, these Red Indians probably made overtures of peace by offering gifts of sable and other fur clothing to the strangers. Peaceful relations, if of a tentative nature, were established. The Norse began trading, although the Beothuks may not have realized that this is what was happening. They probably thought they were engaging in an exchange of gifts.

The Beothuks were greatly taken by a piece of red woollen cloth which a Norseman offered them, and this material instantly became the thing they most desired to possess.

While trading (or gift exchanging, depending on the point of view) continued, one Indian woman, bolder than the rest, dared to peek through the door of a booth where the Norse women had been told to remain for safety's sake. She saw Gudrid, Karl-sefni's wife, sitting beside the cradle of her eighteen-month-old son, Snorri. Gudrid tried to make friends with the alien woman by asking her her name, and by repeating her own. The Beothuk woman responded by trying to imitate the unfamiliar Norse syllables, whereupon Gudrid, who seems to have been a lady of parts, beckoned the strange woman to come in and join her.

One wonders what might have happened if the Beothuk woman and Gudrid had managed to establish a rapport. The saga literature tells us of many proud Norsemen who hearkened to the outspoken criticisms of their women, and sometimes even acted on their wives' advice. It is by no means impossible that if the Beothuk woman and Gudrid *had* become friends, the story of the Norse attempts to plant a settlement in North America might have had a different ending.

The history of later contacts between whites and Beothuks establishes the fact that the Indians *wanted* peaceful relations with Europeans, and went to extraordinary lengths to achieve this. They never succeeded, but only because of the stupidity and barbarism of the successive invaders, were they French, Basque, Spanish, Portuguese or English. The Norse were no exceptions. Even as the Beothuk woman was about to enter Gudrid's house, there was a "loud noise" and the woman vanished—not into thin air, but in flight, for blood was again flowing in a Norse camp in the New World.

With the striking of that first blow – not accidentally, or by a Beothuk, but deliberately, and by a Norseman – panic erupted among the Indians. The saga says that in "the battle" which followed, many of the natives were slain while the rest ran wildly for the shelter of the woods. That many of the Beothuks were slaughtered can be believed. That there was a battle, in any real sense of the word, is questionable. The saga makes no mention of any Norsemen being killed or even wounded.

Immediately after this (the first of many massacres of Beothuks by Europeans), Karlsefni and his people got themselves aboard their ship and hurried back to Straumfiord because, as the saga says, they were "unwilling to risk men's lives any longer." By which we are to understand that they were anticipating retaliation –and with the best of reasons. Nor did they linger long at Straumfiord. Within a few days Karlsefni and most of the rest of the Icelanders sailed for their homelands. The Greenlanders held out until the following spring, then they too sailed away. And so the first European attempt at colonizing Newfoundland came to its end. Nearly five centuries would elapse before European settlements, armed this time with guns, would successfully establish themselves upon the Rock.

III

The Outport Way

The Heritage

The island glimmered in the consciousness of European men long centuries before the darkness obscuring the rest of the Western Hemisphere began to light with knowledge. It was a reality to the Greenland and Iceland Norse who tried and failed to colonize it at the turn of the first millennium. Their discovery of it was never lost but was passed to the wide-ranging fraternity of mariners, including Basque seamen who fished and whaled along its shores perhaps a century before Columbus sailed west. By 1436 it had appeared, if dimly, on European maps as The Land of Stockfish. Well before the end of the fifteenth century Portuguese fishermen knew it as *Terra de Los Bachalaos* (Land of the Cod Fish); Breton and Norman fishers knew it as *Terre-Neuve*; Bristol fishermen of that same distant period called it Newland or the New Founde Land.

These men of earlier centuries, fishing at great distances in time and space from their home ports in Europe, had needs that only solid land could satisfy. There was the need to shelter from the great Atlantic storms; the need for snug harbours where ships could water, repair and take on wood for fuel. Stockfish (dry cod), whether it was preserved with salt or dried by wind and sun, could only be "made" on shore. The blubber from whales and seals could only be "tried" (rendered into oil) at crude factories constructed on the land. So from the first days of the fisheries off Newfoundland, men were making at least seasonal use of the coasts. Skippers who came back year after year had their chosen harbours where semi-permanent structures came into being. Inevitably the owners had to take measures to protect their shore bases, not so much against the presence of the native Beothuks as against thievery and malicious destruction by crews of other ships of their own and foreign nations.

The only certain way to protect a shore base was to leave men to winter there; and with the first such successful winterings (probably by the end of the fifteenth century), the seeds of permanent occupation were sown.

It was a short further step to the decision by certain hardy seafarers to "plant" themselves in the New Founde Land. The advantages were obvious: men permanently established in a convenient harbour, near good fishing grounds where they could use small boats, could fish for eight months of the year off the northern coasts and almost year-round off the southern shores.

There was more to settlement than that. During those early centuries the common man in Europe was in peonage – if not in outright bondage. His very life was forfeit at the whim of those who governed him. The poverty of the damned was the general lot of most except the uppermost ranks. The hardships and uncertainties of hacking out a free life even on the granitic coasts of Newfoundland were no greater than those a man had to face at home in Europe and, in all likelihood, were considerably less. And in Newfoundland, as in no other part of North America, there was only the natural wilderness with which to deal; the human inhabitants, the Beothuks, made no attempts to resist the alien interlopers.*

One thing was needed before the slow swirl of Europeans along the Newfoundland shores could begin to clot into real settlements – and that was women. Historians say nothing about where the women came from, but come they did. In the beginning some were taken forcibly out of the tents of the Beothuks. Others accompanied fishing ships from Europe. The latter were women without homes, without men to keep them – women who perforce kept themselves the only way they could. Aboard ship they served the dual purpose of entertaining the crew and slaving at the job of making fish. Such women were happy to abandon servitude in order to build a life with a free man, even in a remote cove in Newfoundland.

---

*For reasons unknown, the Eskimos had disappeared from Newfoundland before the new European invasion began.

A popular myth implies that the people who first settled the outports were criminals, outcasts and fugitives attempting to evade justice and punishment. In truth, many may have been law-breakers according to the oppressive regulations of their times; certainly a number deserted from ships whose crews were treated little better than galley slaves; while others fled from a European justice so barbarous that it thought nothing of having a man drawn and quartered for minor theft – but criminals they were not. They were the strongest and bravest of the oppressed; and their only real crime was that they dared risk everything to gain the freedom to live or die by their own efforts.

The birthdate of the first settlement on the Sou'west Coast, the region with which I became most familiar, is, typically, unknown. Written history holds no record of it. However, although the Basque peoples of the fifteenth century left no documentary record of their early venturings, Spanish scholars later chronicled a Basque tradition which stated matter-of-factly that their seamen had been whaling off Newfoundland a full century before Columbus sailed. So it could well be that these mysterious and ancient people provided the first successful European inhabitants; and it is surely no mere coincidence that the harbour which is now Newfoundland's navel, and which lies at the western extremity of the Sou'west Coast, still bears the name Port aux Basques.

The first documented reference to settlement on the Sou'west Coast comes from the Portuguese. It is a fragmentary notice of a voyage made just before 1500. After this date the pattern becomes a little clearer. Until about the middle of the sixteenth century, Portuguese, French and Spanish Basques, and Normans and Bretons, had as many as six hundred ships in Newfoundland waters in any given year, mostly on the southern and eastern coasts.

As the years slipped by, Basque and Portuguese interests and influence in southern Newfoundland declined while those of the French grew. This shift was a continuous one – not an abrupt replacement of one people by another. Earlier settlers who were already well established before the French drifted westward remained where they were and blended their blood with that of the newcomers, eventually adopting the French tongue as the general language. The change was slow, spanning most of the seventeenth century.

In the train of the French came a new infusion of Indian blood as Micmacs from Nova Scotia, close allies of the French, were encouraged to migrate to *Terre-Neuve*. Whites and Indians intermarried. Thus, by the early eighteenth century, the Sou'west Coast was home to a people of mixed Basque-Norman-Breton-Portuguese and Indian heritage. The race—and it was in reality a race—took on further admixtures, for this was a famous pirate coast where Dutch, English and Spanish freebooters made their headquarters, secure from interference since not even France attempted to exercise sovereignty over it.

The Sou'west Coast remained remarkably free from involvement in the wars, skirmishes and raids that grew out of the bitter struggle between France and England for possession of Newfoundland, and of Canada. It was largely by-passed by the warring fleets, although visited by peaceful fishermen and honest pirates with profit to themselves and to the inhabitants. In consequence of this continuing freedom both from war and from official interference, the little clusters of families that inhabited every suitable cove and harbour from Cape Ray to Fortune Bay felt no real allegiance to any European nation. They were a people united within themselves in a society that had no name, no flag, no boundaries. The sea was their common country, and the way of the sea was their community of life. Each outport lived not only remote from the turmoil of the outer world but also from too-close propinquity with neighbouring settlements, since each group of human beings in its cliff-girt cove was insulated from all others by the dark wastes of ocean. Nevertheless, the coast dwellers were all as one people, for the sea had made them one.

Through the generations further changes came almost imperceptibly. In the main these were superficial and did not deeply affect the lives men led. Even the Treaty of Utrecht in 1713, by which France was forced to cede the whole south coast to England, caused no dislocation in the centuries-old way of life. The

English sent a naval officer, Captain Taverner, to cruise the newly acquired shores and to demand an oath of allegiance from the settlers on pain of expulsion if they refused. He met with no resistance. The people took the oath. After all, what was a nominal change of allegiance to them? They went on about their age-old business with the sea.

But change was heralded by the arrival of carpetbaggers representing powerful merchant companies based in southern England and in the Channel Isles. These newcomers seized some of the best harbours and proceeded to introduce the same mercantile system under which outport fishermen in the English parts of Newfoundland (the English had settled the east coast as early as 1600) had been mercilessly exploited for generations. These merchants controlled all imports, which they sold on credit to the outport people. In return they demanded exclusive rights to the fishermen's catch, the value of which was applied against the man's debt. If there was a credit to a fisherman's account (and the merchant was the sole judge of this since the people were illiterate), it could only be "taken up in trade" at the merchant's store. The outport men were no longer allowed to sell fish to visiting English ships or those of foreign nations, or to buy goods from them.

This system, once established, continued in full force until the late 1940s. Profit on the goods sold to outport fishermen sometimes exceeded five hundred per cent, while profit on the salt fish "bought" from them regularly amounted to three or four times the sum credited to the fishermen's accounts. It was a rare fisherman indeed who ever succeeded in getting out of debt.

The English and Jersey merchants affected life on the coast in other ways. For one thing, they used indentured labour. Each year their ships brought out cargoes of so-called "youngsters" (men ranging in age from fourteen to sixty years) recruited mostly in the counties of Devon, Dorset and Somerset, and on the island of Jersey.

These "youngsters" were obliged to serve their masters for a period of from three to five years, in exchange for their keep. If the masters so chose, the indentured men were then obliged to make a payment of three or four pounds in order to gain their freedom. They were used as crews for the fishing boats owned by the merchants; as brute labour; and sometimes were hired out to entrepreneurs who had established themselves as masters of certain small outports which they ran as minor principalities.

Hundreds of the "youngsters" reached the Sou'west Coast during the eighteenth and nineteenth centuries, and few ever returned, or wished to return, to the starvation lot of the poor in the England of those times. Some served out the full indenture period and then slipped away to take up the outport way of life. A great many others drew the breath of freedom early and ran off to hide themselves in bays and inlets where they became "livyers" (people who "live here").

Chauvinistic English historians have claimed that after Utrecht the French mysteriously vanished from the coast, to be magically replaced by an entirely English population. Nothing of the sort occurred. But the intermarriage of Englishmen with French girls gradually brought about an apparent anglicization of the population. The language changed and the surnames of many families were anglicized. But other things did not change. Most of the old names for the bays, the settlements themselves, mountains and rivers remained, as indeed they still remain. And the pattern of the coast dwellers' lives did not undergo any essential disruption.

English officialdom showed little interest in the Sou'west Coast, leaving it to be run as a fiefdom by the merchant companies, whose only real opposition came after 1800 when Americans from New England began fishing offshore. In 1818 a treaty between Britain and the United States gave the Americans the right to fish anywhere along the coast, and also allowed them to make use of any "unoccupied" harbours, creeks or bays. This treaty remained in force for almost one hundred years.

The Americans' freedom to come and go as they pleased (a freedom shared, illegally, by the French fishing fleet operating out of the nearby French islands of St. Pierre and Miquelon) was bitterly resented by the English merchant companies. But it was a blessing to the people of the coast; it offered them an escape hatch, no matter how narrow, from complete servitude to the merchants. They could and did engage in an illegal bait trade, selling squid and herring to American and French fishing vessels and getting paid in cash. And they could and did engage in an equally illegal trade with St. Pierre and Miquelon, smuggling loads of lumber, fresh caribou meat and other produce to the French islands – in exchange for rum, sugar, flour, clothing and similar essentials at a fraction of the price charged them by the merchant monopoly at home. American vessels harbouring on the Sou'west Coast bought fur and fish from the local people and sold them cheap New England goods, while the merchant princes raged and sent delegation after delegation to England demanding that this poaching on their preserves be stopped by force.

Without the presence of the "foreigners," life on the Sou'west Coast might have become intolerable. For centuries the people had endured adversity, had overcome and thrived on it; but that had been natural adversity. The ruthless exploitation (there is no other word for it) they had to endure under the rule of the English and Jersey merchants strained the fabric of their lives to the breaking point.

Conditions became worse in the first decade of the twentieth century, when the merchants at last succeeded in persuading the government to cut off the American trade. Left with a free hand, the merchant companies and the smaller independent merchants then tightened their grip to such an extent that they very nearly throttled the life out of the Sou'west Coast. It became nearly impossible for a man to obtain or cling to much more than a fingerhold on existence. It became virtually impossible for the population to grow either in numbers or in spirit.

These were the years that are still starkly remembered by the old people as The Hard Times. And they were hard indeed. Starvation was a constant spectre. Malnutrition was something men and women were born to and died of. It is perhaps the surest measure of the qualities of the coast people that they survived this period at all. They were helped by the two world wars which brought so much prosperity to the fishing business that a little of it managed to spill over from the merchants' grasp. After 1933 the new colonial government (a commission established by Great Britain after Newfoundland's merchant princes had run the island into bankruptcy) began to offer some assistance to a forgotten people. Cottage hospitals were built and a free medical service (even if of a rudimentary nature) was provided. By the time the Second World War began, the people were on their feet again. True, the merchants still dominated the scene, but their grip had slackened sufficiently so that life could renew itself.

In the last hours before confederation with Canada became a reality, in 1949, the coast was a land of vigorous human life. Its people were a unique and fascinating breed; quick, confident survivors of a rigorous evolutionary winnowing process. As fishermen they were unparalleled. As seamen they were unsurpassed. Although their homes were remote from the outer world, they were by no means backward in thought or in experience. There was hardly a family that had not sent sons, brothers, uncles and fathers abroad as seamen, or as skippers, in the great overseas carrying trade which before the Second World War had made the Newfoundland mercantile fleet one of the largest (in numbers, if not in tonnage) in the world. London, Lisbon and Genoa were names familiar in the mouths of most of the coastal peoples. Largely illiterate as they may have been, their understanding of and empathy with strange peoples with strange ways was deeper and embraced more tolerance than most of us can claim today.

Newfoundlanders were always much more closely linked to the seaboard people of Europe than to those of North America. Prior to joining Canada they had no real political, little social and cultural, and not even much commercial affiliation with this continent. When confederation with Canada was first mooted, in the latter part of the nineteenth century, Newfoundlanders lustily sang this song:

> Hurray for our own native land, Newfoundland!
> Not a stranger shall hold an inch of her strand.
> Her face turns to Britain, her back to the Gulf.
> Come near at your peril, Canadian Wolf!

Many of them were still singing the same song when confederation finally came upon them in 1949.

The man who engineered confederation was Joseph Smallwood, a one-time labour organizer and pig farmer, but always a highly political animal, who combined messianic visions with essential ruthlessness. He became the first premier of Canada's newest province, and remained its premier for twenty-three years. "King Joey," as he was called (sometimes affectionately, sometimes with bitterness), tried to transform his island kingdom into an industrialized principality, dependent on and imitative of the Admass society of Canada and the United States. "Off with the old and on with the new" was his guiding principle, and he applied it with a vigour and haste that made no reckoning of the psychic and spiritual havoc it created in the lives of his own people.

The day that Smallwood came to power, the continuity and evolution of the Newfoundland way of life was disrupted, probably forever. Newfoundlanders were directed to reject the sea which had nurtured them through five centuries. Fishing and fishermen, ships and seamen, were deemed obsolete. Progress, so the new policy dictated, demanded the elimination of most of the thirteen hundred outport communities that encircled the island, and the transformation of their people into industrial workers. Progress dictated that the men of the sea forswear their ancient ways of life and move, as rootless migrants, to the alien milieu of inland industrial or mining towns. The entrepreneurs of the new industries wanted abundant labour and, of course, they preferred it cheap. The outport people had to be induced – and if not induced, then forced – to abandon the ways and the world they knew.

The tactics used combined both methods. The first step was to wither the fisheries and the mercantile marine by withholding the support which would enable them to make the transition into effective economic enterprises of the twentieth century. With their underpinnings knocked out, the outports began to totter; but they did not fall, for their intrinsic strength was greater than the politicians had anticipated. So the next step was to reduce basic services, or to fail to maintain them. Outport schools found they could no longer obtain teachers; those regions whose communications were by sea found that the government-run steamer service was deteriorating. But the heaviest pressures were brought to bear through reduction in medical services. On the

Sou'west Coast many outports found themselves going without a visit from a doctor for as much as ten months at a time, even though two government doctors were resident on the coast.

In conjunction with these "deprival tactics" the government devised a centralization plan. Outporters were to be subsidized into moving to a few "growth centres." At first people were offered $500 per family, *provided that every family in an outport agreed to move.* The size of this "assistance grant" was later substantially increased, but still fell far short of compensating the people for their abandoned houses, or for the cost of buying or building new homes in the new towns.

Whatever the tactic used, the aim itself was dubious in the extreme. The *raison d'être* for the centralization plan was to create viable new economic and social units. Yet Burgeo, a typical growth centre, and the outport where I made my home for several years, suffered a massive expansion in its population without any increase in ways to provide its people with a decent way of life. To this day the one fish-processing plant in Burgeo employs only a fraction of the employable people, and pays them only minimal and intermittent wages. Many of the younger men can find work neither at the plant nor in the fish company's ships and are forced to seek work as far away as western Canada. Burgeo is *not* a growing community, despite the increase in size resulting from the influx of refugees from other outports; it is a dying community, and it may be that this too is part of the plan, for a people uprooted once can more readily be forced to move again.

The heritage of the outport inhabitants at the time of confederation ensured that a strong, venturesome and viable people could move into our modern world with no loss of their own sources of strength (something that the isolated fishing folk of Iceland, the Faeroe and Shetland Islands have successfully done), and perhaps with advantage to the waning strength of other men elsewhere. It was a potential that had little or no meaning to the apostles of instant change.

I remember a summation of the outport people made to my wife and me by a woman doctor of the new order employed by

Smallwood's government. We were aboard the coastal steamer as she nosed into Burgeo harbour. The ship blew a long and lugubrious blast on her whistle and, as the sound echoed amongst the islands, men, women and children began to appear from the scattered houses and move towards the wharf. The doctor, standing beside us at the rail, gestured contemptuously towards them. "These people are scum," she said. "They are descended from scum, and they are still scum."

But I also remember a stormy evening in February in the snug kitchen of a fisherman's home in the outport of François. Present were three men who had spent most of the day hand-lining for cod from dories pitching in a gale of winter wind. Now the time had come for rest and talk. The talk ranged wearily over the problems of a people who seemed to have no future; of a way of life whose end could not long be postponed.

After a while there was silence; the silence of men who, for the first time in their lives and perhaps for the first time in the lives of their people, were experiencing the ultimate bewilderment that had come upon them with recognition of the truth that they were completely helpless to save themselves.

The wife of the house brought a pot of fresh tea to the table where we sat and filled our mugs. As she returned to her seat by the stove to begin combing her daughter's hair, her husband broke the silence.

"It's been fine you came to visit. I hopes you found some yarns to write, and you'll make a good voyage out of it. But still and all, I'm wondering could you do one thing for we? Could you, do you think, say how it was with we? We wouldn't want it thought, you understand, that we never tried the hardest as us could to make a go of things. I'd like for everyone to know we never would have left the places we was reared, but . . . we . . . was . . . drove!"

The last word burst into the quiet room with a terrible intensity. The little girl, who had been half asleep as the comb slipped through her long, dark hair, stared up at her father with astonished eyes.

He slowly lowered his head until he was looking with an unseeing gaze at the splayed hands with which he clutched the table top before him. Unconscious of us all he spoke once more, no louder than the half-heard murmur of the black waters gentling the pilings of the landing stage outside the door.

"Aye, Jesus, Jesus God, but we was drove!"

The Cove

The brooding barrier of rock towering out of the sea along the Sou'west Coast is kinder than it looks. It is pocked by scores of fiords and coves, some big enough to shelter a fleet of schooners, and others only large enough to protect the boats and stages belonging to a handful of families. These were the places where men settled, always within a few hours' sail or row of good inshore fishing grounds.

There are fifty or sixty such refuges along the coast, and a hundred years ago they were all occupied. Together they formed a frieze of human habitations from Port aux Basques east to Bay d'Espoir along the line of demarcation between the surging sea and the rock ramparts. Their names sing a strange litany: Foxroot (it was once Fosse Rouge), Isle-aux-Morts, Rose Blanche (Roche Blanche), Harbour Le Cou, Petites, La Poile, Gallyboy, Grand Bruit, Our Harbour, Messers (Messieurs), Ramea, Burgeo, La Hune, Cul de Sac, François, Rencontre, Dragon, Mosquito, Bonne Bay, Pushthrough, Goblin, Lobscouse Cove. But the song they sing is much shorter now, for most of the coves have returned to silence.

Not all of the havens were on the main shoreline. Shelter was also to be found on some of the islands. Of these the Burgeo group huddles close up under the coast and was evidently settled in the sixteenth century. Ramea, five miles offshore (and originally called Ilos Santa Anna), apparently knew no permanent human inhabitants until a mere two hundred years ago. The Penguins, a scattering of spume-swept islets fifteen miles off the towering headland of Cape La Hune, were never permanently settled, although families from La Hune and François summered on them, camping in makeshift huts and fishing for cod from two-man dories. In times far removed the Penguins were the home of a vast breeding rookery of great auks. These huge, flightless birds furnished the transient fishing fleets and the local fishermen with countless tons of meat, most of which they used as bait, until the day came when the great auks could no longer withstand the slaughter and disappeared forever from this earth.

Most of the early comers eschewed the naked islands and sought out sheltered coves on the main coast. The sites they picked were hardly determined by aesthetic factors (although many are spectacular in the extreme), nor for the creature comforts they could offer; they were chosen solely because they were the best possible places from which to carry on the inshore fishery. Some—such as François, Richard's Harbour, Cul de Sac and Dragon—were built against such precipitous and rocky cliffs that there was hardly a square yard of level land to be found, and the houses clung precariously to steep, scree slopes, like so many seabirds' nests. At more exposed, if less rugged, coves the houses perched on spray-drenched foreshores of almost-naked rocks behind which small boats could shelter.

These settlements had to withstand such ferocity of wind and water that the buildings were sometimes bound to the rocks with ring bolts and iron cables. Churches posed a special problem since anything that reached upward, whether towards God or an empty sky, was fair game for the wind. The Anglican church at Burgeo blew down three times in sixty years, with the result that not a few of the parishioners prudently transferred their allegiance to the Methodist faith. Burials posed a problem too. Often there was not enough soil in which to dig a grave and thus the rough plank coffins had to rest on the surface rock, precariously protected for a few decades by mounds of peat and gravel.

It took indomitable persistence for an outport to root itself at all upon this coast and everything about the surviving settlements bears testimony to this strength. The houses stand as square and solid as blocks of basalt. They are so strong that they can be levered off their foundation posts, trundled to the water's edge, set afloat and towed miles across open water to be hauled up on shore at a new site. When the outports were "closed out," many people refused to abandon their houses and shifted them in just this way. Scores were "launched off," and one of the most remarkable sights I have ever seen was a flotilla of such houses being towed by a gaggle of little motor boats. One house, whose lower rooms had been filled with oil drums to give additional buoyancy, carried the family as passengers in the upper storey. Its owners had even rigged the kitchen stove in one of the bedrooms so the wife could "bile the kettle" during the voyage.

Many of the coves were devoid of soil; but even that drawback could be, and was, overcome. Over the generations people patiently made things grow. They built potato patches by collecting baskets of detritus that had lodged in crevices amongst the rocks. By manuring this sterile stuff with seaweed and rotting fish they gave it a measure of fertility.

The wheel had little utility in most outports. The houses grew like barnacles, strewn every which way among the boulders; and the paths that linked them were often so steep and rough that even a wheelbarrow was of little use. That did not matter either. Strong arms, strong legs and two-man hand barrows served the purpose of the wheel.

The settlements were not purely functional. It was a monochromatic world that the first settlers knew, so they gave it colour by planting seeds gathered long ago in European gardens. The cerulean iris (the *fleur-de-lis*), the wild briar rose and other hardy, elder flowers adapted so well that many still persist at settlement sites from which houses and people have now vanished.

In the early times there was no paint to buy (supposing men had had the money with which to buy it), so outporters made their own by mixing red ochre with cod liver oil. Although the resultant mixture stank to high heaven for a year or so, it gave warmth and colour to the buildings.

Until confederation most families kept a cow and spent summer days gathering salt grass which grew in protected places, turning it into hay against the long, wild winters. Sheep and goats, which were imported so long ago that they developed into distinctive breeds, also learned to prosper where previously only caribou had been able to find sustenance. Then there were the dogs – the "water dogs" – black, smooth-haired beasts with massive forequarters, otter-like tails and webbed feet – dogs almost as much aquatic animals as they were animals of the land. Nobody knows where they originated, but they were on the Newfoundland coasts when history first begins to speak about the island. It is from this aboriginal stock that the famous breeds known as the Labrador and the Newfoundland were developed.

On a foundation of sterility and desolation the men and women of the coves built their small, strong worlds–bastions of courage and endurance wherein there dwelt a resolute and prideful race.

Between Wind and Water

In winter the small world of an outport appears somnolent. Even on those days when no storm wraps the settlement in an obscurity of driving snow and spume, there is so little movement to be seen that a stranger might conclude the inhabitants were hibernating. But this is an illusion. Within the narrow compass of the cove, "between wind and water" as the people say, life is being lived with undiminished vigour.

The harbour comes alive well before dawn light as the first fishermen board their boats and start their engines. The slow, heavy beat of the single-cylinder "make-and-breaks" is a sound felt rather than heard, and it used to be the heartbeat of the settlements before the coming of the raucous outboard motor. Throughout the short day life flicks its fingers intermittently across the cove. A dory dawdles in the narrow run between two islands as its owner hauls his herring nets. Someone is shovelling snow from the deck of a little schooner. There is always work to be done aboard the moored or anchored vessels – knocking off the ice after a "glitter" storm; pumping the bilges; replacing chafed mooring gear; or repairing a recalcitrant engine. The arena of the harbour is seldom crowded in the winter; but it is never empty.

It is the same along the landwash where men spend the balance of their lives when they are not at sea. The landwash is the indeterminate region where the water meets the land. It is a domain of docks, flakes, stages, fish stores, upturned boats and tidal wrack. The skeletal structures of the "stages" (wharves) dominate the landwash, brooding over the scum of cat ice that forms during the winter nights and breaks and flows away as the tide falls. Behind, and often attached to each stage, stands the fishstore, known simply as "the store," where gear is stowed, lines baited, nets repaired, boats built; and where, in the glow of a little stove, those who are too old or too young for the fishery foregather to wait until the boats come home from seaward.

Each man's store is each man's club. It is ill lit and cluttered, redolent with the smells of stockholm tar, of salt bulk fish, of pickled herring, of old net twine and of spruce sticks snapping in the stove. The store is a museum too, for it contains the memories of a man and of his father's fathers. Here, in dark corners, lie conch shells once used as foghorns; worn, red sealskin boots from Labrador; a broken "swile" (sealing) gun of gargantuan proportions; inscrutable objects of brass and copper that are the finite wreckage of some long-lost ship; a pair of homemade "racquettes" (snowshoes); and the phallic mass of an antique jump-spark engine. Men gravitate from store to store. A stranger may never see them either come or go, but if he pushes open the strap-hung door and steps inside, he finds the club in session – if not in Garge's store, then sure to be in Sam's.

This is the place where the slow, casual gossip of the sea is heard – and old stories, sharp jokes and subtle drolleries. And hands are always busy mending twine, baiting gear for the morrow's trip to the "grounds," playing the intricate cat's cradle, known as "the schooner game" – doing a thousand things; for until the heart is stilled, the hands of an outport man are seldom idle.

The landwash embraces the steamer dock, and when the ship lets go her long, visceral rumble from outside the farthest headland, men, women and children appear mysteriously, drifting down towards the dock. The crowd does not gather, it seems simply to grow and swell. The people stand about and watch the freight coming ashore. They gossip with passengers aboard the ship, exchanging news about old friends in other coves. They come to greet the steamer not out of idleness but to share the continuity of life along the coast. The steamer is the link, not only between the outports, but to the capital, St. John's, and to even more distant places in the outer world.

The houses crowd close to the landwash, and to one another, in cheerful propinquity that owes nothing to the mathematical mind of a town planner. Their arrangement and alignment appear to be wildly haphazard; and so they are, if one thinks only of the neatly patterned and deadly-dreary streets of mainland towns. The pattern of an outport is not dictated by man; it is dictated by the vagaries of the riven rock to which the houses cling. This may be an offence to the eye of a planner, but the effect is a delight to the eye of anyone else, a delight that is enhanced by the boldly individualistic and lavish use of paint in wild and brilliant hues that has been one of the more spectacular results of confederation with Canada. The brash colours flow together in the random pattern of the buildings and, against the sombre backdrop of the winter cliffs, acquire beauty not by design but by happy accident.

Linked by a meandering web of pathways twisting and twining uphill and down, the houses with their gardens and wooden-fenced enclosures form a different arena; but it too is seldom empty, though never crowded. Children on their way to school run leaning into the wind. A woman emerges from her house and scuttles to the merchant's store to buy a pound of salt pork. A brisk young man goes by, accompanied by his water dog hauling a country "slide" (sled) which carries a suspicious-looking lump of something wrapped in canvas that may well be, and probably is, a quarter of illegal caribou meat. Old Uncle John swings past on his way up from the landwash, a string of cods' heads, destined for his supper, bumping against his legs. Clem comes along the path to meet his cow who is waiting impatiently for her evening feed. Girls who have worked a long shift in the fish plant, red-faced and red-nosed in the evening chill, tramp wearily homeward. And all day long there is someone going to or coming from the well. Even when darkness falls, leaving each house alone but glowing outwardly through its frilled curtains, the slow and easy flow of human activity does not cease entirely. The lithe shadows of young people slip past and into greater darkness, melting and clinging as the night grows old.

Oil lamps burn in every kitchen; sweet wood smoke or rank coal smoke staggers from the chimney tops as snow begins to fall, obscuring all the cove and waking the guardian foghorn on the outer head, so that its heavy voice begins to boom above the never-ending mutter of the sea, calling, calling into the black night.

Within These Walls

The home of an outport Newfoundlander is no man's castle; it is the woman's. It is at once the core and the boundary of her existence. Once she has come to it as a bride (when she is perhaps no more than sixteen years of age) she rarely leaves it voluntarily for more than a few hours, not because she is imprisoned in it but because for her it is the centre of reality, the cave of ultimate security. Within these walls she is mistress of the world, accomplished in a score of skills and at ease in her fulfilment.

The outport house has evolved to suit its environment as surely as any animal evolves to suit its world. Built four-square, with the flexible strength that belongs to wooden ships, it makes total use of the space its walls enclose. The roof is pitched almost flat, since in this land of winds there is but little chance of it being overloaded with accumulated snow. The ceilings are low and heavily beamed, and the rooms have the snug and comfortable feeling of a vessel's cabin. Essentially the house is a land-berthed ship. Its upper deck contains the bedrooms, usually four in number and unheated. Big beds – soft sprung and mattressed with down ticks – almost fill them, for in these homes a bedroom is exactly what its name implies. The lower deck may have a parlour and perhaps a bedroom too; but the main cabin is the kitchen, the heart and essence of the house.

The kitchen is the largest room – bright, warm and welcoming. It always contains at least one daybed (a combination sofa and single bed) which provides a place for the man to stretch out for a few minutes before his meal; a place for the woman to sit as she knits, sews or spins; a place for a gaggle of neighbours' children to perch in owl-eyed silence; a place for a grandfather or an aging aunt to rest and reminisce; a place where young lovers come together when the rest of the household lies sleeping.

The stove is central and looms large; it glitters with nickel trim, and its top shines like a black mirror with the accumulated polish of the years. Above it hang thick woollen mitts, socks, outer clothing – all swinging and steaming. It is a room where everything is neatly in its place, ship-fashion; and it is kept scrupulously clean. The kitchen is colourful to such a degree that the eyes of a mainlander can be dazzled by the brilliance of high-gloss paints upon the walls and by the gleaming, painted linoleum or canvas on the floors.

The kitchen windows usually look out upon the cove and over it to the grey sea beyond. During the long hours when the husband is away at the fishing grounds, the woman's glance is forever reaching out beyond this room so that the eyes of the house–the salt-streaked eyes of glass–become her eyes as well.

As for the man, he spends so little time in his own house that he sometimes seems to feel uneasy in it. He often leaves before dawn. If it is a good day, he may be at sea until late afternoon, after which he will be preoccupied at his stage or store until suppertime. On a "looward day," when the weather "ain't fittin'" and the boats stay in the harbour, he spends most of his time down at his store. The house is where he eats his meals, sleeps and procreates. But it is only when he is very old, "no good for it anymore," that he at last enters fully into the house he built, or that his father's father built before him.

So the house belongs truly to the woman, and she gives of it to her children born within its walls; to young lovers; to her husband and to aged relatives; and, as often as circumstances will allow, to the entire settlement. There is no single thing in their lives that outport people value more than what they call a "time."

Almost anything will serve as an excuse to have a time and to fill the house with people. The arrival in the harbour of a fishing vessel from another port, a member of whose crew is perhaps a fifth cousin of some local householder, can spark a time. During the Twelve Days of Christmas (the outports still celebrate both old and new Christmas days, together with the twelve days between), every night is a time in its own right. Masked and costumed mummers come thumping at every door: "Is mummers allowed in?" Once inside they pound the kitchen floor with sea boots and rubber boots to the shrilling of a fiddle or the whine of an accordion. A time can happen quite spontaneously when three or four neighbours drop in for a "gam" (gossip), or it can be made to happen with the miraculous appearance of a bottle of "white stuff" (pure alcohol), imported without the blessing of the Custom's Officer, from the off-lying French islands of St. Pierre and Miquelon on foggy nights when the Royal Canadian Mounted Police patrol boats are drowsing at their moorings.

Here there is gaiety. But there is also pain and fear and darkness in the spirit. This is the place where women watch and wait through the interminable night, while the house shivers in the tearing talons of a winter's gale and a boat is too long overdue. It is the place where people sit in silence, but not alone, while in an upstairs room a pulse flickers fitfully and a heartbeat slows. The outport home rejects no one and no emotion. It accepts all that there is of life and death. It provides a place where those who have outworn their flesh can wait the hours down. For them there is no banishment to an old folks' sterile dying place where they must endure the pervading chill of death, preceding death, that freezes the spirit of the world's unwanted. Until their last breath fails, those whose present has become their past are nurtured within the haven of these walls. And at the going out at the end of it, they pass in dignity and in simplicity. And they are mourned.

Within these walls there is a sustaining certitude that is proof against disaster, against hardship, against the darkest hours of adversity, and against loneliness. Here there is a quality to human sharing and an unspoken understanding that is proof against the very fates themselves. Here there is a unity that has no name. And here there is quiet at the close.

The Country Path

The world of waters looms foremost in their minds, but the land beyond the sea's reach also plays its part in the life of the outport people. From every settlement there is a trail leading inland. It is often called the Country Path, a strangely gentle sobriquet for a track that may lead up a precipitous cliff face for a thousand feet and can demand of the traveller that he use his fingers as well as his toes. The Country Path is not always an exercise in mountain climbing; from some outports it winds inland up the pitch of a river valley; but it always leads into a hard land.

A few men in most outports preferred the interior plains to the rolling plains of ocean. These were mainly men who carried within them the instinctive predilections of Indian ancestors. Leaving the settlements in October, accompanied by their dogs and laden with all the supplies they could carry, they traversed the windswept sweep of the high barrens until they came to the edge of the Big Woods. Here they would build tiny cabins, called tilts, and spend the winter trapping fox and wolf and mink and marten. They were seldom seen again until late February when they emerged from the wilderness with the season's catch. They were called "the countrymen"; but now they are mostly gone and those few who still survive are old men living with their memories.

The country casts a lesser spell on almost every man in the outports for at least a part of each year. In the past it was the country that gave them fresh meat, fuel for their hungry stoves, and wood with which to build their boats and homes and stages. Meat meant ptarmigan, hares, caribou and, in later years, moose as well; but caribou was by far the most important game. In the old days caribou roamed the winter barrens in "companies" of thousands. Those days are gone, and so are most of the "deer," slaughtered by sport and commercial hunters who used to go out by the trainload from St. John's and intercept the herds as they migrated south across the trans-island railroad tracks. Some small herds still remain, and the first heavy snows bring a restlessness to the outport men as their eyes turn briefly from the sea towards the land, and their thoughts go to the southward-moving herds. Caribou are forbidden to them now, by ukase of a government which wishes to reserve the remaining deer as targets for wealthy mainlanders; but the peoples of the coves are not to be deprived so easily. On a December day when the west wind whips the snow into driving billows across the inland world, white-clad figures drift quietly out from amongst the houses and take the Country Path.

When they return, they do so in darkness; and the creak of the loaded slides on brittle snow is all that betokens their approach. In the morning, life in the outports continues in its accustomed patterns; but the merchants note with disgust that for the next few weeks the housewives show remarkably little interest in purchasing salt beef or pork.

The World of Waters

The world of the outport man is the world of waters. He has eyes for little save the sea. His constant thoughts lie with it. When he steps outside his door his glance lifts unconsciously towards the sky, then drops to the line between sky and water, and finally interrogates the face of the sea itself. Weather and water are preoccupations ingrained in him since childhood. His proper existence is aquatic; all else is peripheral to him. Because he is of the sea, he does not sentimentalize about it. He neither loves, hates nor fears it; but holds it in abiding respect. And it is perhaps this, as much as anything, which gives him his enduring respect for himself.

The world of water is a complex one even for those who only know its surface. Men from the outports may ship as seamen on coasting vessels; aboard an ocean-going freighter; on tugboats; on icebreakers or cable ships; or they may go as fishermen in every kind of vessel from one-man dories to the giant new steel draggers. They may even go afoot, upon the frozen world of the pack ice, as the sealers do in the spring of the year.

The outport man comes to his marriage with the sea slowly, but certainly. As a child of three or four years he comes to know the landwash, to recognize and be familiar with the sounds and smells of the sea's edge in quiet and in storm. A year or two later he has found his way to the stage-head where he will spend hours fishing for little tomcods or sailing model boats. At seven or eight he goes with an uncle or with his father in a dory to jig for squid; or perhaps to wade knee-deep in the breakers on some gravel beach dipping up capelin in a wicker basket. By the time he is ten or eleven he will have his own lobster pots and will think nothing (nor will his parents) of rowing single-handed in a dory for several miles to jig for cod. In winter he will join his fellows playing the dangerous game of "copying" – leaping from floe to floe across the salt ice, as the grown man must do when he joins a sealing ship. In late summer and early autumn the youngster learns to make fish by helping members of his family split and salt a few quintals (a quintal is 112 pounds) of cod – not to sell, but to eat at the family table. By the time he is thirteen or fourteen he has done almost all those things which have comprised the life of fishermen and seamen on these coasts for hundreds of years. The recapitulation is complete, and what began as pastimes have become the man's way of life. He has become one with the world of waters.

In the beginning the liveyers fished from small skiffs or shallops. The fish were "plenty" then. A man rowed or sailed his boat to the nearby grounds, dropped a light anchor and set about jigging to such effect that he would soon be knee-deep in fish. Then he rowed home, gutted his fish, split it, salted it and finished his work as the day finished. If he had a bumper catch, his wife and children would help him split and salt. During the day, if it was fine, the women and girl-children would spread the salt fish on the flakes to cure.

This was a way of life the antiquity of whose origins escapes the reach of our inquisitive probings into the past. The jigger, a decoy fish suspended by its snout with large hooks embedded in its tail, has a known history extending back for six thousand years. A version of it in my possession, carved in soapstone by fishermen two thousand years ago, is nearly identical with the leaden jiggers that are still being cast and used by the outporters of the Sou'west Coast.

Jigging was the way it was done in the beginning, and there are still a few old men who stubbornly retain it as their preferred fishing method. But for most men it was pushed into the background by the development of hand-lines. These consist of long, heavy lines to which "sudlines" (short leaders), each carrying a baited hook, are fastened at intervals of a fathom. Working from a dory, two men can set several "tubs" (perhaps half a mile) of line, anchored and buoyed at both ends. When the line is all out they return to the starting point to "haul their gear" and, with luck, may take a fish from almost every hook. "Fish," be it noted, in Newfoundland means codfish and nothing else.

With the switch to hand-lining came an increased need for bait. During the course of the year a fantastic variety of bait is used as, when and if it becomes available. Mussels and clams will serve when nothing else can be found. During the late winter and early spring the bait is herring, taken in shimmering thousands from nets set off the headlands and in the runs between the islands. In early summer the capelin – small, sleek, brilliantly coloured little fishes – storm the beaches in untold millions to lay their eggs at the high-water mark. In summer the squid strike into the shore and men fill their dories with them. Seine nets are used to catch the primitive sand lance. In older times sea birds, both young and old, were used extensively. Fishing for bait was an important and highly specialized skill among Newfoundlanders.

Hand-lining is still done from two-man dories. Some men simply prefer the open boats, the heave and thrust of the great seas, the cut and slash of wind and spray, to the relative protection offered by bigger craft.

One January day when the temperature was down to 20 degrees and the salt spray froze on the oars and on the dory's gunwales, I went hand-lining with Uncle Tom, a man almost seventy years of age. For hours he worked his gear barehanded while I huddled in the stern sheets and slowly perished. When we got back to the cove that evening I was in a state. "By God," I told him angrily, "it's bloody well inhuman for a man to have to get his living like this. It's a crime!"

Uncle Tom turned to me with mild surprise in his faded eyes. "Not human did ye say? Why, me dear man, 'tis the finest kind of life. Think of they poor fellows on the draggers now, gone from home a week and maybe two. But we'uns gets home each evening, and there's the woman waitin' and the fire roaring up the stack. A crime you calls it?"

All the same, hand-lining is dying. It has been supplanted by long-lining, which is essentially the same thing except that bigger, enclosed and much more powerful boats are used. They carry crews of from two to eight, and can work far out at sea, many miles from their home ports, setting miles of gear each day. Two men in a small long-liner can bring in as much as four thousand pounds a day when the fish are plenty; and if they received a fair price for their catch, they would make as good a livelihood as a man could wish for. But there's the rub. Cod, gutted and delivered to the door of the fish plant, may fetch only a few cents a pound, although it sells to the consumer on the mainland for twenty times as much.

A low price for the catch is and always has been the noose around the necks of Newfoundland fishermen. Before the Second World War, most of the offshore fishery (deep-sea, as opposed to the inshore fishery carried on from small boats fishing close to home) was done by schooners equipped with fleets of dories, owned and outfitted by large and small merchants and merchant companies. Men often went out for months aboard these vessels; they starved and froze and all too often drowned while hand-lining or jigging from open dories far out of sight of land. If they survived they were lucky to get starvation pay. Nowadays diesel-powered draggers with huge otter trawls (big nets that are dragged along the bottom) catch whatever may be there and, in the pro-cess, rip up the spawning beds as well. Those outport men who manage to get berths on the draggers must spend a week or ten days at a time at sea. But their share of the returns is by no means commensurate with the value of the catch. Life on a dragger is demanding and exhausting, yet this is not a matter for complaint. A mate from the Burgeo fleet described the draggermen's feelings in these words: "Nobody minds rough weather and hard times at sea. We're used to that. It suits us, you might say. Nobody stays ashore because of that. But times has changed, and these times people wants their fair and proper share. I'd never blame them if they stays ashore once they finds out there's nothing in it if they goes to sea."

The sea is the abode of riches, but precious little of that wealth has ever rubbed off on the hands of Newfoundland fishermen. It is a point modern politicians and bureaucrats carefully avoid when they cite the poverty of the outports as an excuse for closing them down. They would do better to admit what they know all too well: that this is the poverty of exploitation. They would do well to alter the imbalance between the earnings of the fishermen and the earnings of the plant owners and middle-men, as a just and honest means of maintaining the viability of the outports. They would also do well to acknowledge that the outports are not, and never have been, dependent on a single type of fishing.

The sea at their door offers the outport people a tremendous diversity of gainful work. Apart from the cod, redfish, sole and haddock fisheries (which is where the interests of the big operators lie), the outport men can and do take halibut, herring, mackerel, turbot, swordfish, salmon, lobsters, shrimp and many other creatures of the sea.

"St. John's just wants to be clear of we," a middle-aged fisherman in Ramea told me. "Little them fellows care if us has to leave all that's dear to we. Why don't they give we the chance to work here where us belongs? There's still fish in the sea, and we'se the byes could catch 'em if us had the half-a-chance."

There is no doubt that he is right. I have visited many comparable coasts in other parts of the world whose small fishing communities faced survival problems similar to those of the outport people of Newfoundland. There has been no depopulation of those coasts. People who have always been fishermen and seamen and who wished to continue in that way of life have been given the chance to do so. In Norway, Iceland, Shetland, the Faeroe Islands, Finland and the U.S.S.R. it is government policy to provide meaningful assistance to the coastal dwellers so that they can achieve a way of life compatible with modern standards, but in a manner of their own choosing – and from the sea. And this humane and rational approach has brought big dividends to the nations concerned: ships flying their flags ply the world's seas; their fisheries are important economic assets. Those countries have put themselves in the forefront of ocean transport and of the harvesters of the oceanic farms to which we must turn with increasing need if we are to feed the human species.

Newfoundland had the men. The men had the skill and the will. All the advantages were theirs – save one. Those who held their future in their hands turned contemptuously away from the world of waters. And so it is the fleets of other countries which now sail the world's oceans – fleets belonging to nations which were able to distinguish between the illusion and the substance of progress; to nations which gave *their* seafaring people "the half-a-chance."

IV

Men, Seals and Ships

Although the patterns of human life along the several coasts of Newfoundland were similar in many ways, they were not all of a piece. Those who dwelt in the northern bays and coves found themselves barred off from the sea for several months each year by the southward-flowing arctic ice. The ice denied them access to the cod for much of the winter and well into the spring so that their summer fishery had to be particularly intense. The ice brought them a special opportunity as well. It provided them with the seal fishery . . . and therein lies a story unique to the annals of man and sea.

Apart from material credited to a specific source, this section of the book is derived from my own researches and from many gams with Newfoundland sealers. For literary purposes, I have presented much of it in the first person and have given fictional attribution to some of the narrators. However, the story itself is in no way invented but is the remembered and recorded truth about the sealers of Newfoundland.

The Northern Baymen

I was born out of them – and into them – part of the seventh generation to make a new beginning within an old continuity in that great bight of Newfoundland's northeast coast called Bonavista Bay.

Ours was a timeless way of life. Three centuries ago when our ancestors crossed the Western Ocean they had already been committed to the sea since time out of memory. They neither knew, nor wished for, any way of life not of the sea. Because the land meant little to them, except as a place to rest, build one's vessel or repair one's gear, they did not greatly care what kind of land it was. As long as it was washed by fruitful waters, any bald lump of an islet or rocky cleft on the mainland shore was good enough.

The off-lying islands in the northern bays were favoured by our people because they lay handy to the fishing grounds and that was where our lives were centred. When men had to row, or depend on a little lug sail to get them to and from the fishing, it counted more to be near the grounds than to live in a fine, snug place on shore. The offer islands were stern, unfriendly lumps of rock naked to the pounding seas from the North Atlantic, half-drowned in spindrift when the nor'easters blew, and cut off from the mainland for weeks and months when the arctic pack drove down amongst them. Yet, wherever they offered any kind of shelter for the boats, there our settlements took root and grew, clinging like limpets between wind and water.

I remember how the little settlement on Braggs Island, where I spent much of my childhood, would come alive before daybreak on a summer's morn. We woke to no belated cock-crow but to the bark of the single-cylinder "make-and-breaks." The slow, heavy explosions were the pulse of the place. Skiffs and punts would dawdle a while in the narrow runs while the men hauled herring nets for their supply of bait.

The inshore fishery was the way of life for a good many Braggs Islanders but not for all. My father and his brothers mostly left the inshore fishery alone. "Small boats," they used to say, "is for small men." For them the fishery meant a summer voyage to Labrador for cod. June saw the schooner fleet sail out from every little cove along the northern coast. From Trinity, all round the shores of Bonavista Bay; from Fogo, Twillingate, from Notre Dame, and west to Cape St. John, two or three hundred vessels flying free! All punching to be first upon the cod-fish grounds that ran all the way down north from Belle Isle Strait nearly a thousand miles to Chidley Cape. Hundreds of white-winged ships all racing for the prime cod trap berths at Domino, Groswater Bay, Wild Bight, Cut Throat, Cape Harrigan and Makkovik, Nain, Manvers, Mugford and Saglek, Ramah and Iron Strand . . . And, when the cod struck in, then the long northern days—short nights—hauling the traps; cutting and splitting fish on deck; salting it down, until the vessel had her "saving crop" and, with good luck, a bumper voyage. In September month the ships drove south like birds, dispersing to the myriad coves from whence they came.

That was one-half of it. The other was the late autumnal voyage taking the "made fish" (salt bulk or dried) past Baccalieu and south around to St. John's town. The fish would there be sold; with luck, the merchants' debts repaid, and then renewed as men bought the winter's grub: cases of tea, barrels of flour, 'lasses and butter, and salt pork. When all was stowed below, the schooners cleared for home. November it would be by then, with winter storms already battering a snow-smeared coast. Those were hard times to be at sea, and every year the Widow Maker took her toll. One June when I was young, my Uncle Thomas shipped as second hand to Skipper 'Lias Glover, bound down the Labrador with fifteen sharemen in the schooner *Kindly Light*. Many's the time he used to tell that tale.

Me sons, they never was such plenty of fine fish before! We loaded her right to the hatches, penned a hundred quintal more on deck and then bore up for home – the twentieth day of August month it were. The weather was nor'west and so we made the passage home to Braggs in just five roaring days. Having no long delay in Bonavista Bay we cleared again for St. John's town and ran her down in one long reach.

The price of fish was something wonderful that year. When we had settled up, we took our sharemen's bills and near bought out the place. Plenty of grub, me sons! Yard goods and ribbands for the women and the maids. Twine enough for to knit a hundred nets. It looked to be the bestest voyage we lads had ever seen.

We bore away for Braggs before a sou'east breeze. Next day we raised the white snow-duster on the Nor'ard Head and altered for the cove . . . but as we come about on the new tack the ship heeled over to a sudden heavy gust; lay down until her rail was under and the scuppers running green. Up in the fo'c'sle head the galley stove – red hot it were, for 'twas a bitter day – tore loose, plunged thwartship into a drum of kerosene.

Then come a dreadful sight! Enough to make a dead man stand and stare. The flames run up to heaven in the time it took for we to man the boats. We just got clear, and nothing but the clothes we stood up in. Like a great torch, she went, and not a single thing that mortal man could do. Up on the Nor'ard Head the people gathered, and they stood and watched her burn. By the Lard Jasus, byes, it were a cruel cut. Our whole year's voyage condemned. Hard times for Braggs that day, when we folk watched the *Kindly Light* burn down and sink away.

In November of the year when I turned ten my father put to sea from Wesleyville as master of the topsail schooner *Elsie Blake*, bound foreign with a lading of salt fish for Genoa. Mother and I spent that winter with her kin, Ephram and Gramma Glover, out on Braggs. Only a dozen families clung to that bald rock but they'd been rooted there so long we were knit up together tight as a school of capelin in a net. What pleasured any one of them gave pleasure to them all, and pain for one was pain for everyone. I well remember how, early in January – the bay already running thick with drifting ice – my young first cousin, Millie Feltham, "felt her heart." All hands knew that she would likely die unless we could get help. 'Twas easier said than done. The wind was blowing half-a-gale sou'west, heaving the ice like moving mountains on a freezing sea. But all the same, five men agreed to take a big trap skiff twelve miles across that grinding waste of ice to Wesleyville. There was a travelling doctor somewhere on the mainland coast, and fetching he was her one hope.

They were away three days, and no one did a tap while they were gone; could think of nothing but the men out there among the floes. Grandfather Glover – he was one of them. It was his boat. As hour followed hour, day followed day, Gram Glover waited silent by the landward window glass, still as a monument, her mind bound out across that heaving wilderness of ice 'til, out of pity, Mother tried to shift Gram's mind to something else. "Don't fret yourself so much, me dear. They'm be all right." Gram Glover turned and took my mother's eye, and softly said: "A woman's thought has *got* to fly beside her man upon the sea. Her thought, aye, and her prayers as well. It is the least as we can do for them as cares for we."

Cousin Millie Feltham was fifteen when the Braggs Island men brought the doctor back and saved her life. And the very next year Josh Barbour "took her walking," as the saying was. He had come out to Braggs from Greenspond for a Christmas visit, being related to the Glovers on his father's side. My grandfather, Skipper Ephram, remembered how it came about.

He were a wandering lad, were Josh, but when he struck onto Millie, why he just took root. We couldn't get clear of he at all. He was still under our roof in March when sealing time come round. Evenings he'd sit by the kitchen stove polishing up his big black boots with our best butter and molasses, and then away he'd go, a-courting.

He would sit in Feltham's kitchen helping Skipper 'Lias knit up twine for salmon nets, but his eye was mostly on the maid, and he spiled a powerful good lot of twine. Going on past midnight, the family would give it up and go off to sleep, leaving Millie and Josh on the two ends of the daybed; and all hands knowed where that was bound to end. Come the time Josh left for a sealing berth aboard the *Ranger*, 'twas all fixed up for they to be married in November month. After Josh come back from the Labrador fishery in the fall of the year, he shipped for St. John's in a Fogo schooner to buy what gear he needed to set up on his own with Millie. But, homeward bound, that schooner run into a living gale. Took the sticks right out of her and drove her out to sea. 'Twas near two weeks afore the wreck was sighted by a steamer and the crew took off. Trouble was, that steamer was bound for the Argentine and, between the jigs and the reels, Josh never did get home 'til January come around again.

'Course, Millie had got her baby by then – a right strong boy, born with a hood over his head. The finest kind of luck, that was, for a baby born with a hood can never drown. Josh come home too late for the christening of his boy, but in plenty time for a proper wedding!

'Twas a good year for all hands. Lots of fish and a high price, so they was more'n a drop or two on the go. You'd never sniff it in ary house, for the women wouldn't have it; but all we fellows had a bottle hid away. Skipper 'Lias had laid in a keg of black rum against the wedding, and Josh carried home a couple of gallons of that white stuff from St. Pierre . . . like dynamite it were!

The wedding was called for the first Sunday the minister might happen to visit the island. He'd come two or three times a year for marryings and baptizings. But some folks was not contented to wait for he, and so the corks come out well afore sailing day! One evening down in me own fish store, Uncle Abe Oram and Skipper 'Lias set out to find which one of they could jig the longest and the bestest. 'Twas never settled 'cause Uncle Abraham bursted clean through the floor of the room and lost his rubber boots into the landwash.

'Twas dirty weather on the wedding day, with a good breeze blowing off the water and the snow drifting like smoke. Millie wore her Da's big coat over her wedding rig, with her veil a-drawing like a t'gallant sail in the wind. The banging of them old swiling guns when the men give her the salute was something for to hear, and the smell of the black powder sticks in me nostrils yet. Aye, 'twas the finest kind of wedding Millie and Josh Barbour had that day. Skipper Elias and Aunt Maggie Feltham was some proud of they!

Skipper 'Lias, now, he were a high-lining fisherman and swiler all his life – there was none better as we knew. 'Lias were *good* for it. His woman, Maggie, come from the same mould as he.

They was no lighthouse out on Braggs, those times. Come thick o'fog or starm o'wind and snow, 'twere hard enough to make the land. Many's the vessel and her crew was lost because of that. Aunt Maggie's poor old dad, skipper and owner of the coasting schooner *John and Jericho*, was inward bound for Braggs one winter ev'ning from St. John's and missed the offer isle what marks the run. 'Twas thick o'snow and no man seen the land until it were too late. The vessel drove onto the sunkers off the Popplestone. And not one soul was saved.

Maggie was only half-ways growed, those times, but old enough to know her mind. Next day she rousted out we island men and made us set a spar and tackle on the top of Nor'ard Head. From that day on, summers and winters, every ev'ning time she'd fill a lamp – kerosene-fired, with a red glass globe – then, with her gert cloak swirling in the wind, she'd take her way in sickness or in health, come starm or sleet, and hist that light to help poor sailormen steer homeward through the night.

Skipper Elias and Aunt Mag were married forty-seven year and raised a won'erful fine crowd of lads and maids – five daughters and six sons – and never a one as knew a time of want. For 'Lias was a driving man, as would have worked the devil to his grave. Thirty spring seasons to the ice and forty summers fishing down the coast of Labrador. He stayed right up 'til, in his seventy-seventh year, he took the cancer in his throat. They carried him away to finish out his voyage in hospital in St. John's town. For the first time in her life, Aunt Maggie quit our rock to go along of he, leaving her youngest son to tend the Nor'ard light.

The skipper wasted for a month. His flesh went clean away to nothing on the last of it, and then Aunt Maggie brought he home. She travelled with the coffin up to Gambo on the morning train. Six of we met her there, carried the box aboard John Oram's boat and thought to leave for Braggs at once, 'til Aunt Mag spoke: "I'd take it kindly, could you bide 'til dark," she said, "so he can see the light shine out once more on Nor'ard Head."

I supposes 'twas a hard life, accordin' to what they says nowadays, but it never seemed so to we. We was all into it, men and maids together. It took strong hearts and hands, but it give us strength in the doing. And 'twas not all work and no play. By November month the year's voyage was wound up – gear stowed away, fish made and shipped, schooners all laid up and gone to sleep. Was nothing for it then but to snug down for the winter. Then come the dances and socials and weddings and concerts in every place,

and visiting back and forth all round the bay. Bonfire Night –
some calls it Guy Fawkes Day – was always a gert time, with folk
from all around coming to Braggs to act out something for the
big concert.

Aunt Rene Sturge now, she was the rale one! Belonged to
Pinchards Bight, she did. She'd clumb onto the stage and do her
skit, and 'twould make a dogfish laugh hisself to death. She'd
stand up there with a scrubboard and a bucket full of suds, and
Uncle Peter Sturge's dirty underclothes, and wash away at they,
all the time carrying on about the poor old fellow, making him
out to be a proper bosthoon, getting it out on him for the troubles
he'd give her all year round.

But the bestest time of all was Christmas. The fun began New
Christmas Day, December 25th, and run right on to Old Christmas Day, January 6th. That was the jollification! For twelve nights
there'd be a time at someone's place, a different one each night.
And all the while the mummers was on the go. They was dressed
up in every sort of guise, with their faces hid so's none would
know them. Crowds of mummers would go along from house to
house, knocking on the doors and bawling in them squeaky mummers' voices. Once inside they'd start a dance. They'd snatch up
the women in the house and dance them 'til their legs give out.
People would try to guess who they was, and if they guessed
a'right, the mummers was bound to throw back their hoods and
show up. Then they'd all drink a drop of stuff wih hot water and
sugar, and tramp off into the dark again. Ah, yiss, me sons . . .
them was the enjoying times!

Sails to the Ice

During the summer and autumn ours was a world of water, but
for most of the rest of the year it was a world of ice. In late
November a great tongue of the polar pack began thrusting southward out of Baffin Bay and by Christmas time had pushed right
down the coast of Labrador to Belle Isle Strait. By late January it
had engulfed all of northern Newfoundland and was even swelling out over the Grand Banks. Then the whole of the seas we
sailed in summer were hidden beneath ice fields. Nor'east gales

drove the pack tight to our unyielding coasts until the floes began to ride over one another, forming mountainous ridges and compacting the fields until they became one vast, unbroken plain stretching to the farthest horizon. Then westerly gales might drive the ice offshore again until the great white plain cracked and split, allowing leads and lakes of open water, smoking and steaming in the bitter cold, to form between the floes. At night new ice skimmed over the leads, was crushed by the wheeling motion of the pack and formed its own fields of shattered slob. Here and there, towering bergs ploughed through the thickest pack as if it was no more than brittle candy. When the long Atlantic swell set in, the icy plain heaved to the motion until mounded hills and deep, rounded valleys began to crawl slowly across the fields, setting up a terrible conflict that growled like steady thunder, and the cold air glittered with shattered ice crystals.

To those who do not know them, the northern ice fields appear to be a world that life abhors. Yet it is truly a living world. Long, long ago two kinds of seals, the harps and the hoods, discovered that the ice world offered everything they needed. The rich underlying waters sheltered millions of small fishes upon which the seals could feed. The ice gave them a place to rest, and to bear and nurture their young, secure from any dangers which might threaten from the land. The harps, who once numbered many millions, lived in great companies, hundreds of thousands of them sporting together in the open leads and lakes between the floes, or bearing their young together in vast nurseries that stretched for miles across the wheeling pans. The hoods, larger and not so many, preferred to live in family groups consisting of an old dog hood, his bitch and their single blue-backed pup.

The pups of both kinds were born in early March on the southern stretches of their floating world. Three weeks later the young, grown roly-poly on the rich milk of their mothers, were weaned and took to the sea to begin their own independent lives. This was the time when the ice edge had reached its southern limits and was beginning to shrink northward again under the warmth of the spring sun. The seals drifted north with it, travelling right the way to the Arctic Ocean. But when the ice surged south again in autumn, the harp and hood nations swam in its vanguard, repeating an age-old migration which every year took them many thousands of miles.

It was the annual visit of these mighty herds that, as much as anything, led my forebears to make their homes on the bleak coasts of Newfoundland's northern bays. My grandfather used to tell us how it came about.

'Tis often said, and a good many believes in it, as codfish was the whole backbone of Newfoundland. Maybe 'twas so for some parts, and maybe 'tis mainly so these times, but 'twarn't always so.

On the first of it, the people as come to the northern bays was only summer liveyers who sailed up in their boats in the spring of the year from eastward – from Trinity and Conception bays for the most part – and were gone out of it again in the fall of the year. They was only after cod; but back two hundred years ago some of them fell onto the swile fishery and once they had it they never let it go. They took to staying in them little places in the north right through the winter so as to be handy to the swiles, and in the end 'twas the swile fishery as built up all them places right round from Cape Bonavista clear to Cape St. John.

It was the French who first took up the seal fishery, although of course the Eskimos and Indians of Newfoundland and Labrador had been catching seals with nets and harpoons for thousands of years before Europeans first came this way. The English were slow to follow the French. Cod was their prime quarry and they were single-minded about it. It was not until some of them, encroaching northwestward into French fishing grounds during summer voyages, found that seals could be a better source of livelihood, that real settlement of the northern bays began. That discovery, and the consequent need to overwinter in order to be on hand when the seals arrived, resulted in the eventual English settlement of the northeastern coast by nearly four hundred little clusters of our people. In summer and early autumn they mostly fished cod and salmon; but early in the new year seals became the centre of their lives.

January was the time when tremendous herds of old dog seals and pregnant bitches came streaming south along the coasts and into the bays, in advance of the ice that was their abiding home. They came in unbelievable numbers. About 1760 a French seal-fisher, wintering on the northern tip of Newfoundland, wrote of seeing a "string" of old seals that filled the sea from the landwash seaward to the limit of his vision, and took ten days and nights to pass.

As soon as the first outriders of these herds were sighted, all the able-bodied men of the northern bays turned out in small boats to set long, heavy seal nets – some of them five hundred feet in length – reaching seaward from the headlands, or strung out between the offshore islands. The commander of a British naval squadron who visited our coast late in the eighteenth century reported the inhabitants then owned at least two thousand of these nets and that seal oil and sealskins accounted for at least half their harvest from the seas.

Not much time passed before our forebears went the French one better and began gunning for seals in the open leads near shore. In the beginning they went out in open rowboats, but soon they began using larger craft and venturing farther and farther into the ice. By about 1780 they were using shallops – sail boats about thirty feet long with a shelter deck fore and aft, but open amidships. In these little vessels a crew of a half dozen men would sometimes cruise the leads in the bay ice for a week at a time, hunting the old seals with muzzle-loading swiling guns.

Although the hunt with nets and guns was aimed at adult seals, occasionally the people reaped a windfall of a different kind. Once or twice in every generation the pans of whelping ice, laden with newborn whitecoats, would be driven by nor'east gales into contact with the land. Then men, women, children, even dogs, rushed pell-mell out over the raftered ice to reach the nurseries where they made a slaughter of the young seals. They still talk of one such foray over the shorebound ice of Bonavista Bay that yielded 140,000 whitecoat sculps – a sculp being the pelt with the underlying layers of fat still attached.

Happenstances such as this whetted the appetite of the more daring men and they began trying to reach the whelping ice in their shallops. Sometimes they were lucky. Other times both men and boats were crushed and lost. The answer was bigger, stronger vessels and, about 1795, such ships were being built–and so the ship seal fishery to the ice was born.

In the beginning the ships were small schooners, heavily timbered and strengthened. They were rough, tough little vessels, and their crews, who were also their builders, were just as rough and tough. A dozen men would set out into the ice in one of these little ships for what might turn out to be a month-long voyage, most of it to be spent drifting helplessly with the pack, their vessel jammed and likely to be crushed at any moment. They rarely even had a stove aboard but lived cold and wet, eating uncooked food and drinking melt water from pools on the ice.

The losses suffered by these early men and vessels were terrible. Sometimes a quarter of the ships were lost in a single season. However, those that did reach the nurseries and managed to return home brought such rich cargoes that it was not long before the whole of Newfoundland began to go seal-crazy. Thousands of vessels were built all along the northern and eastern coasts to "prosecute the sealing game." These gradually increased in size until brigs of 150 tons were being built for the ice-hunt. The top of it all came in 1884 when 360 sailing vessels carrying nearly 11,000 sealers (which was the biggest portion of the able-bodied men of the island) went to the northern ice and brought back 700,000 seal sculps–most of them whitecoats.

The swiling frenzy mounted with each succeeding year–bringing with it appalling losses of ships and men. Between 1810 and 1870 more than 400 sealing vessels were sunk at the ice and, although nobody bothered to keep account of how many men were lost, there must have been well over a thousand drowned, crushed or frozen to death. They did not die alone. Between 1838 and 1870, the sealing fleet brought in more than twelve million sculps!

The odourless, tasteless oil refined from seal fat commanded premium prices in Europe where it was used for lighting, cooking fat and lubrication. It was as valuable as whale oil, but the sculps had an additional worth since the de-fatted skins made excellent leather. When gas began to replace oil lamps, seal oil continued to increase in value, being used in many industrial processes including the making of high explosives.

Until about the middle of the nineteenth century, swiling remained mainly a local business with the people of each settlement sharing in the ship-building, the hunt, the preparation of the fat and the skins; and all hands sharing in the returns. Then things began to change. As the profits mounted and the cost of building and outfitting bigger ships also increased, one or two families in each settlement began to engross the business to themselves. In short enough order they came to own the seal fishery, and the old, communal way of life was lost forever. The sons and grandsons of the men who brought the Newfoundland seal fishery into being–who built it with their hands and their hearts . . . and their lives–sank back to the level of hired men, and underpaid and maltreated ones, at that. A description, written by one of the new outport aristocracy built on seals, gives something of the flavour of how things were in the swiling game during the last half of the nineteenth century.

St. Stephen's Day, December 26th, was the day the crews all gathered at the homes of the captains and owners to sign on for the spring hunt. Early in February the crews would begin hauling firewood and logs from the forests, ready to be turned into fuel and into spars and punts for the vessels that would soon be ready to leave for the ice. Their labour was not paid for but was considered part of the sealers' duty. All the men got out of it was their grub.

About February 25th, the captains began to get things ready. March 1st was sailing day. At the first crack of dawn windlasses were manned and sails were hung on the yards ready to sheet-home as soon as the anchor was hove short, each captain eager to be in the lead.

It often happened that the harbour was frozen over with from two to four feet of solid ice. All the crews joined together and began sawing a channel to open water. This meant a good deal of labour and occupied ten days or more. As the blocks of ice

were sawn they were sunk under the edge of the floes and the
ships moved down the channel. With sometimes forty or fifty
ships and sixteen hundred men in the parade, it made a great
sight. Sometimes when the mouth of the harbour was reached
the whole outer bay would still be frozen over. Then there was
nothing to do but wait for a swell to heave in and break up the
ice. Some years a month went by before the swell would heave
in. Mutiny was often at hand in those times due to skippers trying
to save on food. Captains were martinets. There was old Bill
Whelan, master and owner for many years of the brig *Hound*.
Some declared he had sold himself to the devil. He always began
his day with a toddy of rum. Every half-watch he'd have another
or so. Blow high, blow low, rain, snow or frost, from dawn to dark
he always kept the deck. When he went below at night he had
his skin full, but the next day he was back again, fresh as a rose.
His officers were hard as nails, and the Old Man was iron, but
with the constant driving of ship and men, he always got the
seals.*

The passing of the old, egalitarian way of life in the northern bay
settlements and the growth of local aristocracies based largely on
wealth from the seals did not go unremarked. In the 1860s a St.
John's clergyman, born well ahead of his age, wrote what was,
for those times, a bitter denunciation of the new system.

Even when death at its most fearful puts not a sudden period to the
sufferings of the sealer, the toils and hardships and perils of the
voyage are indescribable; while he has nought to sustain him but
the fond hope of being able to realize a temporary provision for the
affectionate wife and children. The seal fishery is a lottery where
all is risk and uncertainty, but the risk, we must confess, is not
equally distributed. Take for instance a vessel of 120 tons. Her
merchant-owner may gain a profit of a thousand pounds or more if

*Adapted from The Log of "Bob" Bartlett by Captain Robert A.
Bartlett.

the voyage prospers. But also involved in her success are some thirty fishermen – they may each gain twenty pounds. The merchant, to gain a thousand, has risked a capital of perhaps two thousand. The sealer, to gain twenty, has risked his all – his life. If the voyage fails, the owner still has his ship, but the poor man returns with the loss of his labour and his time, penniless. If the vessel founders or be dashed to pieces in the ice, insurance relieves the merchant, but if thirty lives are lost, then thirty widows and perhaps a hundred orphans shriek their curses on a fishery that gave them no compensation and was the grave of all their hopes . . .

Upon the successful return of a vessel, one-half of the proceeds is handed over to the owner, the other half divided amongst the men whose toil and daring produced it. But the merchant's half is clear, while the poor man's half is clipped. He is obliged to pay hospital dues and is taxed by the merchant to pay not only for the tools and materials used in the fishery, but a further sum of £3.10 berth money for the privilege of being allowed to hazard his life to secure a fortune for the merchant.

By about 1860 the pattern of the seal fishery as an organized exploitation of both men and seals had become firmly established. It was not to change significantly until the sealing game was finally played out. Yet here and there, in the most isolated of the northern settlements, a very few men continued to play it by the old rules up to the very end, thereby providing a living memory of the way it used to be in the time of my forebears. Neddie Budgel was one of those who stuck to the old ways.

They says my great-great-grandfather was the first Budgel come to Cottrells Cove, and he settled there because of the swiles. Nets was the thing in them early times and wonderful big nets they was. But a good many of them old people would rather go gunning. They'd go off in rodneys – four-oared open boats – in January and February before the field ice filled up Notre Dame Bay entirely. They was after the old swiles, the big old harps, but was always glad for a try at the two-year-olds, the bedlamers, for they was best in the pot. They had them old Poole guns, as some calls them, swile guns eight feet long, and firing a charge would kick you clean out of the boat if you didn't mind.

Later times they took to using bigger boats with a lugsail as well as oars. They'd go right into the ice with them boats, March-month when the swiles was whelping; but mainly they went swatching – shooting the old swiles on the edge of the ice and in the leads.

Two hundred year and more, I suppose, Budgels has swiled hereabouts. Me brother and me, we'm still at it, and just about the last to give it a lick. The spring of 1962 they was a good patch of whitecoats not forty mile off Cape St. John. Heard the ships talking about it on the ship-to-shore radio. So we set off in our twenty-eight-foot trapboat – wide open she was, except for a bit of a cuddy in the head, but good power into her. They was lots of loose ice but nary a swile until we got near the Grey Islands, and then the wind come easterly and the ice got so tight we had to haul the boat out onto it. And blow! She blew a living starm for five days. We was snug enough on the ice. Had a little ile stove to bile up the kettle. Course, it warn't exactly like being home . . .

Ten days we drifted. At last the wind come westerly again and the ice opened but we daren't put the boat into it. 'Twas all broke up. She'd have been chewed to pieces like a crackie dog chews up a bone. Ten days more, and we reckoned we'd drifted eighty mile or more afore the ice got good and open. Then we launched off, and bejasus if we didn't strike into old swiles. Leads was full of them. We spent the next two days swatching and filled her up. Put 206 sculps in that little boat and she loaded down till every little slop of water come over her gunwales.

'Twas time to make for home. We cut a sou'west course till we raised Fogo Island light, and after that it was nothing but a pastime to run the forty miles back to the cove. The merchants in St. John's got nary smell of our fat. We trucked it to Port aux Basques, shipped it off to Halifax and cleared $1,070.00. That's swilin', bye! That's the way to do her!

When my grandfather was a boy there were still a few people living on the Wadham Islands, although these are nothing more than a pile of bald-headed rocks, wide open to the Atlantic from the north and east. It was a terribly wild and lonely place but handy to the cod grounds as well as being right in the way of the old harp seals when they were coming south from Labrador.

The Wadham men were sealers first and cod fishermen second. They thought nothing at all of rowing miles offshore into the open ice in two-man punts, and sometimes they would get caught in a blow and be driven away. One spring three of the little boats were blown eastward in a sea of broken slob until they sighted the Funks, a desolate and dangerous rock forty miles out in the open ocean and the last land before you reach Iceland on a northeast course. The seas were breaking clean over the Funks but the Wadham men knew they had to land or be swept away forever, and so they took the chance. Two of their boats were smashed to pieces, but all the men scrambled ashore and hauled the third boat to safety.

Three days later, when the wind dropped out, they piled all hands into the remaining boat and made for home, but a southeast blizzard caught them and they were adrift for two more days and nights and nearly perished from the cold. Although they were tremendously tough, no human flesh could stand that sort of thing indefinitely, and they were close to giving up when, during the second night, a great white bird, such as none of them had ever seen before, came out of the howling night and began circling their boat. It stayed with them until dawn and then flew off, mewling like a cat. They set their course after it and late that same day raised the Wadhams. The Wadham people were sure the bird was a sign sent to save their men; and as long as they continued to live on those islands, none of them would ever shoot any white seabird.

In my time people still told the story of the Wadham "sign," but it was a tale with a happy ending. Many other stories about the inshore sealers end in stark tragedy. Few of these are to be found in Newfoundland's written history, but the Trinity Bay disaster is an exception.

The morning of Saturday, 28th of February, 1892, ushered in a lovely dawn. A soft, bright, balmy air blew from the land over the treacherous ice fields. Small boats were out by early dawn, gunning for seals which had been seen in numbers the previous evening. From Trinity, Ship Cove, Trouty, English Harbour, Salmon Cove and many other small places, the daring ice hunters set off with high hopes to chase the wary seal. In this most exciting and daring of pursuits the Newfoundlander recks not of danger. Difficulties and perils that would afright one not accustomed to the ice fields are mere sport to the hardy native.

On this day seals were few and scattered. In the fierce excitement of the chase many boats rowed far out into the bay heedless of the signs of a coming tempest. A few of the older fishermen, more wary and perhaps less vigorous, noticed the first signs of storm, and before the icy blast came down full force they gained the lee of the land and could row in.

Two hundred and fifteen men were out that day. Many got safe to land only after many hours of tremendous struggle; but the rest, in spite of their heroic efforts, were finally overpowered. The freezing ice tornado swept down upon them and paralyzed their efforts. One bold crew from English Harbour, seeing that all their attempts against the blizzard were in vain, made for the fields of ice. They managed to climb on a pan higher than the rest, where they made a rude shelter out of ice hummocks. Their boat was broken up to make a fire, and with this and some seals they managed to live through the awful night.

Thirteen fishermen were found frozen to death in their little punts. Eleven others were driven up the bay and perished in the bitter dark. The agony of suspense for the dear ones on shore and the sufferings of those poor humble souls in their hour of agony is known only to the Almighty Power who rules the raging of the seas.*

It was the men from the offer islands who were the great seal swatchers in small boats, but it was those from the inner coves,

*Adapted from *History of Newfoundland* by D. W. Prowse.

deep in the bays where good timber could be found, who brought the schooner seal fishery into being and who built it into the burgeoning enterprise it had become by the mid-1800s – burgeoning but fearfully costly of men and ships, as these two letters tell.

> Job Brothers,
> 3rd April, 1862.
> St. John's
> At Sea
>
> Sirs,
>
> I regret that I cannot write to you so encouragingly as I would wish.
>
> After leaving St. John's on the 12th of March I succeeded in getting out through all the ice and kept beating to windward until the 17th evening after I left. When I was 3 miles north of Partridge Point in Green Bay in consort with the Margaret we entered the ice with a heavy breeze of wind from N.N.E. to E.N.E. and a tremendous sea running. Both our ships were leaking and our pumps have been going ever since.
>
> As for seals, I have 430 old Hoods and 460 young Hoods.
>
> As to losses of ships, I am afraid the number will be fearful. I have seen six or eight go down the last few days among which are the Emily Tobin, the Melrose and the Margaret, besides several others I cannot name.
>
> While I am writing there is so much sea, and the ice is so heavy, I cannot tell the moment the sides of my own vessel will be driven in. Since the 20th of March I have drifted from the Funks and we are now off Cape St. Francis and expect to drive to Cape Race before getting clear of the ice. I have Captain Cummins and crew on board since Sunday when they lost the Margaret.
>
> I am yours, sirs, respectfully,
>
> Edward White, Captain

The Manse,
St. Albans Church,
May 12th,1872.

My Dearest Sister:

A heavy sorrow has fallen on us for the loss of the brig *Huntsman*, 120 tons burthen, owned and commanded by Captain Robert Dawe, with a crew of sixty-two. She was wrecked off the coast of Labrador on the night of April 28th while prosecuting the sealing; and therebye was lost her Master and his second son, with forty-one of the crew. The survivors were brought in aboard the brig *Rescue*, Captain Samuel Dawe, from whom we learned particulars of this dreadful event.

On the morning of the 28th, in the vicinity of Cape Charles, a heavy gale with rain sprang up from the northeast which forced both the *Rescue* and the *Huntsman*, who were in company, to seek shelter in the ice. They had not long entered it, and were tightly encompassed when they found it was running very fast in the grip of the tide and was likely to take their ships over some very shoal and dangerous ground. Nevertheless, they did not anticipate danger to life since the land was not far off and the ice lay thick and solid between them and the shore. The wind, however, increased and there was a heavy swell in the ice, and incessant rain, so that the night closed in very dark and gloomy. Yet they still hoped to drift clear of the shoals. They saw no sign of breakers until these were so close they could neither avoid them nor dared they then abandon their vessels.

Suddenly a reef broke directly under the bow of the *Huntsman* sending up such a tremendous sea that the ship was thrown on her beam ends and shattered against the rock, which stood just below the surface.

The *Rescue* was so close that her bowsprit almost overhung the ill-fated vessel. Her crew saw the huge wave rise, heard the shrieks of the poor fellows and the crash of timbers. Some of the *Huntsman*'s crew leapt overboard and were at once crushed or drowned. Most of them, however, took refuge in the rigging. Their Captain was seen from the *Rescue* clinging to the halyards. Twice he was swung far out over the ice and back to the stricken ship. The *Huntsman* then took a final roll and the masts went out of her with a terrible crash and those who had taken refuge in the rigging were flung upon the churning ice where, sad to relate, most of them perished. Only eighteen were rescued and, of these, all but three of the poor fellows were grievously injured from breaking their legs and arms with their fall upon the ice. None of them can tell how they got to safety at all.

When this dreadful news reached us I caused the church bell to be rung; and although it was but Monday morning, many were the sorrowing men and women who came to me seeking some comfort in their terrible affliction. We remain in the deepest distress and hardly know how our small village shall bear the loss which has been laid upon us . . .

Steamers to the Ice

The first sixty years of going to the whelping ice belonged to sail and to the outport settlements, but that began to change when, in the spring of 1862, the sealers were astounded to see billowing black plumes of smoke appear on the horizon. These signalled the beginning of a new age – the coming of steam, and the death knell to sail. The smoke came from two Scots steam-auxiliary whalers taking a look at sealing possibilities before proceeding on their annual voyage for whales in Davis Strait.

Polynia and *Camperdown* could hardly have chosen a worse spring to try their luck. Ice conditions were awesome. A succession of nor'easters had raftered the arctic pack so heavily that the whole sailing fleet was jammed and scores of ships were crushed and lost. The two auxiliary whalers, clipper-bowed and high-masted, belching clouds of coal smoke from their tall, narrow stacks, butted their way into the pack but took such a pummelling they had to withdraw – without having killed a single seal between them. That year it was "landsmen's luck" and the whole population of the Green Bay settlements had gone out over the floes from shore to make the largest kill of whitecoats ever taken from the land.

In May the two steamers continued north and it seemed that their *future* business would not include sealing. However, there was one St. John's merchant-prince-in-the-making, Walter Grieve, who was very thoughtful after the whalers left. True, they had taken no seals, but their performance in the ice, even with tiny steam engines rated at a mere 60 horsepower, had seemed almost miraculous compared with what vessels under sail alone could do.

Walter Grieve did more than think. He sent an agent off to Dundee and bought the little SS *Wolf*, 200 tons, powered by a 30-horsepower auxiliary engine. The bustling St. John's firm of Baine, Johnson and Company got wind of the move and bought a steamer too, the 40-horsepower SS *Bloodhound*.

Between them, the two little wooden steamers brought in 4,300 seals in 1863. It was a small enough showing but it sparked a rush by St. John's merchant firms to buy up any sea-weary steam-auxiliary whalers they could find. Within a decade twenty-six old whalers had been purchased, and in 1873 twenty-two of them brought back 300,000 sculps. The other four had been lost at the ice. *Bloodhound* and *Wolf* were both gone–*Bloodhound* in an incident which was a clear enough indication that the new ships could be almost as vulnerable as their sailing predecessors had been.

. . . The steamers were caught in the same storm with the brig *Huntsman* and, in the dark of the night, the *Bloodhound* struck, or was flung upon, an island of ice and was so much damaged that it was only by the greatest efforts her crew was enabled to keep her afloat until dawn, half an hour after which she suddenly went down. Marooned upon the moving ice, her crew spied the SS *Retriever* jammed in the pack about two miles away, and they made haste towards her. Imagine their feelings when, upon arriving alongside, they found that she too had been shattered by the ice and was fast sinking. There was then nothing for it but for all the men, numbering more than three hundred, to try and make their way over the shifting ice to the distant, rocky shore of Labrador. That they were enabled to do this without great loss of life can only be attributed to the Grace of the Lord.

On reaching the frozen coast they struggled along it to Battle Harbour where the few poor inhabitants did what they could for the destitute sealers. Presently they were joined by the crews of two large sailing vessels, which also had been crushed while pursuing the elusive seal. These distressed men then endured great hardships for some days, being in want of food, clothing, shelter and other necessities, until some of the men spied the SS *Nimrod* at a distance. They tried to attract her attention by making signals. When that failed, our sealers, who are not easily discouraged, finding an ancient and rusty cannon lying on a hill, filled it with a tremendous charge of powder and applied the match. The explosion blew the cannon into a thousand pieces, but those on the *Nimrod* saw the flash or heard the concussion and drew near enough to send men in over the ice.

It was the Scots who first put steam power into the whaling ships and, from the first, the steam auxiliaries built in Dundee were a great success. They were built so strong they were nearly as solid as an ironwood log; but there was precious little space left in them for men. It was hard lines for the whaling crews. Thirty or forty whalers would be packed into one of those small ships like birds in a barrel, but they had luxury accommodations compared to what our fellows got when the whaling ships were bought up by the St. John's merchants for the sealing game. The new owners thought nothing of jamming as many as *two hundred* men into each ship, and keeping them there for weeks on end.

To save on coal, and to increase their power, the whalers were all ship-rigged and, to tell the truth, could often make better speed under a full spread of canvas than under steam. It was said of the little SS *Kite* that whenever she blew her whistle she would come to a dead stop, not having steam enough for whistle and engine both. Still, it was steam power that made these ships cunning in the ice.

Their strength, and the way they could take punishment, was hard to believe. Some of those built in the early 1870s were still afloat, still battling the ice, in the late 1930s. They were such wonderful ice ships that arctic and antarctic expeditions setting out as late as the 1920s still chose the old "wooden walls," as they became known, in preference to modern steel vessels. The wooden sealer SS *Terra Nova*, built in 1885, carried Captain Robert Scott's ill-fated party to the antarctic in 1910. She was one of the last wooden walls ever built and one of the most powerful:

One hundred and eighty-six feet long, her tonnage is 450, and her engine is of 120 h.p. . . . Oak, ironbark and greenheart are the principal woods used . . . her bows are protected by a very heavy stem strengthened with iron ice plates, and the bolts securing the stem plates pass through about ten feet of solid wood . . . the fortifications in the bows consist of huge oak diagonals, two feet in cross section, and two tiers of ice beams almost as heavy extending backward a distance of fifty feet. The planking throughout is over two feet thick.

By the time *Terra Nova* was launched, the arctic whaling game was practically played out. The bowheads were nearly finished and the battered old steam whalers were not wanted anymore in Scotland, so they were bought up for a song by the St. John's merchants. Steam took over at the ice almost completely and, as a result, the St. John's merchants – the Pirates of Water Street, as many of our people still call them – took over the whole sealing business, and the settlements where it had all started were cut out. There was only one thing left for our men to do–work for the St. John's owners aboard the steamers under conditions that were just a bit better than slavery. It was a great time for the Water Street crowd. A good many of them became millionaires, and it seemed they didn't much care how they made their millions. Right from the first, the way they ran the ships was nothing short of criminal.

They was the finest kind of ships, when they was built. Aye, there was none better on the sea. But they got no care from the owners and when they went to the ice some of the skippers used to bate them up something terrible. 'Twas a wonder any of them ever

did come back . . . yet back they come, year after year, some of
them for as long as a man's lifetime . . . I've seen them come in
through the Notch at St. John's so log-loaded the water was
sluicing over their decks and them leaking so bad all hands was
at the pumps or bailing the water out with buckets. They never
had no load lines. Some skippers would fill them to the hatches,
then put near as many sculps again on deck. Oftentimes they'd
start home from the ice, get into the smallest little starm, and
have to run back into the ice for shelter, or down they would
have gone–they were that overloaded. One time Captain Edward
White brought the *Neptune* in with 32,000 seals on deck and
below, and another 6,000 towing on a cable off her quarter! Her
second hand told I: "If an ice-bird had squirted onto we, we'd
have gone down like a stone!" Aye, 'twas cruel the way them
ships was treated and cruel the way the men was treated too . . .
but what fine names they had! *Panther, Tigress, Nimrod* and *Esquimaux* . . . *Proteus, Hector, Lion* and *Eagle* . . . *Polynia, Viking* and
Aurora . . . *Falcon, Hope* and *Ariel* . . . 'twas as good as music just
to say them over to yourself . . .

If the ships were famous, their skippers were even more so, for
they became the supreme folk heroes of Newfoundland. My
father sailed with many of them, and he would talk about them
as if they had been members of his own family.

On the first off, the steamer skippers were mostly Scotsmen,
captains of the Dundee whalers as brought their ships into St.
John's in the spring of the year to take up a crew of our sealers.
That was afore our skippers got the hang of them new kind of
ships. The Scotsmen was the finest kind and they taught our
skippers a good deal.

However, 'twarn't long afore our own skippers took hold of the
steamers, and when they did, my dear man, didn't they make the
seal scutters* fly! Early times, most of the skipper-men hailed

---

*The webbed, compressed hind feet with which seals swim.

from Trinity and Conception bays, but 'twarn't long afore we northern bay men come to the top. As the sailing ships went out and the steamers come in, there was twenty skipper-men for every ship, and didn't they fight for to get hold of a command! That was a fine thing for the owners. They could take their pick, and if a skipper didn't come in top dog, why out he'd go, for there was plenty begging to take his place. The competition was good for the catch but hard on the ships and hard on the men.

The biggest part of the skipper-men run in families. There was four Jackmans, four Blandfords, five Winsors, seven Dawes, eight Barbours, ten Keans and ten Bartletts. Mostly they come to command without any foolishness about master's certificates. A good many of them had no learning and some couldn't read or write. The most of them was no great hands at deep-sea navigating either. Old Captain Peter Mullowney, talking about his ship, used to say: "Me sons, I don't know where this one's at and I don't care, for by the Lard Jasus, I knows where the swiles is to, and I can find 'em in me sleep!"

They was a powerful hardy lot. Had to be. And they was God so far as the men was concerned. A skipper might go in charge of the same ship twenty springs to the ice, and likely the most of his men would stay with him, for they was as staunch to a good skipper as they was to the King in London. To call another man's skipper down was always good for a row.

William Bartlett, who belonged to Brigus, went forty-two springs to the ice as master. He was a jowler true enough . . . a skipper as got the seals. He would bring his ship home log-loaded and a big pay bill for every man aboard. Sam Blandford was another, a proper wildman he was – would pound a man one minute and give him his shirt the next, but no better fellow ever went to the ice.

The one I remembers best was Skipper Henry Dawe. Now there was a swiler! Went to the ice as a common hand in 1863 and by 1875 was a skipper-man of the finest kind. I went with him in 1914 in the *Ranger*, the year of the big disasters, and that was his fifty-first spring to the ice, but he never lost a man in all his time. Lost plenty of seals because he wouldn't put his men to the risk, and always watched the barometer and kept an eye on the weather.

Too bad they warn't all the like of Skipper Henry. I supposes Captain Abraham Kean was top dog for the number of seals. Forty-four trips to the ice, and he brought back a million sculps. My, my, my, *what* a swile killer that man was! Course, some says he was a man killer too. Fair crazy to get the seals, he was, and never a one to worry overmuch what happened to his men.

They were a quare lot, certainly. Some used to burn down in the ice – drop the steam pressure to save coal – at midnight on a Saturday and every man aboard would have to go to prayer meeting next day even supposing they was in the middle of the whelping ice and it fair crawling with whitecoats waiting to be sculped. Then they was others would spend Sunday cruising the floes, stealing the panned pelts other ships had left behind to pick up at a later time. They was some as took the men's condition to heart, and more that wouldn't give them a thought. Some as would sooner lose a man than a seal. A quare lot, indeed they was, but proper men for all o' that. 'Tisn't likely we'll see the like of them again.

Skipper Ned Bishop were a gert pillar of the church. 'Twas more'n you was worth to bring a drop of rum aboard *his* ship. He was a hardy man, as only spoke to we on Sunday when he led us in the prayers. When we was in the ice he almost never left the bridge. There was just one thing in his head – to get the fat! Find where the main patch lay and load the *Eagle* up. If seals was scarce, he'd stay at sea until hell froze. When all the coal was burned, he'd make we hist the sails; and when the grub run out, he'd make we dine on swiles!

I mind one loo'ard spring the whole fleet missed the patch. Most of the vessels give it up and come home clean. Not Skipper Ned! We stayed out nine tormenting weeks; cruising the ice edge till all hands was wore to death. 'Twas more than flesh and blood could bear, so I was chose to tell the Old Man that we'd work the ice no more.

He and his officers was on the bridge when I come aft. They heered my footsteps on the ladder; turned their heads. The Old Man spun around. *He* knowed why I was there! His eyes was harder than the ice. "Captain," I says, "we'd best heave up and cut for home. We's all bate out . . . " And then me throat went dry. He only stood and glared until I thought I'd hang there till me eyeballs froze.

At last he roared: "Go forward now, me son, and tell the men what Captain Neddy said:

Before I takes me orders from a slinjing lot like you, we'll all be damned well dead!"

The traditional date for the departure of the sailing fleet had been March 1st, but with the coming of steam the ships were able to reach the whelping ice so quickly that the newborn seals—"cats," they were called – were still too small and thin to be of much value. It was not until their mothers had nursed them for at least a week that they became layered with the thick coating of fat that was the sealer's prize. However, rather than let some other ship get them, the steam sealers would kill the very young and almost worthless whitecoats anyway. Finally the owners agreed to postpone the departure day for steamers to March 10th.

Each spring as that day drew near, the steamer skippers forgathered in St. John's where they prowled around each other like suspicious mastiffs. Soon enough each of them would be trying to cut out his fellows, to find the main patch of seals without being followed, to get his men on ice before anyone else; or, if he had bad luck, to steal the fat killed and panned by more successful men; and finally, to come home first, log-loaded, to the plaudits of the St. John's population.

But that was for the future. In the last few days before sailing, these hopeful jowlers would at least pretend to be boon companions, since they were, after all, the most famous men in our island, and a class apart.

So they would gather to have a "time" and engage in competition of another sort as each captain sought to out-drink, out-sing and out-dance his peers.

While the captains enjoyed their "times" ashore, the wooden walls lay at the owners' wharves in St. John's harbour, taking aboard their niggardly allocation of provisions, coal and other

supplies, and awaiting the multitudes of men from distant outports who were then converging on the capital city.

The roads leading to St. John's begin to be enlivened by the
appearance of the swilers, each with his bundle of spare clothing
on his shoulder. This light wardrobe he carries on a stick six or
eight feet long, which is called a gaff; it has a hooked iron head
and serves also as a bat to strike the seals on the nose, as an ice
pole in leaping from pan to pan, and as a tool for dragging the
skin of the seal over the fields and hummocks of ice to the side
of the vessel. Some of the men, in addition, carry a long sealing
gun. These rank before batsmen, or common sealers, being the
gunners who will kill old seals after the whitecoats have been
harvested . . . The outfit of the sealers is of the simplest description: sealskin boots, called skinnywoppers, that reach to the knees
and have a thick leather sole, well nailed with iron sparrables or
frosters, to enable them to walk over the ice; coarse canvas or
cotton jackets, often showing the industry of wife or mother in
the number of patches that adorn them, which are worn over an
undershirt; and sealskin caps and moleskin trousers – the reverse
of handsome or picturesque.

Thus, an account written by a well-bred St. John's townsman
about 1870, as if he was describing an invasion by a crowd of
rather unsavoury savages, and this is how the "townies" *did*
regard the outport sealers.

   The point of view of the sealers themselves was somewhat
different, as my father's old shipmate, Captain Llewelyn Kean of
Greenspond, described it.

In 1910, when I was just turned sixteen, I made up my mind it
was time to make my first trip to the ice. Right after Christmas I
began looking for a berth, but it was near as hard to get a berth
ticket as an invitation to the Governor's Ball in St. John's. Times

was hard and there was only about fifteen steamers going sealing that year, carrying from a hundred and fifty up to two hundred and fifty men aboard of each; and for every berth ticket there was three men wanted it. You'd wonder at that, sure. The food was so bad, so wonderful scarce, it would hardly have kept a crackie dog alive . . . two men or more in every bunk, jammed down in the hold among the pens of coal, and bare boards for your mattress . . . no heat, barring a little bogey stove that would hardly bile a kettle; and one oil lantern to light a hundred men. Dirty, dark and cold it was, and the slaving out on the ice would nearly take your life away.

When you did get aboard you took your crop from the owner – a sheath knife, snow goggles of celluloid, and a bag of raisins and oatmeal. Together it was worth maybe three or four dollars, but you got cropped twelve dollars for it from your share of the seal fat. The way the shares was worked was different from the sailing days when there was a small crew of men, and they got half the value of the voyage. On the steamers there was always a terrible big crowd, but the owner took two-thirds of the voyage, leaving only a third for all them men to share. You were some lucky if you cleared thirty dollars after your crop was took out, and that for six or seven weeks of the devil's own work.

Didn't seem to matter. A berth to the ice was what you *had* to have, supposing you had to lie down and beg for it. Only a few years back, a man had to *pay* for his berth. When Job Brothers brought the old *Neptune* over from Dundee, she paid for herself in fifteen years from berth money alone! In my time the owners would give out tickets for half the berths and the captain give out the other half. You'd stand no chance to get one unless you as much as guaranteed to sell all your fish to, and buy all your year's grub and gear from, that merchant or his outport dealer.

But still you had to go. Oft-times I asks myself why we was so foolish. Perhaps it was like going off to the wars. Certainly there was risk enough and blood enough. It seemed like you weren't a proper man at all unless you'd gone to the ice and, of course, when you'd gone once, odds was you'd keep on with it until you was froze to death or was getting too well-up to stand the gaff.

Anyway, it was the number one excitement of the year, and there was the gamble that kept you at it. Always the chance your ship would make a bumper voyage, fill to the hatches, and every man would bring home a big bill. But it was a poor sort of gamble because the merchants set the price for the fat, and if it was a good year at the ice, they'd drop the price of fat down to nothing at all.

I got my ticket, on the last of it, from Skipper Jobie Kean who was my mother's brother. We was to join our ships in St. John's by the fifth of March. The first day of March there was four hundred and more men from all along the nor'western shore of Bonavista Bay ready to get under way. That was a sight to see! Our crowd started off before dawn from Wesleyville, bound for Gambo about sixty mile away over frozen ponds, through the woods, over the barrens, and across frozen bays. There was no roads them times, so it was all shanks' mare. Some fellows carried their bags on their shoulders but more pulled them on little wooden slides. There was some made it straight through, never stopping except to bile the kettle now and again. Others used to hang up in Hare Bay the first night and go on again in the morning.

When that great string of men started across Dark Cove to Lower Gambo, all the local youngsters would be waiting. They'd run out on the ice and take the slides and haul them to the railroad station. They kept the slides for their pay.

Men come into Gambo from all sides. I've seen close to a thousand sealers jamming the town, and no place to sleep except in the cars on the siding. They had special cars for sealers – the oldest, dirtiest they could find. We never cared about that. It might be two, three days before the train pulled out for St. John's, but every man had his own grub, and it was a grand enjoyment to be along of that big crowd. A scattered fellow would get drunk, and a scattered one might start a row. Great fun it was for all of we.

It was an island festival that embraced the townies too. Even in St. John's it was the milestone of the year. The fleet was going to the ice! Long before dawn on sailing day the docks and hills were skeined and clotted dark with people drawn to the harbour side from miles around. The bleak March sky was threaded with great veins of smoke as the old ships stoked up to get the biggest head of steam their worn old boilers could withstand. At each gang-plank the master watches stood, close-written crew lists in their hands to check off every man who'd had the luck to get a berth. Wild laughter and great shouts of merriment rang out so loud you would have thought this was the greatest day in all our history – a celebration of unrivalled joy and vast excitement. So it was . . . and yet, the voyage ahead, fate-freighted for the ice, might bring them death, disfigurement – was sure to be a time of hard-ships that you'd think only demented souls would voluntarily embrace.

Aboard the ancient, grimy ships they searched for stowaways; youngsters who were so drunkenly enthralled by the cold fire of the ice they'd risk their unlived lives, struggle and curse like savages when they were caught and hove ashore. At eight they sailed. The cheers rang back from ship to ship, from ship to shore and, from the cliffs, old muzzle-loading guns blew out black puffs of smoke and roared like God. The rusty blast of the ships' whis-tles raised plumed serpents of white steam. Old die-hard ships! Yet so majestic. Out they swept – to wage their war against the seals on the white ice.

Fifty years going to the ice should have been enough for any man. It would have been for most, but Skipper Alpheus must have been born with seal's blood running through his veins. When the hard northern ice swelled south towards the Funks, and Paddy's Brush brought in the first spring gale, not wife nor devil could have held him home in Greenspond. A proper jowler was Skipper Alph.

Year after year the same Bonavista crowd came to him for berths aboard the old *Neptune*. There were long faces the spring when word went round that Skipper Alph was sick. He'd found his heart; could scarcely breathe; lay white-faced in his bed in his big house upon the hill. The doctor shook his head when sealers stopped him on the road and asked the news.

The *Neptune* fitted at St. John's that spring, though no one knew who'd take command. Her owners sent word to Skipper Alph, asking who he'd recommend. The Old Man's answer was: "Let her come on to Wesleyville. I'll find your man." On March the 10th that good old wooden wall steamed down the bay. Her barricade was lined with men, all wondering who the Old Man would choose. Agape, they watched the shore where a trap boat was putting out, pounding her way into a steep head-sea. A whisper started . . . mounted to a roar! "By the Lard Livin' Jasus, byes, 'tis him! 'Tis Skipper Alph hisself!" And so it was. They hoisted him aboard strapped to a chair. Gentle as women, carried him below where, from his berth, through five long weeks out in the ice he held to his command, then brought the *Neptune* home, log-loaded, to the land.

Next to the captains of the sealing ships – Olympian figures, closely linked to the owners and almost as unreachable – came the master watches. There were four such aboard each steamer, and the entire crowd of sealers was divided equally among them into four watches. On ice the master watch was as much in command of his thirty to fifty men as if he had been the master of a vessel, and they his crew. However, since he was not possessed of the magic cloak of authority which enfolded the actual ships' officers, he had to reach and maintain his position by being superlatively good at everything he did – and this among a crowd of men who vied desperately with one another to kill the most seals, copy on the worst ice, drag the heaviest tows of sculps, venture farthest from the ships, take the greatest risks, and endure the worst hardships. A master watch had need to be a veritable Titan.

He also had to be a man who could bear a terrifying responsibility. The captain was responsible for the safety of the men as long as they were aboard the ship, and for finding them and picking them up after they had gone out on the ice, but it was the master watch in whose hands their lives lay once they were away from the vessel. And it was away from the ship, far out on the ice, that the most deadly perils lay.

The master watches were truly men of heroic stature, and it was because of them that the roster of human victims of the seal fishery was not infinitely greater. It was little wonder that, while great captains were worshipped from afar, it was the master watches who became the living legends of outport Newfoundland.

Jacob Kelloway, who belonged to Greenspond, was a master watch for thirty-seven springs. He was also a great storyteller, and he remembered what seemed like every last detail of his long life as a sealer. He never tired of telling us his history, and we youngsters never tired of listening.

The steamer fleet always made a grand display, hightailing nor'ard along the coast from St. John's, making to round Cape St. Francis with all sail set and smoke a-pouring out of every stack. Aye, and every man aboard desperate anxious to get into the swiles. But there was never no telling where the whelping pans might lie – might be anywhere from off of Hawke Harbour on the Labrador, right away out to the Grand Banks, four hundred mile to the sou'east.

I remembers one time I shipped in the *Adventure* with Captain Henry Dawe. There was eighteen steamers in the fleet that spring, and they was all mostly in sight of each other when we run through Baccalieu Tickle. But we was in the fore, and Skipper Henry hauled off for the Funks and when we took the ice that evening there was nar' sign of any other ship, only a smudge of smoke on the horizon, for they was all still holding to the land.

Once into the ice it was every skipper for himself. Unlucky ones used to dog the better men, sometimes so close they'd come right aboard with their big bowsprits. That used to drive Captain Abe Kean right wild. One time when he was in the *Terra Nova* he was dogged by the little *Kite*, and he undertook to put a stop to that by running the *Terra Nova* into a field of old arctic ice, the thick blue sort as is as hard as iron. He calculated the *Kite*

would get jammed and he could leave her far behind. But 'twas
the *Terra Nova* got jammed herself. Kean couldn't free her, even
with dynamite, for three days and nights. When the *Kite*'s skipper
saw what was up he backed out of the hard ice, took a cut to the
eastward, fell onto the main patch, loaded to the gunwales in
them three days, and was the first ship back into St. John's.

'Twas wonderful how news got around amongst the ships, even
before they had the wireless. A vessel might look to be all alone
in the world the day she struck the patches, but by next morning
there'd likely be a half dozen ships butting into the floes all around
her and putting their men on ice.

We struck a corner of the main patch late on March 14th, but
before 'twas full dark the *Terra Nova* hove in sight and hard in
her wake come the *Ungava*, *Neptune*, *Thetis* and *Beothic*! Skipper
Henry was vexed to death, but there was nothing to be done.

I don't say as any man slept much that night . . . all hands
waiting for daybreak to get in among the whitecoats what was
bawling every which way, all around the ships. When it come
light we see the *Terra Nova* so close on our starboard bow you
could almost hear her smoke rushing overhead. All the ships was
getting up steam and starting to put their men over the side. And
what a wonderful sight it was – close to a thousand men spilling
out onto the ice with their gaffs and their pan flags. 'Twas like
some old-time army going off to war.

If some sadistic prison commissioner had set out to design the
ultimate hell-ship, he could hardly have done better than to take
as his model one of the old wooden walls of the Newfoundland
seal fishery. Any unfortunate prisoners sentenced to serve time
in such a vessel would soon have been driven to riot or suicide.
And yet every spring thousands of freeborn islanders would *vol-
unteer*, and even fight for the *right*, to serve on these ships. Why
they should have done so remains a mystery, for I never knew a
sealer who could give a reasonable explanation. "'Twas the
excitement of it," some might say, if hard pressed. Or: "'Twas a
great lark for we bay fellows." It could hardly have been the
money involved, for the men got precious little of that. Part of it

may have been the need to stick to established tradition, and it had been traditional almost from the first that going to the ice entailed almost unimaginable hardships and dangers. Some "experts" have said the whole thing was akin to what anthropologists refer to among primitive tribes as the rites of passage, when youths earned the right to be called men by deliberately accepting physical agony and courting the possibility of death. That might help explain why youngsters *first* went to the ice; but how to explain why a man would continue to endure those agonies every spring of his life until he died of them or became too old to get a berth?

My grandfather went to the ice for nearly half a century. He had no illusions about the life, and yet he returned to it, spring after spring.

The first wooden wall as ever I shipped aboard was the SS *Esquimaux*. She was a little thing, only about a hundred feet overall, and had been a whaler for thirty year before being bought up for the sealing. She was soaked through and through with whale and seal oil and the stink of her was enough to make a goat lose his dinner. She was built with accommodation for maybe twenty men, but she carried a hundred and sixty the spring I went in her, and we was out ten weeks, most of it in the ice with northerly gales and the coldest kind of weather. I don't suppose I was dry half the time, for there was no place to dry out your clothes, supposing you dared take them off. We worked in the same clothes, lived in them from the beginning to the end, and them soaked in seal fat and blood and dirt till they was so stiff they'd crackle. We slept in them too, for there was no such thing to be had as any sort of bedding. The only time I warn't chilled half to death was when I was on the ice working seals, and then I was on the go so hard I *had* to get warm.

As for the grub, 'twas hard to believe a man could live on it, let be work like a darkie slave. Five days a week it was nothing at all but hardtack and black tea. The hardtack – ship's biscuit, some calls it – was likely full of weevils and harder than tenpenny nails. The tea was made up in the morning by the galley-

bitch – one of the sealers serving as the cook – in ten-gallon cop-
pers. A handful of tea and a scoop of 'lasses was throwed into
the water and left to boil away all day with more water added
as the men drank it up. Water? I suppose you could call it that.
The tanks on them old ships was so foul we mostly used water
melted from ice we hauled aboard across the decks, sometimes
knee-deep in seal sculps, blood, coal dust and ashes. Twice a
week, Tuesdays and Thursdays, we got duff, made out of condemned flour put into bags and boiled in a slut – a big kettle –
with a bit of salt pork. The cook would sling them out, half-a-
duff to a man, and you *could* manage to glutch them down while
they was hot, but let them get cold and they was turned into
cannon balls. Sundays we got a bit of salt fish to go with our
hardtack. Small wonder most of us learned to eat raw seal meat.
The heart, when it was fresh cut out and still warm, was as good
as steak to we fellows.

Some men brought along a bit of grub of their own. The crowd
from Trinity Bay used to bring potatoes and eat them raw. Most
of us had a little bag of oatmeal and another of raisins, but we
kept that for when we was on the ice.

The queer thing about it was there was no complaints. The
men took it all for nothing. Before we got into the patches you'd
think they was having the finest kind of holiday. You never heard
so much yarning and singing and carrying on in your life. Of
course, once we got into the fat, all that went out. There was no
time then for anything but work. Out to the ice you'd go before
dawnlight, and you'd be on ice all of the day and maybe all the
night too if the captain didn't happen to get back for you. When
you did get back aboard, your supper was hardtack and black tea,
and then you'd work on deck, icing and stowing down seal sculps
maybe till midnight or later. Or you'd be shifting coal, carrying
it in baskets to the stokehold or hauling ashes up on deck for the
firemen. If there was plenty seals the bunks would be tore up to
make pens for the fat 'tween decks, and the men would be
crowded out and have to sleep on deck, supposing they had time
to sleep. Many's the time I've laid down on a pile of steaming
seal sculps. They was softer than them old plank bunks at any
rate.

Things got a mite better after 1914, when William Coaker, the man as started the Fishermen's Union, made the government pass a law to improve the food. After that the men got dried pea soup twice a week. I remember Captain Abraham Kean was right wild about that. "Mark me!" I heard him say. " 'Twill be the death of the sealing game. Too much luxury, that's what! Why, I remember when we never even had stoves aboard 'cause the owners thought the men would stay and warm theirselves 'stead of going on the ice . . . Now sealing's a pure luxury, with engines to do the work, and bunks and hot food . . . it ain't a man's game any more!"

Skipper Abe was the hardest kind of a man, and maybe that was why he got so many seals. His men was right feared of him, aye, even his officers was. They'd do anything at all, take their lives in their hands day and night, rather than chance being called a hangback afore the rest of the crowd. A man *had* to keep up with the rest, put up with whatever was going, or he'd be ruined, certainly.

Aye, it was hard times, but if you lived through it, sure, you could look ary man in the face afterwards. And 'twasn't the hard times you remembered. What I recalls the best was the times we used to have 'tween decks when the ship was jammed or there was no seals about. Good times, me son. Aye, they was that.

Death on Ice – Part I

Finding the whelping patch among those thousands of square miles of drifting, heaving ice was the vital element in the hunt. Sometimes the patch was never found and the ships came home empty. Sometimes it was found and could not be worked because of ice conditions. Sometimes it was found on a Sunday and, if the skipper of the ship was a practising Christian, that could be a special kind of disaster. Jacob Kelloway used to tell of one such occasion.

'Twere coming on duckish Saturday evening, and we'd been butting around in the ice for a week, and the ship was pretty well jammed, and not a sign of a patch of young seals had we seen when the scunner, up in the foremast barrel, lets out a whoop:

"Young fat to star-r-r-r-r-b'ard!"

All of a slam all hands was on deck and lining the rails. Skipper Tom was out on the wing of the bridge with his spyglass, pointing it all round the ice like an old brass cannon.

"How many and how far?" he bawls back to the barrelman.

"Scattered few 'bout a mile off nor'nor'east," comes the answer, "but I t'inks they's a gert patch a mile or two 'yond that."

All eyes was on the skipper. He paced up and down, chewing on his lip, as we waited to hear him give the order: "Over the side and make a rally, men!" But he never give it. 'Twas too dark and the sky was looking for weather. It must have near choked him to keep quiet, knowing the next day was Sunday, for Skipper Tom was a church-going man. There was nothing to be done but burn down where we was at till Monday morning and hope the patch wouldn't go abroad, and none of them other ships would heave in sight.

That Sunday was the most tormenting day ever I spent. The whitecoats was all 'round and singing so loud they near drowned out the hymn singing down below. Uncle Absolom Kelloway was our preacher, and he was so vexatious about them seals, he gave the Lord the rate word.

"Lard God," he hollers. "Blessin' on your name! But what in hellfire's the use of puttin' we into such a pickle? We been a right lang time aboard o' this one and nary a pick o' fat to be had. Well, now Lard, we don't say 'tis all your fault, certainly, but we t'inks 'tis a wunnerful cold smack for ye to put we onto swiles on a Saturday night, and Sunday no more good to we than legs is to a fish! 'Tis an awful muckery ye got we into now, and we'm hopes you's all t'roo wit' trashin' we around like dat!"

Uncle Absolom laid it heavy enough, but the Lord never held it against us, for Monday morning come fine and warm and we killed and panned near three t'ousand seals that day.

The impression of an army setting out to do battle as the sealers streamed onto the ice was more than skin-deep, for they were organized almost on military lines. Before the ship reached the ice the men would have been divided into their four watches, each under the command of a master watch who, in turn, divided his group into three sections. One of these he kept under his own control; the other two being commanded by his two junior officers – a bridgemaster and a scunner (more often called a deck robber).

As soon as the ship got into the whelping ice – into the fat – the four watches would muster on deck and await the captain's orders. As the vessel steamed along, he would call for a rally by one watch, and the men involved would scramble over the side, leaping wildly to get clear as the ship continued on her way, sending the floes spinning and cracking in her wake.

The master watch would lead his crowd to the first good patch of young harp seals and there detach the scunner with his section. The bridgemaster and his group would be left at the next good patch and finally the master watch would pick a patch for himself and his men at "the end of the line," perhaps three or four miles from the point where they had gone on ice. By then the ship herself might have steamed clean out of sight, dropping the other watches along a course ten or fifteen miles long.

Each leader would disperse his men in pairs so that if one plunged through the ice his chum could come to his rescue. Two or three particularly strong floes in each area being worked would be selected and marked by numbered flags sporting the colours of the company that owned the ship.

So the men were scattered, often over a hundred square miles of ice, to kill and sculp the whitecoats wherever these were to be found. A good man could sculp a hundred young seals in a day, but the real work lay in making the heavy fat-layered pelts into tows of four or five and then dragging them to the nearest flagged pan, which might be a mile away across broken, hummocked, shifting ice.

Ideally the ship would retrace her course in the evening to pick up the pans of fat and the sealers, but conditions at the ice were rarely ideal. It was all too common for pans of many hundreds of pelts to be left adrift for days – or to be lost forever when a storm came down. And it was no uncommon thing for sealers to be left out overnight as well.

Written accounts of what it was like to be a sealer in those times are rare because most educated Newfoundlanders took care to have nothing to do with that dangerous aspect of the business. There was one remarkable exception: the Reverend Doctor M. Harvey, who was born into one of the Water Street families that had come to the top in the sealing game. At one time or another A. J. Harvey and Company owned a dozen sealing steamers and made a fortune out of them. Like most of the Water Street crowd, however, they gave a good deal more thought to the money than to the men, and it was a surprise for all hands when the Reverend Doctor joined one of the family ships in the spring of 1895 to see for himself what it was all about. The way the men and seals were treated upset him so much he published an account of it which nearly made him an outcast from his own family and from the rest of St. John's society.

Let us suppose the steamer has at last got sight of the seal patch. The whimpering of the young seals is heard, gladdening the hearts of the hunters . . . It is like the sobbing or mewling of an infant . . . No sooner is it heard than the vessel is laid-to, the men eagerly bound on the ice, and the work of destruction begun. A blow on the nose from a gaff shod with iron fractures the skull of the young seal. In a moment the knife is at work. The skin, with the fat adhering, is "sculped" from the carcass, which is left on the ice still quivering with life.

The work of slaughter goes on without cessation. The hunters scatter over the ice in all directions and often wander miles from their ships. The ice is soon stained with gore and dotted with the skinless carcasses of the slain. The deck becomes slippery with mingled blood and fat. Bloodgouts cover the hands and arms of the men. The shivering seals' low moans fill the air. What a scene, amidst these icy solitudes of the frozen ocean, with the bright sun lighting up the glittering pinnacles. The poor mother seals, now cubless, are seen popping their heads up in the small holes in the ice looking for their snow-white darlings and refusing to believe that the bloody carcasses on the ice are all that remains of their tender offspring. With a moan of distress they plunge into the sea as if anxious to escape from the ensanguined trail of the hunter.

As for the sealers, the perils of the ice field are neither few nor small and the hardships and exposure are such that only men of iron could endure. These men seem to have an absolute contempt for the terrors of floes and sea. They leap from pan to pan where it would seem a child could hardly be sustained, and think little of passing a night on ice far from the steamer. Should a fog or snowstorm set in, there is a terrible risk of losing their way and perishing miserably in these ice deserts, or of falling through the openings, which are covered with floating snow.

Sometimes the field ice on which they work separates without a moment's warning into fragments, and they are floated off to perish by cold and hunger. The greatest danger of all is when a violent storm rages, breaking up the ice fields and driving before it the larger floes intermingled with fragments of arctic ice as hard as granite.

Woe to the vessel that is exposed to these ice giants. When the wild nor'easter rises, the great swell of the Atlantic, rolling in continuous ridges, heaves the pavement of ice into mighty folds. The whole mass contracts and expands and the broken fragments are dashed up on one another in hills of ice. Fragments rafter over each other in layers fifty feet thick. The thunderous crashes of the ice giants, combined with the roaring overhead of the gale and the blinding snowstorm, make up a scene of awe and terror. Then, at times, an iceberg takes part in the fray, sailing remorselessly forward, rending and tearing the ice field and scattering its fragments.

Such are the scenes amidst which the sealers gather in the "precious things of the deep."*

---

*Adapted from *Newfoundland in 1897* by Rev. Dr. M. Harvey.

One of the few educated men I ever knew who went to the ice was a Wesleyville boy who grew up to be a teacher. Here is his account.

After my father and his older brother died in the *Greenland* disaster in 1898 – they froze to death with so many other sealers – my mother made a vow that, come what might, none of us boys would ever go to the ice. Although hard times followed for our family, she not only kept her word but was very reluctant even to let my three brothers and me go fishing on the Labrador in the summers to make enough money for our schooling. "The sea took too many of our folk," she used to say. "It'll take no more of mine!"

She herself had been a teacher when she met my father, and she was determined I would be one too, for it was almost the only work a man could get in those days that did not take him on the sea. I won a scholarship finally and went to St. John's for teacher training. Then in 1928 I took the school at Newtown – that used to be called Pinchards Bight. That Christmas I got married and was in a fair way to being a happy man, but a few years later the hard times came again and things got very bad. There was no money to pay the teacher, and we had a small baby to keep. So I determined I would have to go sealing and hope to make a few dollars. That was in the spring of 1931.

For old times' sake, Captain William Kennedy, who was going navigator on the *Viking* with Captain Abraham Kean, Jr., son of the famous sealing captain of that name, procured a berth for me. Away I went to Gambo with the rest of the local men. It was a great thrill, indeed, for me, and I did not mind going in the least; but my poor old mother was heartbroken, being certain only bad would come of her broken vow.

As I recall there were about a hundred and fifty of us aboard the *Viking*, and we were mostly northern bay men. There were some jokes made about a man thirty years of age making his first trip to the ice, and I was known as Whitecoat, but it was good-natured, and I did not mind.

We put out on March 9th and were the last ship to sail for the front, being delayed by some American motion picture men who were to sail with us and make a picture of the hunt. Two days out from port we ran into a terrible storm in open water, the "blue drop," as the men called it. It was really a hurricane and seas were soon boarding the ship and sweeping her end for end. She laboured very heavily and began to take water so badly the engine-driven pumps could not hold it. A huge wave swept away our galley with all the cooking gear and the stove, and the cook barely escaped with his life. All of our boats were swept away as well, except one nest of dories, enough for perhaps a dozen men.

It was a bad lookout entirely, and I began to fear my poor old mother had been right, and I should have stayed ashore. However, with all hands at the pumps we somehow kept her afloat while Captain Kean worked her in to the lee of the land under Flowers Island, which was uninhabited then and lay less than twenty miles from Newtown, which we could see in the distance but could not reach because of the ice. Here we rode out the storm for three days and made what repairs we could. I thought it would have been entirely likely the captain would give up the voyage because of the damage, but he was a Kean, and he had his father's reputation to maintain, so on Saturday, March 14th, we steamed out of the bay bound nor'west. We found the main ice near the Horse Islands and by evening were well into very heavy pack.

When I turned in that night I had a difficult time to go to sleep although I was done-in from working at the pumps. I could not get the thought of home and Newtown out of my head, but it was not my wife and child I thought about so much as my mother. At last I fell asleep, but I seemed to hear her as plain as I could hear the rasping of the ice against the hull. She was weeping and moaning the way she did for a long time, at night, after father's dreadful death.

And then, it seemed to me, I was wide awake and out on the ice in a terrible blizzard, searching for survivors from the *Greenland*. Suddenly two figures emerged from the drifting snow in front of me. I knew they were my father and my uncle. But they were not alive. They were dead men – frozen white – and stumbling towards me holding out their frozen arms . . .

I had no more sleep that night. I don't believe in ghosts and spirits, but, as the Lord is with me, it was a true warning from the other side.

The *Viking*, built at Arendal, Norway, in 1881, to the same design as the Scots whalers, was a 500-ton, ship-rigged wooden wall powered by an 86-horsepower engine. In 1904, when the Norwegians had no more use for her, she was bought by Bowring Brothers of St. John's and for the next twenty-seven springs went to the ice for that company in the sealing game. By the spring of 1931 she was a half-century old and showing her age. Decades of neglect and hard usage had, in the words of one of her last skippers, "fair taken the good right out of her." Nevertheless, she was still considered good enough to carry one hundred and fifty men into the most dangerous waters in the North Atlantic and into the violence of the pack ice.

In early March she put to sea under command of Captain Abraham Kean, Jr. Like so many of the sealing skippers, young Kean knew little navigation and was not a qualified master. So Bowrings had been forced, by law, to ship a certified master as well. He was Captain William Kennedy, age twenty-nine, who had just been accepted as a seagoing officer by one of the large British freighter lines. Since he was not to take over his new job until summer, and because times were hard, he was glad to earn a few dollars shipping aboard the *Viking* – although the orders of the owners, that he was not to interfere with the operation of the ship, did not please him. He was, in fact, little more than a passenger aboard.

In addition to her sealers, the *Viking* carried an unusual extra complement, an American film crew led by Varick Frissell, who was making a romantic film about sealing to be called *Northern Knight*. They were all young men and, in truth, the *Viking* was a young man's ship that spring, for the great majority of her officers and men were in their twenties, driven to the ice by the urgent financial need of those depression years.

Having barely weathered a hurricane on her way to the front, the *Viking* finally took the ice late on Saturday, March 14th. The pack was exceptionally heavy and after a few hours Captain Kean decided to burn down for the night in a polynia, or open lake, among the floes. He went early to his cabin, leaving his officers and the film-makers to sit a while, drink tea, and yarn in the tiny saloon where the bogey stove glowed red-hot as protection against the bitter night. Under the saloon table slept a massive black Newfoundland dog named Cabot, belonging to Varick Frissell. The dog kept whining uneasily until one of the Americans, Henry Sargent, bent down and fondled its head. Frissell was busy printing large letters on a piece of cardboard. Clayton King, the *Viking's* 22-year-old Marconi operator, peered over his shoulder and read the words aloud: "Notice! DANGER! POWD. . .er." The final two letters had not yet been added, but Clayton voiced them anyway.

The Newfoundlanders in the saloon – with the exception of Kennedy – were amused. What was the danger in powder? Every ship going to the ice carried as much as a ton of blasting powder and dynamite, together with dozens of cases of rifle ammunition for the adult seal hunt. When a ship got jammed, the men freed her with explosives which they treated as casually as they treated most other things aboard those ships.

The *Viking's* magazine was a small room just off the saloon. It was too small for its job, so several cases of powder and ammunition had been stored across the narrow hall in a tiny, doorless cubicle that also held the vessel's only toilet. It was perfectly normal for a sealer to be seated on the throne smoking his pipe or knocking the glowing dottle out against one of the cans of blasting powder. This spectacle had appalled the Americans and, after discussing it with Captain Kennedy, Frissell had decided to put up a warning sign.

The sign was never completed. The ship suddenly lurched violently to starboard, heeling over so sharply that the bogey fell on its side, spilling burning coals all over the floor and down the alleyway. The men slid off their benches into a heap against a transverse bulkhead. While they were sorting themselves out, Captain Kean burst from his cabin and, only half-dressed, stumbled out on the bridge as the ship gradually righted herself.

He saw at once what had happened. The wind had changed; the "ice claw" anchor holding the ship to the edge of the floe had torn loose and the *Viking* had gone charging across the polynia to bring up hard against the further edge. Captain Kean was just about to call the bo's'n to put another ice claw out and make fast when the whole stern of the ship buckled beneath his feet. He was flung far out over the ice in the red glare of a tremendous explosion. The *Viking's* magazine had gone up in a pillar of flame with a colossal roar!

Of the dozen men in the saloon, only three survived. One of them was Clayton King, who wrote a pamphlet about his experiences. This excerpt from it begins after he had crawled to what was left of the stern of the burning *Viking.*

Looking around me I saw nothing but wreckage. The ship had been blown apart almost to the water's edge . . . the ice was aglow from the flames. Cries for help were everywhere. On one ice pan I saw a man in a pool of blood – a deep gash in his head.

"Who are you?" I cried.

"Kennedy. Come and help me."

"Can't make it. My legs are all smashed up."

Another explosion shattered the hull and a body came hurtling out of the wreckage to land on an ice pan close to the ship. The man's head split open to his neck. With a few convulsive movements his body slid off the pan into the sea.

I felt the cords on my neck drawing taut with the heat. Get clear, I must. I either fell or threw myself and landed in the water. Henry Sargent came to my rescue and pulled me out. After heroic work he was able to move Kennedy and myself from danger. As the fire reached deeper into the hull there were more explosions. Black clouds of smoke belched from her deck. Figures, grotesque in the light of the flames, were falling over the side . . .

We three drifted away from the wreck . . . Sargent got me and Kennedy on a piece of wreckage from the *Viking's* stern. This, supported by an ice pan, was the safest place for a while at least. As the night wore on, the wind came howling out of the north. The hours went by. The dawn came and the sun shone brightly with a blue-white glare. We were drifting fast. For twenty-two miles from where the *Viking* went down we drifted in the ice of the desolate Atlantic.

Monday I was only conscious intermittently. Tuesday I heard Sargent raving: "God! What am I going to do? Kennedy is dying and King is dead!" Later I heard Kennedy breathing very heavily and guessed he had pneumonia.

In my next conscious period I heard Sargent shouting: "Hurrah! Hurrah! It's a steamer . . . I can see her hull!"

As a rescue boat from the SS *Sagona* reached the ice pan I heard one of the crew exclaim: "Look at King's legs!" I looked at them myself. My right one was twisted up alongside my body, the bone exposed and the frost shining through the lacerated flesh. I drifted off into a coma and when I woke again someone patted me on the shoulder, saying: "King, you are all right now."*

King was all right—if losing both legs to the hip from gangrene is "all right," but at least he lived. Kennedy did not, nor did twenty-eight others of the *Viking*'s crew. The survival of many of the rest was survival only, for a great number suffered crippling injuries from which they never recovered. The majority managed to make their way over the ice to the isolated Horse Islands, where the local Marconi operator, Otis Bartlett, became a Newfoundland hero by reporting their terrible plight to the outer world and by directing a rescue fleet of sealing ships and other vessels to the disaster area. The film-maker, Varick Frissell, and Cabot, the big black dog that had whined uneasily under the saloon table, were among those who were never seen again.

The wooden walls did not always die by accident – sometimes they were murdered.

---

*Adapted from *The Viking's Last Cruise* by Clayton L. King.

The *Diana* began life in 1869 as the whaler *Hector*. A whaling ship's life in arctic seas was hard enough, but in 1871 her Scots owners decided to squeeze even more work out of her by sending her to the Newfoundland seal fishery each spring. In February of each year thereafter she fought her way across the winter North Atlantic to St. John's, took on a crowd of sealers, and headed out to the whelping ice where she butted and pounded about among the floes, often until early May. Returning to St. John's she would discharge seals and sealers and then shape her course northward to spend an icebound summer cruising for bowheads in Davis Strait and Baffin Bay. When the autumnal gales began she would go labouring homeward to Dundee again, a weary ship, worn with the travail in the ice. This was her life until 1892, but at least her Scots owners gave her some kindness in midwinter when she was laid up, and kept her in good condition.

Things changed for her when she was bought by a St. John's firm in '92, renamed *Diana*, and given over completely to the sealing game. During each of the remaining years of her life she seldom came alive except for the two or three months when she went sealing. For the rest, she mostly lay, dirty, neglected, dying by degrees, moored with her sister wooden walls at the south side of St. John's harbour.

In the spring of 1922 she was fifty-three years old and for years past had received only the most cursory attention and minimal repairs. Her ancient engine was little more than a pile of junk. Her masts and spars were brittle and cracked with age; her sails were not much better than patched dusters. Below the waterline, rot and sea worms had finally begun to win their victory over her massive timbers and planking. She leaked at almost every seam; her too-few lifeboats were baskets that would have filled instantly had they ever been lowered. Everyone knew she was unfit to go to sea, and this included her owners as well as the one hundred and sixty-seven men who were to sail in her, one of whom had this to say of her:

She war no better nor a death trap, and we'm all knowed it, sure. But what was we to do? Was no other berths for we in ary other ship. 'Twas the devil's choice, bye. Five or six older chaps left her, certainly, and went ashore. 'Twas all right for they, but we knowed as any man refused to sail would never get another berth on ary vessel out of St. John's. The owners would see to that. So the most of we stayed aboard she for the voyage.

She sailed on March 10th under command of a hardcase skipper of whom it was said that he valued a good fat seal over any sealer who had ever lived. Perhaps that was a lie, but it was true enough that he did not seem to value human life very highly, and it was his boast that he would sail a log to the front if there was no other command available to him.

It was a bad spring for ice, with the floes close-packed and spiked with innumerable bergs and growlers. Heavy easterly gales kept the field compacted, jamming most of the vessels of the sealing fleet but sending the big bergs plunging through the raftered ice as if it had no more substance than tissue paper. Twice *Diana* found herself jammed and in the path of one of these blind behemoths, and once a cliff of ice ripped through the pack so close alongside that it snagged the end of her main yard and splintered it to bits.

The ice was bad, the weather ferocious – but the sealing was good. Most of the ships were in the main patch and, because of the tight ice, the men could hunt far and wide among the white-coats. By March 21st the *Diana*'s hard-driven, half-starved and increasingly sullen crew had stowed away something between 14,000 and 19,000 pelts (the true number was never known), and the men were praying for the ice pressure to ease so that the leaking, creaking old hulk could make her cut for home.

The pressure did not ease. Instead, it grew worse. The floes began to rafter into ridges thirty and forty feet high that came hard against the sides of the old wooden wall. She groaned, and her timbers writhed under the mounting pressure. She began to open up until her pumps could hardly cope with the inflow.

Now even her hardcase skipper grew apprehensive that the old ship could not endure and so he secretly arranged by coded wireless with a sister ship owned by the same firm to have her take on as much as she could carry of *Diana*'s cargo of prime young fat. Then he ordered his crew to begin putting the sculps back on ice and to pan them at a safe distance from the ship. At the same time he assured them the vessel was in no danger.

The men were not stupid. They were convinced that when the ice slackened *Diana* would go down, whereupon the sister vessel would pick up the fat and claim it as salvage. That way the owners would suffer no loss, but the sealers of the *Diana* stood to lose the handful of dollars their unimaginably hard labours had earned for them.

So there was a "manus"—a mutiny. The men refused to unload a single pelt unless the captain guaranteed them their share when the fat reached St. John's. The captain would promise nothing. He and his officers armed themselves and held the bridge.

The impasse lasted for two days while the sister ship, which had been unlucky in the hunt and only had a few thousand sculps of her own, lay waiting like a jackal several miles away. She kept her distance, and the *Diana*'s crew believed this was deliberate —that she would not rescue them until they had put their seals on ice. On the morning of the third day of the manus they made up their minds to break the deadlock their own way—or at least some among them did.

Shortly after dawn the fearful cry of "FIRE!" rang out. There was no more than enough time for all hands to gain the ice before the old vessel, her every plank and timber soaked through and through with oil and her holds filled with seal fat, became a roaring pyre. She burned so fiercely that men on the *Terra Nova*, fifteen miles away, were awed by the pillar of smoke that towered into a white and cloudless sky.

The fire was so terrible hot we was feared the ice would melt under we. That was foolishness, of course, but 'twas such an awful sight to see her burn, with all that fat aboard.

How did it happen then? They's none as ever would say for sure, but this I knows. Yiss, by the Powers, we was all agreed that if we was to lose *our* voyage, the merchants in St. John's would never take a nickle profit out of it! Nor did they. No, they couldn't even sell she to the insurance companies, for none of them was daft enough to place a dollar on the old *Diana*.

So the *Diana* died at the hands of her own men. But perhaps murder is too hard a term for what they did, for it was a true Viking funeral they gave her at the end of her long years.

Disasters at the ice were so commonplace that most were soon put out of mind—except by those who survived, or by the families of those who did not survive. Those who went to the ice lived with the near certainty that they would be involved in a disaster sooner or later, and in some masochistic way they almost seemed to embrace the prospect. " 'Twas as if a man never felt hisself to be a proper swiler 'less he'd been on talking terms with death a time or two."

If the sealers had come to a fatalistic acceptance of danger, disfigurement and death among the northern floes, those who exposed them to it – the owners of the sealing industry and the autocracy of Newfoundland – were equally unconcerned. St. John's *was* Newfoundland to them, while the outport people dwelt somewhere in limbo. The writers of the island's history were *of* St. John's; and so, during the nearly one hundred years that the seal fishery was conducted under sail from the outport settlements, most of the men and ships that were lost achieved no mention in the records. They lived in limbo, they died in limbo and were conveniently forgotten. It was not quite the same with the steam fleet and their crews, for these ships were owned in St. John's, sailed from there and, when they failed to return, could not be so easily ignored. Consequently, records of the steamer losses still exist, even if these only consist of a few words in the St. John's newspapers.

During the thirty years between 1870 and 1900 the sealing steamers *Bloodhound* (first), *Wolf* (first) and *Wolf* (second), *Retriever, Osprey, Ariel, Tigress, Hawk, Mic Mac, Tiger, Resolute, Winsor Lake* and *Mastiff* were all crushed and sunk in the grinding pack. The *Lion* disappeared without a trace, with her entire crew, while heading for the ice. The year before the *Tigress* was crushed; her decrepit boiler had exploded and killed twenty-one men. In 1889 the *Walrus* lost twenty-five men who went adrift in the pack and were never found. Five years later eight more men were killed, and the *Walrus* was nearly sunk, by a powder explosion.

Because the sealing industry was by this time concentrated in St. John's whose merchants sent a number of sailing ships to the ice, some of the sailing fleet casualties did manage to find their way into the written history of the seal fishery. They included the *Huntsman*, lost with forty-five men; *Dundonald*, thirty-three men lost; *Village Belle*, eighteen drowned; *Deerhound*, forty-four lost; *Emerald*, thirty-eight lost; *Northland*, thirty lost.

These were but a few of the sealing disasters during these three decades, and the near-disasters were even more numerous. One March day in 1890 the *Terra Nova*, *Eagle* and two other steamers had their entire crews, totalling more than five hundred men, on ice in dubious weather when a blizzard swept over the floes. In their ferocious competition with each other the steamer captains had spread their men for twenty or thirty miles over the pack and, with the onset of the storm, had no chance of finding them again until the storm ended. It did not abate for three days and nights and, but for a miracle, most of the sealers would have perished.

The miracle was the presence on the scene of the little *Kite*, under-powered, ancient and unable to dash off through the pack scattering her men broadcast as her bigger rivals had done. She lay jammed in the middle of the main patch. Her own men were out, so the *Kite* kept her whistle blowing all through the balance of that day and far into the night to guide them back to safety. Fortunately she had a disproportionately loud voice, and the abandoned sealers from the other ships also homed on it. Dawn found the *Kite* playing host to her own one hundred and fifty-six men plus five hundred and forty freezing strangers! Unable to take them all aboard, the *Kite*'s master provided coal and wood for fires on the ice, canvas for rough shelters, and a supply of tea and hardtack until the storm ended and the men could be picked up by their own ships.

That was a desperately near thing, but it had no perceptible effect on the behaviour of the ships' owners. The Newfoundland government, which the merchants effectively controlled, continued to refuse to enact any significant legislation to prevent further additions to the long list of sealing disasters, on the grounds that any such laws would interfere with the owners' God-given right to make the greatest possible profit from the seal fishery. As one official publicly stated: "The financial stability of our island home depends to a large degree upon a flourishing and successful seal fishery. It is our bounden duty, therefore, to ensure that nothing interferes with the gathering of the great harvest of the ice fields, whose failure must inevitably work fearful hardship upon the lives of all our people."

He was, of course, speaking of economic hardship. The other kind could be disregarded or, when it was brought to public notice, could be hailed as evidence of the sealers' patriotic qualities.

After one particularly horrendous disaster, the mayor of St. John's, a prosperous merchant with sealing interests, piously proclaimed:

"These fine fellows died at duty's call . . . They are in God's keeping and there they will rest with the Merciful Father who does not permit even a sparrow to fall unnoticed, and who was with them in their darkest hour."

The newspapers would also sometimes publish an inch or two of memorial tribute to the dead, praising the hardihood and courage of the sealers who were prepared to "die gallantly, in duty's traces." The following appeared in a St. John's paper after the SS *Newfoundland* disaster:

INDUSTRIAL SOLDIERS
GO DOWN IN FIGHT

We ask: why did you, knowing the hazardous occupation of sealing, face its perils and dangers? The answer is one that inspires our Faith in Man! It was Duty's Call, and you obeyed. Were a monument to be erected to your memory, the epitaph could be inscribed: Sacred to those brave and hardy soldiers of the Industrial Army who struggled, suffered and died on the Frozen Battlefield for their Captains of Industry, and their loved ones at home. R.I.P.

Memorial poems were also sometimes written and published by the English-educated offspring of St. John's merchants. Presumably these were intended to bring comfort to the widows and children of our dead, although most outport people never saw a paper and couldn't have read one anyway.

> Away far out on the Northern Floe
> Labour the men of our Isle,
> And they fight the grim Boreal blasts
> With their cheerful native smile.
>
> And when the Storm King reigns supreme,
> They honour their native land,
> And give their lives on the stormy floe,
> Those heroes in heart and hand . . .

Perhaps these effusions were not really meant for the sealers or their families. Perhaps they were meant, instead, to ease the consciences of the St. John's elite who were responsible for the disasters. They may have served this purpose, but certainly they did nothing to prevent further tragedies from taking place. Death on the ice for the outport men was something the owners and rulers of our island could easily take for granted even when, in the spring of 1898, just eight years after the near-loss of over five hundred men at the ice fields, there occurred an event that ought to have shaken their placid conviction that human sacrifice was quite in order so long as commerce prospered.

It was the great dream of every Newfoundland boy to make a voyage to the ice, and the youngsters of St. John's—"carner byes," we used to call them contemptuously – were not immune. Few of them ever got berths because they weren't really fit for the life, but I knew of one exception – a young man apprenticed as a pharmacist's assistant, who got the chance to ship aboard the SS *Greenland* in the spring of 1898.

The law called for a doctor to sail on every sealing ship, but of course the owners would not pay for a real doctor, even if one could be found who would have gone. Instead, any man who could read the label on a pill bottle or who claimed to be a hand at doctoring would fill the bill. Compared to most, I was pretty well trained and Captain Arch Davis, commanding the *Greenland*, was right content when I agreed to sign on with him.

The fleet sailed from St. John's on March 10, 1898, and the little *Greenland* was jammed up with one hundred and fifty-four sealers, plus the officers and engine-room crowd that amounted to fifteen more. It was a bad year for ice. The heaviest kind of old arctic pack was pushed south right into the land. Only a few days out, and before ever a ship had got into the seals, the *Mastiff* got nipped so bad she had to be abandoned and went down.

It was a bad start, certainly, but none of the other ships turned back. There was no getting deep into the fields, so the fleet hung on the eastern edge. On March 16th there come a westerly gale that opened the ice up a bit, and all the ships cut westward into it, following the leads when they could. Next day the *Neptune*, in the van, struck into the young seals and by nightfall every vessel was into the patch and all hands was on ice.

All the next week the men were away from the ship from dawn until dark and there was little enough for the "doctor" to do. Most of the sealers, specially the northern bay men, thought it a weakness to admit they was ever sick or hurt. Just the same, a number got "seal finger" and had to come to me. That was some kind of infection they'd get when they nicked a finger with their bloodstained old sculping knives. We treated it with raw carbolic acid poured on after it had been lanced, but often enough that did no good. Then the finger would have to be cut off or the infection would spread and kill the man. One of our master watches had lost four fingers that way, two from each hand. I had to cut off the forefinger of a man myself, without anything to ease his pain except a drink of rum.

Despite bad weather, the sealing was good and all ships were making a good showing. By March 30th we had about thirteen thousand pelts aboard and the men had panned another six or seven thousand. Panning seal sculps was done to save time so the sealers from one ship could kill all the seals in reach and not let other crews get them first. A ship might string her men out over twenty miles, all busy panning and moving on again. But when she came to pick up those pans she might not find the half of them.

The morning of March 31st the ice got loose and the weather mild, and some of our men looked for a storm. Just the same, all four watches was sent out. There was only scattered seals left by then so the men had to go far afield; some of them six or seven miles from the ship and mostly to westward where the ice was tighter.

Early evening, about three o'clock it was, the wind began to blow a hurricane with driving snow, and the temperature dropped right out – well below freezing. The gale was so heavy it caught the *Greenland* broadside where she lay in an open lead and heeled her over so all the loose pelts on deck slid into the lee scuppers and she nearly went right on over! For a time we were in a desperate state because we couldn't get her righted with the few hands left on board, and the stokers couldn't stand up to fire the boilers and keep steam on her.

Luckily one of the watches was close enough to the ship when the gale struck to get back aboard. All hands went at it then, shifting ballast and trimming coal and, after dark it was, the ship was upright and we had steam on the engine and the pumps. By then it was too late to try and pick up the rest of our men, for the wind was a living gale and thick of snow besides.

When dawn came the *Greenland* was jammed in heavy ice that was driving seaward. Westward of us, and between us and the men, a lake had opened near half a mile across. The barrelman could catch glimpses of our fellows on the other side of the lake, huddled up in black patches on the ice, but the ship could not get to them, nor them to us. Captain Davis was pretty near frantic, for he thought to lose them all. The cold was enough to kill a man outright. In the afternoon there come a lull and the captain sent every able-bodied man to haul our boats to the near edge of the lake and try to go for the stranded sealers. The fellows with those boats took some awful risks but they ended up saving a good many men. Most of the fellows in one watch that was off more to the northward contrived to get around the lake and back to the ship. By nightfall we had a hundred men aboard but fifty or more was still adrift. By then the temperature was below zero and we never thought to see any of them live through the night.

Next day the storm let up. The *Greenland* worked clear of the jam and went after the missing men. There was only a few of them alive, and they was in terrible bad shape. We picked up twenty bodies and five men so far gone they died aboard ship. The rest of the forty-eight men as was lost that day was never seen again by mortal eye.

The voyage home was the most desperate time of my life. I had to set-to and try to save the lives and limbs of dozens of men frost-burned almost to death. It was a nightmare to me but must have been all of that again for the sick men crowded into the cold 'tween deck space.

To make all worse, we met another gale as we neared land and the old engine give out and the *Greenland* blew onto the rocks near Bay de Verde and was near a total loss with all aboard. A lucky shift of the wind took us off before she broke up, and we somehow limped into St. John's with a cargo of dead seals under hatches and a cargo of dead men roped in a heap on the foredeck.

John Melendy, one of the survivors of that dreadful ordeal, had this to add:

There was times during that forty-eight hours onto the ice when things wasn't too bad . . . like the feeling that rose in me when the sound of the storm was drowned out by the voices of the men raised in the hymn "Oh God, Our Help in Ages Past." Then there was other times, times when friends and shipmates struggled up to you and asked you into their house for a cup of tea! Then they would just vanish into the storm again before you could even stop them.

On the second day of the storm all of us were seeing things. A group of fifteen, myself included, thought we saw our ship in the ice on the horizon. We set out from the solid ice over the slob ice towards her. We scrambled all day on our hands and knees and in our wake was a trail of blood from our bleeding hands and knees. I realized after a while it was all a dream. There was no ship. I told the men to follow me back to the main ice and four of them did, but the other ten perished there among the slob.

We found a few seals on the main ice and killed them and used their skins for shelter, drank their blood and ate their meat. The next day we really did sight the ship and she finally came up to us . . . only four left out of fifteen.

If anything might have been expected to change the attitude of the Water Street crowd towards the seal hunt and the sealers, it should have been the appalling homecoming of the battered *Greenland* with her gruesome deck cargo in full and horrifying view. But Water Street was proof even against such a shocking sight as this. There were some pious professions of distress in the newspapers, and some of the usual heroic versifying. A subscription was taken up on behalf of the wives and children of the dead men, and each bereaved family got about ten dollars out of it. However, this was a *public* subscription, not compensation paid by the owners of the *Greenland*. They paid nothing, although the bodies of our northern bay men were shipped home at the expense of the owners – in makeshift crates made from scraps of condemned lumber, and the men still clad in the tattered clothes in which they had died. Some of these "coffins" fell apart during the train journey to Gambo and it was said that several corpses had to be hauled out of the boxcars with ropes because they were so badly decayed.

There was no investigation into the disaster and, far from improving, the conditions endured by the men grew worse. This was not the time for reform of the seal fishery – competition for the remaining seals was growing fiercer as the herds dwindled in size. The merchants reasoned that if the high level of profits was to be maintained they would have to reduce operating costs. Sealers were one of those costs and sealing ships were another. Since there was an oversupply of both, it made good commercial sense to treat them as expendable items.

To some extent the sealers could be expected to look after themselves, since they were usually only at the ice for six or eight weeks and had the rest of the year to recover from that ordeal. This was not true of the ships. With the arrival on the scene of the first steel, ice-breaking sealers, in 1906, the wooden walls became even more neglected. Most of them had become so unseaworthy that no insurance company would cover them and, even by the lax standards prevailing in St. John's, they ought to have been condemned out of hand. But it was the policy of the owners to let the ice "condemn" them.

In the five years between 1907 and 1912 the following wooden walls were lost in the ice: *Leopard* and *Greenland* in 1907 (the *Greenland* had survived the death of so many of her men by just nine years); *Panther, Grand Lake* and *Walrus* in 1908; *Vanguard* and *Virginia Lake* in 1909; *Iceland* in 1910; *Harlaw* in 1911; and *Labrador* in 1912. Some of these were crushed when their captains, increasingly desperate to make a good showing for the owners, put their ships into fatal jeopardy. More were lost when they broke down, blew up, or simply opened up and sank as the inevitable result of decades of neglect. As competition for the remaining seals continued to increase, some captains were so careless about the way they put men on ice that it became almost the accepted thing for parties of men to find themselves spending a night or two on the floes when their ship was too busy elsewhere to come and pick them up. Jacob Kelloway remembers searching for one such unlucky party.

We never knowed they was adrift until night fell. By then there was a living starm from southerly with blinding snow. All night the bo's'n kept the whistle moaning through the muck. The master watch burned flares. Two days blew by, the wind veered northerly – a bitter blast. But all the same we thought to try our luck at finding them. Bad ice was all about. Black water smoking in the cruel frost. The ship tight jammed; we walked three mile before the light began to fail; by then she'd almost vanished in the drift. 'Twas time to give it up. John climbed a pinnacle for one last look . . . and spied the figure of a man lurching amongst the clumpers. We fired guns, waved flags, and bawled at him to come. He heard. Stopped for a moment, turned from side to side like a blind child. And then . . . began to run *away* from we! Run? More like a bird he was, the way he flew over the heaving pack; dodging from sight like a black fox; skipping across the slob like he had wings.

We done our best. Chased after he till our lungs was choked, but lost him in the veil of water smoke. We never saw the hide nor hair of him again. No more his chums. He must have been the last one left alive. Poor lad! Went mental in the head. I think he never knew but what *we* was the dead . . . come back to claim him too.

The hypnotic world of ice had peculiar effects on men and there were few sealers who, at one time or another, did not see strange objects and images. Some of the visions may have been due to the agonizing ice blindness resulting from the concentrated glare of sunlight on the glittering plains; but other things they saw were not so easily explained, as with this tale that Jacob Mullet used to tell.

Fifty-one springs to the ice and forty-three a master watch . . . they's not much I hasn't seen out there. Some says the ice's a lonely place, but I never found it so. Lots of life out on the ice. They's the swiles, of course, and what a sight it be when the old 'uns haul out for their enj'yin' time after the whitecoats dips – takes to the water. I been in the barrel on a fine sunny day and they was nothing to be seen far as the eye could go, only swiles lying about on the pans as thick as pepper, sunning theirselves. T'ousands and t'ousands; and more t'ousands leaping and breaching in the leads and lakes.

And one time I was on ice and we come on a white bear, big as a house he was, and he took we for swiles and come for we hell-a-humping till he was no more'n a chain off, and we fellows with nothing but our gaffs. It looked like a tight squeeze, but old Uncle Benjamin Sturges, belonged to Cape Freels, he takes a jump for the bear and gives a shout: "Git out of it now, you big white buggar! Git out, damn ye, or I'll bite the black nose off your h'ugly face!" And would ye believe it, byes? That bear he turned and hauled his wind and we never see him after!

Aye and the little white foxes would be out there, t'ousands of miles from the arctic where they come from; and ice birds; and big black ravens come off from land to look for the carcasses. The sharks liked swile carcasses some good too. I've stood on a pan and gaffed a dozen and hauled 'em out. One time we used to take their livers and put 'em in a puncheon and sell 'em when we got back to St. John's.

Yiss, me sons, I seen it all . . . but they's some things I didn't care about. I remembers the spring of 1911 when I went master watch on the *Newfoundland*. Young Wes Kean, son of old Captain Abe, was skipper of her and 'twas his first command. 'Twas a good spring . . . moderate weather and the whitecoats thick as flies on the flake in August. We done very good.

One morning, near the end of March, Skipper Wes put me and my watch of forty men out in a scattered patch of "rusty-coats" – young swiles getting their dark hair and near ready to dip. Wes steamed away to see could he find more swiles for the rest of the crowd, and the ship was near out of sight when it come on to starm, right sudden. I got my crowd together in a hurry and I says: "Well, lads, us'd best give this up and make for the ship. Skipper'l never find we now, but we might find he."

I thought he might stay where he was to. I had a good compass and I knowed I could lay a cut handy enough to hear the whistle for a guide.

'Twas no Sunday courting stroll we had that day. The ice was open and the leads full of slob and half the men got ducked before we come to a great big lead. There was no crossing she at all. So then there was nothing to be done but find a pan of thick old ice and put up for the night. After dark the wind hauled nor'ard and it got colder than a merchant's heart.

We was all near froze and pretty well bate-out by then. A good many of the men lay down to take a rest in the shelter of a line of clumpers. I lit some flares and sot meself down on a piece of ice and I supposes I dozed off, for the next thing I knowed I was looking up the path from the landwash to my own house. 'Twas clear as the real thing. But the old Union Jack I always used to fly alongside was hauled down to half-mast. They was a big crowd gathered round – people I knowed as well as I knows meself – and they was all waiting for something. Then the front door, as we never uses, swings open and out comes a coffin, with me woman and me youngsters walking behind it, all crying and carrying on. I knowed right away 'twas my own coffin.

Then the quarest thing ever come over I. Up I jumps from that piece of ice, all standing. I'd been near perished when I sot down, but now I felt fit as a young fellow going off to a dance . . . and that's what I had in mind . . . to go to a dance!

'Twas only a minute until I had the whole crowd on their feet. Them as couldn't or wouldn't budge, I kicked them till they did.

"Git up and come to the dance!" I shouted. "Or, be Jasus, I'll kill ye if ye don't!"

Some told me afterwards they was certain I'd gone off cat-crazy, but they was feared to go agin me. The truth on it was, me mind was clear as it is today. But 'twas like some stranger had stepped into me skin and "Dance!" says he. And dance we did till the blood was moving again and there was no more chance we'd freeze to death.

We was still at it, bawling out the old songs and jigging like a proper crowd of loonies, when out of the dark of the starm comes a blare of a steamer's siren. In a minute the old *Newfoundland* hove in sight, all lights lit and shining, and flares lining her barricade till she looked like she was all afire. When we was aboard again they told us they'd have missed us sure, only they heard the hullabaloo we was making from downwind and found us so.

'Twas a quare thing, certainly; for what would make a man dance at his own funeral? And that was just what I done.

Death on Ice – Part II

By 1900 the seal fishery was in the hands of only a few St. John's merchants, of whom the most famous – or infamous, depending on your point of view – were A. J. Harvey and Company, Bowring Brothers Ltd., Job Brothers and Company, and Baine, Johnson and Company. These four set the rules of the game, decided the price of fat, and took the lion's share of the profits; but with the continuing destruction of the seal herds, each was constantly seeking a means of gaining an advantage over its rivals.

In 1906 Harveys jumped into the lead by building a steel ship for the sealing. The SS *Adventure* was a wonder for her time: an 800-tonner with a 200-horsepower engine, specially designed for the ice to a new and daring plan. Her forefoot was cut away so that, instead of trying to split, or butt the pans aside, she could ride right up onto them, breaking and separating them with her weight and her momentum.

At first the old sealing hands, including the directors of the rival companies, thought Harveys had gone mad. "A steel ship like that," they scoffed, "will be crushed in the ice like a sardine can. There's no give to her plates. It'd be suicide, sure, to go to the pack in her!"

This belief was so widespread that Harveys had a job to get a crew for the *Adventure* and she was forced to sail with less than half the men she could have carried. But once in the ice she soon proved herself. She was twice as handy and twice as fast as any of the old wooden walls. She could get along through ice where none of them could follow, and she made a bumper voyage. When she sailed back through the Notch into St. John's harbour, there were some glum faces at Bowrings and Jobs, for she had made it clear that the days of the wooden walls were now numbered.

By 1909 Harveys, well satisfied, had built two more steel steamers, the *Bonaventure* and the *Bellaventure* – 500-tonners with 300-horsepower engines. Striving to catch up, Bowrings built the 2,000-ton, 450-horsepower *Florizel*, and Jobs commissioned the *Beothic*, of the same class as the *Belle* and the *Bon*. In 1912 Jobs added the 1,000-ton *Nascopie*, but Bowrings topped all competition with the 2,100-ton, 600-horsepower *Stephano*. All of these ships were intended to serve as sealers in the spring but as passenger vessels or freighters for the balance of the year.

The coming of the steel fleet brought competition for the remaining seals to a new and frantic pitch. Risks were taken with men and ships that startled sealers who had been going to the ice for half a century. This was especially true with the old wooden walls who, though they were now badly outclassed, still outnumbered the steel steamers. What had been foolhardy daring by captains in the past now became suicidal daring as the skippers of the wooden walls tried desperately to make good showings. By 1914 the competition at the ice had become a kind of madness and events leading up to the spring of that year did nothing to restore sanity. Rumours of war had sent the value of seal fat skyrocketing, with the result that the Water Street crowd dispatched to the ice every vessel they could find, seaworthy or not, and crammed them to the hatches with men who had been told this was the *Eldorado* spring – *this* time they were bound to go home with their pockets stuffed with gold.

That spring, as for many years previously, the honorary commodore of the fleet was Captain Abraham Kean – legendary seal-killer who, before he gave it up in 1934, was to boast of having killed one million seals. He was a hard man, a driving man, and an obsessed man. His ship, the marvellous new *Stephano*, was the unquestioned queen of the fleet, and Kean was determined to fill her up – to bring in the greatest load of fat ever to enter St. John's harbour. With Captain Abe setting the pace it was a certainty that the other captains would risk heaven and earth in order not to be left too far behind in the race for the little silk flag which was the worthless but fiercely coveted prize given by the St. John's Chamber of Commerce to the high-lining sealing skipper of the year.

One of those who sailed to the front in the spring of 1914 was Skipper Llewelyn Kean. Skipper Lew was from Greenspond but was no relation to Captain Abraham Kean. Although he held his master's papers, he was unable to get a vessel of his own that year and so he shipped as a bridgemaster. That was a common thing, for in those years there were always more captains than there were sealing ships for them to command.

That was the first spring ever I sailed in one of the new steel ships. I had the luck to get a berth with Captain Billy Winsor in the *Beothic*; a smart little vessel she was too. Billy Winsor was a smart man himself, a devil-may-care lad, all for the seals and a great hand for taking chances with his ship and his men if it would get him the fat.

That year all the skippers, and the men too, were dead keen. Word had gone round that fat would fetch the highest price for forty years, and all hands looked to make a big bill if we found the patches.

The old wooden ships put to sea on March 10th, every last one of them as was still afloat–*Bloodhound, Kite, Diana, Newfoundland, Terra Nova, Eagle, Thetis, Neptune, Ranger* and *Southern Cross*. Some was bound to the front, but most, like the *Cross*, were going to try their luck in the Gulf. Because the steel ships were so much faster and abler in the ice, it was agreed they would give the wooden walls a start, so we didn't sail from St. John's until March 14th. All the steel steamers were bound for the front, for that is where the main patch lies. It was a grand sight they made, steaming out the Notch all in a line: the big *Stephano* in the lead; the *Florizel* and *Nascopie*, and then the smaller ships: the *Bell, Bon, Adventure, Beothic, Seal* and *Sagona*.

Most of them stuck close to old Abe Kean in the *Stephano*, dogging the Old Man; but Billy Winsor was never a man to follow another skipper's course. When the fleet struck heavy ice off the Funks, and Captain Kean cut in for land to run inside towards St. Anthony, Billy cut north instead into the heavy stuff. My, how he drove that ship! Times I thought sure he'd tear the bows out of her, but in two days we was into the south corner of the main patch and not another ship in sight.

It looked to be the finest kind of spring. By March 20th almost the whole fleet, wooden walls and all, were into the main patch along of we and killing seals for a pastime. The patch was long and narrow—I'd guess it to be fifty miles long and five or six wide. Right from the first we were high-liner, and Captain Abraham was in a fine fret because we were well up on him. By March 29th we had twenty thousand stowed below and another five thousand panned; but the Old Man had only eighteen thousand altogether. Still and all, every ship was doing very well except the *Newfoundland*. Somehow or other, Captain Wes Kean, old Abe's youngest son, had gone astray and got his ship jammed into the worst sort of heavy ice about seven or eight miles from the whelping pans. Try what he would, he couldn't get clear, and his men were taking no seals at all.

There were plenty of seals, but conditions weren't the best. One morning, the 23rd I think it was, we was working a patch when Skipper Billy, from the barrel, saw another big patch way off to the westward. He took back aboard two watches—a hundred men—including the one I was in, steamed out to the new patch and put us on ice while he went back to pick up the panned pelts and the rest of the crowd. Then the weather closed in, thick and wet, and when he started back he couldn't find us.

We didn't think to take much harm, because there were two or three other ships in the vicinity and we expected we could get aboard one of those if we was put to it. The *Florizel*, with Captain Joe Kean (another of the Old Man's sons), came handy to us to pick up some of his own men, and we started for her, but she veered off and went away full speed and was soon out of sight in the murk. Captain Joe saw us well enough but supposed our own ship would pick us up.

Dark come on with wind and wet snow, and it was not the best. The ice where we was, was going abroad and was soft anyway. The scattered fellow was falling in and when we'd haul him out he'd have to take off his boots and stockings and trousers, wring out the salt water, and pull them on again. He'd be so chilled the life was near out of him.

The drift got so heavy a man could hardly see his chum even before it come full darkness. We'd been on ice all day, every day, for about a week, and we were all beat-out. A good many of the men began to lose heart. There seemed to be no ships near us by then, though if there was, it would have been a job to find them anyway.

Sid and Willis White, belonged to Greenspond, came up to me and Willy said: "Lew, we got to get clear of this crowd. There'll be nary one of them alive tomorrow morning." I agreed we should branch off and try to find some tight ice and straighten away for the night. There was nine in my lot and we went off on our own. We found some good ice where there was still some live seals and a good many carcasses, and we set to work to build a circular shelter out of ice blocks and dead seals to keep away the wind.

Now while we was at all this, Skipper Billy was still searching for us. He contacted the *Florizel* on the Marconi and asked had she seen any of his men. Skipper Joe came back and said he had, and Billy asked him to pick them up for the night. Joe agreed to try and, between the jigs and the reels, he did find the main crowd and took them aboard . . . and none too soon for some of them. But he never found us, and we never saw nor heard the ship.

Never mind that, we was all right. We had about thirty seal carcasses at our "door." We tore up our tarred tow ropes and frizzed them out for to light a fire. We fed it with shavings from our gaffs and poles until it was hot enough to melt seal fat and after that we kept it fair roaring with carcasses. They burned like a furnace and gave us all the hot roasted meat we had a mind to eat.

Every man went and got himself a live young seal and this is what we sat on all night. The seals didn't seem to mind. Every now and again they would open their eyes, look around, and go back to sleep. By morning they weren't white any more . . . they was just as black with soot and smoke as all the rest of us.

Morning came and the wind veered west, very strong and freezing cold. About midmorning, in the midst of a heavy squall, we heard a voice yell out: "HARD A STARBOARD!"–and there was the *Beothic* pretty near alongside our pan. Her lookouts had smelled the burning fat – 'tis a terrible strong stink – and she'd steamed up on it until they saw our fire.

I tell you, we had a good time when we got aboard. Skipper Billy gave all hands a big drink of whisky. I never minded being out that night – we was comfortable enough. But Sid White told me afterwards he never thought any of us would come through. It seems just before he come to me on the small ice, he and some other fellows were a bit apart when out of the drift there was the loom of something.

"Looked to I like a big kind of beast with long, sharp horns," Sid told me. "The snow gusted up in a minute, and it was gone when the squall cleared. A fearful bad sign, according to the old folk, for they says if you sees one of them ice spirits it foretells the death of a good many poor fellows."

Perhaps that's all a pack of nonsense, but all the same, what happened to us out there that time was well known right through the fleet, because of the Marconi; and I used to wonder afterwards whether the skippers took proper account of it. Certainly, Captain Wes Kean on the *Newfoundland* was the only man who never heard the news, for his was the only ship without a wireless.

I know one thing, though. Skipper Billy was right heedful where he put his men after that, and we were just as heedful to stay handy to our ship.

By Monday, March 29th, all the ships, with one exception, had been into the fat for ten days or more. Only the *Newfoundland* – the largest and most powerful of the wooden walls – was still out of it, still jammed fast in heavy, raftered ice, about eight miles southeast of the main patch where, in light whelping ice, the rest of the ships were free to move about almost at will.

Captain Wes Kean's frustration and fury at having put his ship into such a situation had mounted to an explosive pitch by Monday night. At dawn on Tuesday the visibility was exceptional and when he climbed to the barrel he could see several ships on the northern icescape. Although unable to talk to them by wireless, he was sure they must be in the seals. He swung his glasses to the nearest one, the *Stephano*, commanded by his father, and saw that her after-derrick was hoisted vertically. This was the signal agreed upon between father and sons to show that the Old Man was working a good patch of seals. The sight was too much for the young skipper. Only twenty-nine years old, he had been made master of the *Newfoundland* four years earlier, largely because his father had pushed him up with Harveys. In order to refute the charge of favouritism, he had to bring in a good load of fat each spring. Now, the way things looked in this most important of all springs, he stood a good chance of having to come home almost clean. That was an intolerable prospect. Peering from the barrel into the beckoning northern wastes, he made up his mind. If the *Newfoundland* could not reach the seals, her men would have to go to the seals on their own feet.

Shortly before 7 a.m. all four watches, totalling 179 men, were ordered over the *Newfoundland*'s side under the leadership of 33-year-old George Tuff, the vessel's second-in-command.

"'Tis a long haul and damned rough ice, Garge," Wes Kean told Tuff, "but the seals is there in t'ousands, sure. Go straight for the *Stephano* and report to Father. He'll put you onto the patches and tell you what to do. Doubtless he'll keep you aboard his ship tonight, and when the ice slacks off I'll steam over and pick up the men and the seals you've panned."

If Tuff had doubts about the wisdom of the plan he gave no sign; but doubts he must have had because, at the age of seventeen, he had been one of the survivors of the *Greenland* disaster. It had taken him months to recover physically from that experience and for years afterwards he had been plagued by frightful nightmares in which dead companions, frozen rigid, implored him to let them into his warm little house at Newtown.

The weather was extraordinarily fine that Tuesday morning – too fine, too warm, too calm by far, or so thought some of the men who had heard from the bo's'n that the barometer was falling. "'Twas a weather-breeder, certainly!" one of them remembered; and many were aware of a vague sense of unease as the long black column began snaking its way through the chaos of pressure ridges and raftered ice towards the tiny shape of the *Stephano*, hull-down to the north.

The going was even harder than Wes Kean had predicted. "I never saw worse ice in all my time," George Tuff remembered. After three hours of exhausting travel the attenuated column had only gone three miles from the *Newfoundland*. Those in the lead now came upon a scattered handful of whitecoats and all the men halted gratefully while these were clubbed and sculped. When the long line moved on again it was incomplete. Some fifty men had detached themselves from it and, in startling defiance of the ingrained habits of obedience *and* amid shouts of "yellowbelly" and "coward" from their companions, had stubbornly turned about and headed back for their own ship.

When they reached the *Newfoundland* they were met by an infuriated Captain Kean who as good as accused them of mutiny and threatened them with the loss of their shares in the voyage. Subdued, strangely silent, they remained on the ice until his rage had run its course; then, muttering something about "bad weather," they came quietly aboard and went below. Not one of them cared to tell Wes Kean the true reason for their return.

'Twas a bright, sunny morning when we left the *Newfoundland*. They was no reason to see nothing as wasn't there. But some of we saw something as had no right to be on the ice or anywhere at all on God's mortal earth! We come round a high pinnacle, and there it was . . . a giant of a man it looked to be, covered all over, face and all, in a black, hairy coat. It stood there, big as ary bear; blocking our way . . . Go forward in the face of that? No, me son! Not for all the gold as lies buried in the world!

It took nearly five hours of exhausting struggle before the remaining 126 men from the *Newfoundland* reached the high steel sides of the *Stephano*, which had stopped to let them come aboard. They had seen no more seals, and a heavy haze had clouded the sky. A few glittering flakes of snow were already beginning to fall. The fine day was quickly coming to an end.

Before we got to the *Stephano* 'twas clear enough there was dirty weather on the go, and they warn't a man of we expected to go back on ice that day. We was certain sure the *Stephano* would be our boardinghouse. While most of the crowd went below for a mug of tea and a bit of hard bread, George Tuff went aft to see Captain Abraham Kean and get his orders.

The *Stephano* got under way again, and about twenty minutes later we was called back on deck. The snow was coming thicker, but the Old Man was up on the bridge waving his arms and bawling: "*Newfoundland* men, over the side!" Oh yiss, I can hear him yet. "Hurry up now, byes! Get out and get your seals!"

We hardly knew what to think about it, but the most of us supposed we was just going for a little rally, handy to the ship, and would be back aboard soon enough. But we was hardly clear of her when the *Stephano* swung hard around, showed us her stern, and drove off full steam ahead to the nor'ard. Young Jobbie Easton was along of me and there was a quare look on his face.

"That one's not coming back for we. She's gone for good!" Those as heard him began to crowd around George Tuff. "That's a lie now, ain't it, Garge?" some fellow asked.

"No, me sons," says George very low. "Captain Abraham's orders is for us to go and work a patch of swiles sou'west from here about a mile, pan the pelts, and then strike out for our own ship. He says as he's got men and seals of his own to look out for."

The snow was getting thicker by the minute, and any man who'd ever been on ice before knew what our chances was of finding the *Newfoundland* that night. Uncle Ezra Melendy pipes up and says: "Us'll never do it, Garge. 'Twill be the *Greenland* all over again." Then there was proper hell to pay. Some was calling on George to lead us back to the *Stephano* or chase after she. John Howlett stuck his chin out and told Tuff to stop wasting time and to start for the *Newfoundland*. "God damn it, Garge. This is no weather to be killing swiles!" Then John turned to us. "Byes," he says, "'tis time for we to give up this and go for our own ship!"

It come near to blows, but there was no changing George's mind. He had his orders from the Old Man, and bedamned if he'd fly in the face of them. So off we went to find them seals and, afore we knowed it, the starm was on full blast.

On Tuesday morning, March 31st, one of the most savage storms of the year swept in over the southeastern approaches to Newfoundland and overwhelmed the island. Within a few hours the city of St. John's lay paralyzed beneath a tremendous snowfall, buffeted by hurricane winds. Ocean-going freighters laboured through towering seas offshore, seeking shelter, or lay hove-to, head to the gale, trying to ride it out.

During the afternoon the storm swept out over the northern ice and that vast plain became a faceless wilderness given over to whirling snow devils that obliterated everything from view. The storm caught nearly a hundred of Captain Abraham Kean's men far from their ship, for he had refused to believe the evidence of his senses, or of the plunging barometer, and had subbornly continued to pile up seal pelts as if there was nothing else in life of any import. His men were lucky. The *Florizel* appeared, as if by magic, close to the *Stephano*'s men and, thankfully, they scrambled aboard. But the storm had caught one hundred and twenty-six of the *Newfoundland*'s men on ice . . . and there was no luck left for them.

Adrift in that raging chaos, on ice that began to heave and grind and shatter as the storm swell lifted under it, they were at least seven miles from their own jammed and helpless ship. What was more ominous, *nobody knew they were adrift.* Aboard the *Newfoundland*, Captain Wes Kean ate a good hot supper and went to his bunk, content in the belief that his men were safe aboard the *Stephano.* On the *Stephano*, the Old Man was preoccupied with wondering whether or not the storm would prevent him from overtaking that young upstart, Billy Winsor, and getting enough whitecoats to make him high-liner once again. If he gave any thought to the *Newfoundland*'s men, it was to assume they had reached their own ship. After all, that is where he had *ordered* them to go.

There was no way for anyone to discover the truth. Although all the other ships were fitted with wireless and could communicate with one another, the *Newfoundland*'s wireless had been removed before she sailed, by orders of her owners, A. J. Harvey and Company. As one of their directors was to testify later: "It did not pay to keep it aboard." Harveys did not feel that its presence added to the profits from the seal fishery.

'Twas terrible . . . terrible, my son! After the starm came on I never saw a better chance for a disaster . . . We started back for the *Newfoundland* 'bout one o'clock, in a gale of wind, with the snow so thick and wet it was enough to choke a man. We struck east-sou'east looking for our outward track and found it, but 'twas too late by then. The ice was wheeling so bad the track was all broke up and there was swatches of open water everywhere. The snow was so heavy it lay thick on the water and 'twas a job to tell it from good ice. Before dark six or seven of the men had fell through and was lost . . . 'Twas no use to go on . . . The men gathered round about on two or three of the biggest pans they could find, and they was none too big at that, and built up shelters out of clumpers of ice. Then the snow changed to freezing rain, till we was all drenched to the skin, but at least it warn't too frosty. I prayed 'twould keep raining, for if the wind backed to nor'ward and brought the frost, I knowed we'd no chance at all . . .

Lew Kean was safe aboard the *Beothic* that night and, as he said: "Thankful to God for it . . . "

I never saw worse weather at the front. I dare say there were few enough managed to sleep sound that night. The grinding and the roaring of the ice was enough to put the fear of the Lord into any man. Wild? I went on deck a time or two, and I don't know the words to tell what it was like. It was all a man could do to keep his feet, and the sleet cut into you like shot.

In the morning it was still blowing a living starm, and then it come on to snow again and the wind veered to nor'west and brought the white frost with it. That killed them altogether! The shelters those poor fellows had built was straight – like a wall – and no good at all when the wind come round. There was no seals where they was to, and they had nothing left to burn. Their clothes was pitiful poor, for it was a warm morning when they left their ship, and the most of them left their oilskins behind, counting to be aboard the *Stephano* for the night. For grub there was nothing but a bit of oatmeal or a pick of hard bread in the bottom of some fellows' nunny bags. A few had little bottles of Radway's Ready Relief – supposed to be a pain killer but, if the truth was out, only flavoured alcohol – good enough stuff, but there wasn't more than a glutch for every man.

Same as a good many sealers, they were mortal feared to lay down and take some rest. Believed they'd never wake again. That was pure foolishness . . . the worst kind! They spent the whole night on their feet, marching about like sojers, running around, pounding each other to keep awake . . . and they beat themselves right out. In the morning, when the frost took them, they were so done in they began to fall dead on their feet. Some even froze to death standing up.

About noon the snow let up and the sky cleared, but the wind was sharper and frostier than ever and the ground drift was like a cloud. If a man climbed to the top of a pinnacle he would be in clear air, with the sun shining on him, but on the ice he was near blind with the drift. In breaks in the storm, the few fellows as had the strength to climb the pinnacles could see some of the ships . . . the *Florizel* away to the nor'ard; the *Stephano* under way, and trying to pick up pans far off to the nor'east. Once the *Bell* come straight for them, close as three or four miles. Six men set out to walk to her, but they all perished, and the *Bell*, never seeing them, turned and steamed away. That took the heart out of the men as was left, like it was cut out with a sculping knife.

The devil of it was that not a one of we on any of the other ships knew they was lost. I tell you, when Harveys took that wireless out of the *Newfoundland* they killed those men better than bullets could have done.

Before dark came on, things was so desperate that George Tuff, with three of the master watches and a few other fellows, undertook somehow to get across that heaving mess of broken ice and reach their own ship. George had spied a glimpse of the *Newfoundland* from a pinnacle. She'd finally got clear of the jam and started steaming towards the *Stephano*, intending, I suppose, to pick up her men as Wes Kean thought was on his father's ship. When George saw her she was jammed again, but a lot closer to the men than before. Those fellows pretty near got to her, though how they stood up to it, the Lord knows. They was coming up towards her lee side . . . but all hands aboard her was looking out to windward where the *Stephano* lay. And then she burst out of the jam and hauled away for the *Stephano*, and those fellows just had to watch her go. That finished them entirely. They crawled into a hole in a pile of clumpers as night come down, freezing bitter cold and blowing a whole gale again.

Back on the two floes where the most of the men still was, it was even worse. When them poor fellows as lived through it told me about it afterwards, it was near enough to freeze me blood.

. . . The weather was near zero and the snow blowing like a whirlwind. You could look up sometimes through the drift and see the stars up there. Down on the ice the men was dying. My first cousin, and best chum, he lay down to die but I wouldn't let him do it. I punched him and hauled him about and jumped on his feet . . . that's how he lost his feet, I suppose. I got them all broken up, jumping on them. "Bye," I said to him. "Don't you die out here! Don't you give it to them at home to say you died out here on this ice!" But I had to go on kicking him . . . I nearly killed that poor fellow to make him live . . .

Some went crazy at the end of it, yelling and squalling and wandering off and never seen again. More died quiet, sitting or lying there, most likely dreaming of being home again . . . They saw strange things. One fellow come over to me and says: "Come in to the house now, me son. We'll have a scoff. The woman's just cooking up a pot of soup." I never saw him after. His eyes was froze shut with the ice caked on his face . . .

Uncle Ezra Melendy, as had lived through the *Greenland* disaster, was an old fellow but he wouldn't give it up. His legs was froze solid to the hips and he was crawling over the ice trying to keep close to we. He'd lost his mittens and his hands was froze hard like claws. He crawled up to me and says: "Me hands is some cold, bye." I went along his back trail a bit and found his mitts, but I couldn't pull them on his hands, all crooked up like they was. So I slit them with me knife and put them on that way. "That's good now," he says and crawls off. His body was never found afterwards . . .

Freddie Hunt never had his cap, and his boots was gone right off his feet. He had only a poor jacket of cotton made from a flour bag, but he was some determined not to die. Wednesday night he started to take the jacket off a dead man, but the corpse rolled over and says: "Don't ye do it, Freddie. I aren't dead yet! . . . "

The worse thing I seen was when I tried to get to another pan and I fell over a clumper. Only it warn't no clumper. 'Twas Reuben Crewe and his son, froze together, and the old fellow's arms tight around the lad, and the lad's head buried under his father's jacket. I recall the drift eased off about then and it seemed light as day and I looked around me and 'twas like being in a graveyard full of awful white statues . . . dead men all around . . .

At the crack of dawn on Thursday morning Captain Wes Kean climbed to the barrel of the *Newfoundland*'s mainmast. The weather had moderated; the wind had dropped out and visibility was good. For some time he anxiously watched the *Stephano*, which was also jammed now but less than a mile distant to the east. He was looking for his absent men who should have been leaving the big steel ship to return to their own vessel. As yet there was no sign of life aboard the *Stephano* so he swung his glasses to the west to see if there were any seals in sight. He was electrified to see a small group of men staggering across the ice towards him in the pale half-light and, with sick comprehension, he knew what had happened. Kean very nearly fell from the shrouds in his haste to gain the deck, and when he reached it he was close to hysteria.

Half an hour later George Tuff and three others were being helped aboard their ship by a rescue party of horrified shipmates. These survivors of the lost party looked more like walking dead than living men. Tuff stood before his captain, weaving from side to side and barely able to mumble through cracked and bleeding lips.

"This is all the men you got left, Cap'n. The rest of them is gone . . . "

At about the same time that Tuff regained his ship, the barrelman of the *Bellaventure*, which was then steaming about looking for lost pans some miles to the northwest, saw what he took to be a small party of sealers belonging to some other ship. As he watched, he realized there was something wrong with them. "They looked right queer . . . like they was drunk, crawling and falling about." He called his skipper, Captain Robert Randell, and in a few minutes the *Bell* was crashing through the pack towards them under forced draft. Two of the figures were much closer than the others and at 9 p.m. the wireless began to crackle.

CAPTAIN SS *BELLAVENTURE* TO CAPTAIN SS *STEPHANO*. TWO *NEWFOUND-LAND* MEN IN PRETTY BAD SHAPE GOT ABOARD US THIS MORNING. REPORTED ON ICE SINCE TUESDAY AND SEVERAL MEN PERISHED.

This report was picked up by almost every ship in the fleet and all those in the vicinity began to converge on the *Bell*. Soon hundreds of sealers were scattering across the pack laden with stretchers, food and rum, searching for the lost party. By nightfall the *Bell*, magnificently handled by Captain Randell, had found and taken aboard thirty-five survivors, all frightfully frostbitten, including several who were thought to be beyond saving. The other ships had found nine more . . . and that was all of the lost party ever to be found alive.

At dusk the *Stephano*, *Bellaventure* and *Florizel* came together alongside the stricken *Newfoundland*. The death ship's roll was read and the appalling scope of the disaster was finally revealed. Then the dead, the dying and those who would survive, although crippled and disfigured for life, were all placed aboard the *Bellaventure* and she prepared to leave the ice for home. She would be the first ship back to St. John's that year, but for her there would be no cheers from the crowded quay, no bellow of gunfire from Signal Hill. Below decks she carried the sculps of many thousands of prime seals – a fortune for her owners. On deck, twisted and contorted into ghastly postures, she carried the frozen bodies of seventy men who would go to the ice no more. Nine others of the lost party remained behind, already buried in the darkness of the icy sea.

The *Bellaventure* departed from the ice alone. Orders from the owners of the remaining ships had been received by radio. They were to continue sealing. Many of the men on those other ships had lost cousins, brothers, even fathers in the disaster, and now they came as close to violence as their natures would allow. When Captain Billy Winsor, whose ship was already log-loaded, tried to put his men on ice they flatly refused orders. "No, Cap'n," their spokesman told him. "Us aren't goin' swilin' in that grave- yard. Not for the king hisself!"

One by one the captains gave up and took the cut for home . . . all save one. Captain Abraham Kean stayed out. He was implacably determined to better Billy Winsor's catch, and even when his own men mutinied he kept the *Stephano* in the ice.

"I seen him on the bridge when the *Bell* pulled away," one of his crew remembered. "Never had no eyes for her. He was spyin' to nor'ard on the lookout for swiles. More like a devil than a man, he looked up there. No doubt 'tis a lie, but they was some aboard was sayin' the Old Man'd think nothin' of runnin' the winches on one side takin' up sculps while he was runnin' em on t'other side takin' dead men off the ice."

In that ill-omened spring of 1914 most of the wooden walls had gone to the Gulf of St. Lawrence (to the *back* of the island) rather than to the front, partly to avoid competition with the steel ships and partly because ice conditions were always easier there since heavy arctic pack was absent. Nevertheless, the Gulf voyage carried its own special risks. Between Cabot Strait and St. John's lay some two hundred and fifty miles of open ocean – as wicked an expanse of water as exists anywhere, and at its worst in early spring when cyclonic gales thunder against the granite cliffs of

Newfoundland's south coast. As old Captain Henry Dawes suc-
cinctly put it at the time: "You only needs to be a sealer to take
a ship to the front, but to take one to the Gulf . . . Mister, you'd
best be a sailor, and a damned good one at that!"

Captain George Clarke, in charge of the *Southern Cross*, was
a jowler of a sealing skipper, but considerably less experienced
as a sailor. He had no master's certificate, and most of his previous
experience had been limited to fishing schooners. Nevertheless,
he was in command of a 500-ton wooden steamer and a sealing
crew of 174 men.

The *Southern Cross*, *Terra Nova*, *Viking* and several others of
the old ships had a lucky passage westward and took the Gulf
ice on March 12th. They found the whitecoats almost at once
and a great slaughter was soon under way. By Sunday, March
29th, Captain Clarke had proved his right to be called a jowler,
for the *Cross* was log-loaded with about twenty-five thousand
seals. Her holds were jammed full and several thousand pelts
had been precariously penned on deck. That afternoon Clarke
sent a radio message to Captain Bartlett, skipper of the *Terra
Nova*, announcing that he was bound up for St. John's that same
night and expecting to be the first ship home. Bartlett, whose
vessel was also loaded, had "no mind to make a race of it." An
experienced master mariner, he had taken thoughtful note of a
drop in the barometer and he preferred to hold to the shelter of
the ice until he saw what kind of weather was brewing.

The weather that was on its way was the same violent storm
that killed so many of the men of the *Newfoundland* on the
northern ice fields. On Monday night it caught the *Cross* in open
water on the dangerous weather coast of southern Newfoundland. Another captain might have run for shelter, but Clarke chose
not to do so despite the fact that his leaking, strained old vessel
was grossly overloaded; was crank in a seaway at the best of
times; and had almost no lifesaving gear aboard apart from a few
flimsy wooden punts which would not have lasted ten minutes
in the great turmoil of wind and water that was already turning
the ocean feather-white. The *Southern Cross* held to her course,
corkscrewing into an increasingly savage sou'easter until she was
acting more like a submarine than a surface ship. That was how

she appeared to Captain Thomas Connors, skipper of the coastal freighter *Portia*, during a momentary and frightening encounter with the *Cross* a few miles off Cape Pine on Tuesday afternoon. The *Portia*, a new steel ship, was having all she could do to hold her own and was trying desperately to work up for shelter into St. Mary's Bay, when out of the driving scud a vessel suddenly hove into sight.

"A big, black, three-masted steamer came hell-bent out of the muck and damn near ran us down. She cleared our stern by no more than a dory's length. I only saw her for a minute, but there's no doubt she was the *Southern Cross*. She seemed half-seas under and so low in the water her decks was running green. Then she was gone."

It was the last time she was ever seen. Not a single trace of the *Southern Cross* or of her crew was ever found, except for a broken life belt bearing her name that washed ashore in Ireland many months later.

So ended the spring of 1914. The merchant princes of Water Street were the richer by the profits from 233,000 seal pelts. And the ordinary people of Newfoundland were the poorer by the deaths of two hundred and fifty-five of their best men.

One time every man, woman and child as could walk would be on the docks and the cliffs to cheer the sealing ships back from the ice fields. This time 'twas all different. The people was there right enough, but they was quiet . . . some of them watching and waiting for a ship, and for men, as would never come home again. It seems to me as something broke in the heart of our old island that spring of 1914, and never rightly healed again in after times.

Last of the Wooden Walls

After the black spring of the *Newfoundland* the government was finally forced to enact regulations giving some protection to the sealers. For the first time, sealing ships had to pass classification examinations. When these were carried out in the spring of 1915 *only three* of the wooden walls scraped through!

The increased costs of keeping the old steamers in what was, at best, barely seaworthy condition cut painfully into the profits, and so most of the owners now began to lose interest in the hunt. All the new steel ships were chartered for war work, or sent abroad, and few of them survived to return to the island when the war was over. In ever-dwindling numbers the remaining wooden steamers continued going to the ice, but they were a dying breed. Between 1915 and 1931 the *Nimrod, Diana, Bloodhound* (third to bear that name), *Kite, Aurora, Erik, Viking, Stella Maris, Nord* and the *Newfoundland* herself (hopefully renamed *Samuel Blandford*) all perished at the ice or on the island's coasts and reefs.

A few new steel ships, including the *Imogene*, were built after the war but they were cargo and passenger ships first and foremost, and they went sealing only as a sideline. The truth was that the sealing game was fast playing out. The harps and hoods had been unable to stand against the loss of forty or fifty million slaughtered during the preceding century. Still, during the thirties, there were a few lucky springs that almost made it seem as if the great days had returned—springs when the handful of remaining ships struck into a remnant of the main patch. It happened in 1933 when the *Imogene* came wallowing in through the Notch, log-loaded with 55,600 seals and all flags flying to proclaim her victory. And for one more time the people of St. John's crowded up on Signal Hill, out on the Battery, and along the harbour quays to welcome the high-liner home. But it was only a last flicker of a sun already set.

At the end of World War II the sealing game passed into the hands of Norwegian interests. Manning new and deadly, ice-strengthened motor vessels, they set out to ruthlessly clean up the survivors of the harp and hood nations. A few Newfoundland coasters made occasional trips to the ice, but theirs were hardly more than scavenging voyages to those northern floes that were being scoured clean of life.

The great seal nations of the northern ice were passing into memory, and the sealers of our island followed, in the fading wakes of their own vanished ships.

The wooden walls, and the men of the wooden walls, had accompanied the seal hunt to its zenith, and they descended with it. By 1933 only the *Ranger, Eagle, Neptune, Thetis* and *Terra Nova* remained afloat out of the nearly sixty wooden steamers which had taken part in the hunt out of Newfoundland ports during the preceding seventy years.

In 1942 the last wooden walls made their final voyage to the ice. The war at sea was then reaching full fury and no modern ships could be spared for the seal fishery; but the price of fat had soared because of the war and so, again, there was money to be made out on the northern ice fields. Some of the St. John's merchants decided to take a chance – with other men's lives – and three grimy, splintered, decrepit old ships were towed from their silent anchorage at the south side of St. John's harbour to the company quays. Here they were superficially restored and fitted out, and one March morning slipped almost unnoticed through the Notch under the long grey guns of newly built coast forts. A friend in the navy saw them go.

I was in a frigate on the North Atlantic convoy run out of St. John's that spring, and we were inbound after a bitch of a crossing. It was foggy, as usual, and I was on the bridge when the Number One called out: "For Christ's sake, come and look at this!" I went out on the wing and there they were, like ghosts out of the past. The wooden walls! Three of them in line – belching black smoke, their lovely old spars still standing and still carrying their yards. There was the *Terra Nova* and the *Eagle*, with the *Ranger* in the van. The *Ranger* dipped her flag to us and we saluted with our siren. I could hardly believe what I was seeing. They looked like they were a hundred years old. It was right out of another age; and I thought, "Bloody good luck to you, old timers. Bloody good luck . . . you'll sure and hell need all you can get!"

Old die-hard ships – commanded by die-hard skippers of a vanished era, for no one else would have dared take those ancient relics to sea, to risk the submarines and, what was far more dangerous, to risk the northern ice once more.

In command of the *Ranger* was Captain Llewelyn Kean. Although born in 1889, Skipper Lew was still in his prime after thirty-five years at the sealing game. Here is his own story of that final voyage – the period that marked the end.

The *Ranger*. Yes . . . she was a grand old boat, you know. Took thousands and thousands of seals in her time. Built in Dundee in 1871 – white oak, greenheart and Australian ironbark. She was only a little bit of a thing, not much bigger than a good-sized tugboat of today, with a 70-horsepower reciprocating engine, and fully rigged when she was young. Towards the end she still could carry sail, and there were times we needed it.

In 1938 I was second hand to Captain Sid Hill in the new *Beothic* owned by Bowrings. They owned the *Ranger* too, and that spring she'd gone to the Gulf with Captain Moses Clarke and got into a devil of a jam, was nipped and pretty near sunk. Clarke got her back to St. John's somehow. Clean she was, with nary a seal on board, and all broke up. He stepped ashore swearing he was finished with the seal fishery, and he meant it. Never did go back. Most people thought the *Ranger* was finished too, and not before time, but when Bowrings asked me if I'd take her out to the front the next spring and try and make some kind of a voyage with her, why I said, "Fair enough, sorr." I doubt they cared if I got many seals. The thing was that if no one took her, she'd have had to be condemned.

It was well on in the season by then. The other ships had been at the ice for near two weeks. All I could get was about twenty-five men to go along of me, with old Skipper Ben Kean as second hand. We run into tight ice off the Funks, but I cut to the eastward and fooled around until I got a line on the other boats by listening in on the Marconi. After that it was all luck. We got into a corner of the main patch and took twelve thousand seals, and that was better than some of the other boats did that year. But we was in such heavy ice and had so little power we couldn't get clear again and was carried along for ten days until we was a hundred and twenty miles *south* of St. John's. Then the ice went slack and I straightened her out, nor'nor'east for the Notch. That night she began to leak like a salt basket. It looked like it was going to be a bad job, and I had a mind to go back into the ice so if we had to take to the boats we would have some chance. But the weather stayed civil, and the pumps wasn't losing ground too fast, so we held on and somehow brought her in.

There was the biggest kind of crowd waiting for us. I suppose nobody ever expected to see the old lady come back again. Women waved their aprons, and men and youngsters were all over the Battery yelling and shouting. When we got docked at Bowrings and they got emergency pumps onto her, I noticed that Skipper Ben looked poorly. I suppose it was the close thing. Anyway, him and me went into the cabin and I poured us both a big drink of rum. We downed it and I went ashore to report to the owners and that was the last time I saw Skipper Ben alive. His heart give out and he was dead within the hour.

Bowrings was well satisfied with what we done, and when I told them about Ben, they said: "I suppose you want to carry him home to Wesleyville?" I said: "Yes, sorr, we got to carry Skipper Ben home." So they told me to buy a coffin and charge it to the company. Real gentlemen, they was.

There was some as thought I was foolish to stay in that old tub, but anyway I took her out each spring after that. Mostly we had good voyages; and I learned her ways. One thing about her, she'd never leak while we was in the ice. But when she got into the blue drop, wouldn't she leak! The safest plan was to get into the ice quick as you could and stay as long as you could.

In the spring of 1942, on account of the war, only three ships went out. There was my cousin Charlie Kean in the *Terra Nova*, Sid Hill in the *Eagle*, and me in the *Ranger*. None of them vessels was fit to be at sea, I suppose – the *Ranger* was seventy-one years old that spring – so we agreed to stay in company. The crowd I had aboard was small, only fifty-five men, and the most of them old fellers or lads too young to jine the navy or the army; but they was yary – a good crowd.

It was a bad spring all round. Almost no ice at all and so, of course, no seals. We went down the Labrador as far as the Round

Hills and found nothing; only we near got beat to pieces in a storm. So we ran back into Belle Isle Strait as far as Red Bay and anchored there a couple of days, pumping her out and trying to repair her a bit. Then we tried the French Shore. Nothing at all. So on we come to the south'ard, looking to find old seals moulting on what ice there was. There was a few around the Funks but the ice was too scattered to put men onto it, so we put out the boats and went swatching. Got a few hundred sculps the first day, but that night the glass began to fall like it had no bottom into it.

"Well, Albert," I says to my second hand. "We're going to have a starm, and that's all there is to it."

The three vessels was close together, but there was no harbour in sight and no heavy ice we could run into for shelter. If the wind come on from nor'east the way it looked, it was going to be hard times. We straightened out to try and shelter up in Notre Dame Bay. The *Eagle* took the lead with the *Terra Nova* astern of us.

By midnight it was a howling nor'east gale and the old *Ranger* couldn't punch it. She began to give out. She opened up and leaked so bad the pumps couldn't come near it. Then, when we was about thirty miles nor'east of Cape Fogo, the headway came off her. She wouldn't answer her helm and swung right around and lay in the trough of the seas. I knowed what had happened, of course, before ever the chief engineer climbed up on the bridge to tell me the water was up to the boilers and the fires was out.

"Bad lookout, Cap'n," he says to me. "Nothing we can do now. The water is into the engine and the steam pumps is finished."

"Yiss, bye," says I. "That's right enough. We're in bad shape for certain."

We put all hands onto the hand pumps or hauling water out of her hold with barrels slung to the fore derricks, but that was only foolishness. She was rolling down to her gunwales with seas coming right across her, putting aboard ten times the water the men could get out. That would never do at all, so we bent on jib and foresail – it was all as her old standing rigging would bear – and that gave us steerage way and we begun to head off before the gale. I says to myself: "Well, Lew, bye. Whatever she's going to do now, she's going to do." We just had to take it, whatever happened.

The men were played out entirely and most of them went below and fell into their bunks, too tired to care if they lived or not. Now the seas was coming right over her, end for end. They knocked down everything; beat up all our boats and swept the galley clean overboard, stove and all. The big greybeards coming in over her stern ran right through her. By dawn she was dead in the water and there was only five or six men still fit to help work the ship, and we needed four men on the wheel all the time. It was a bad enough job, and time for us to try and save ourselves.

I went to the Marconi shack and sent out an S.O.S., but the only one heard it was Skipper Charlie in the *Terra Nova*. He never knowed it then, but *her* time was almost up. In the summer of 1943 she went down in the Greenland Sea – the last of the old wooden steamers – the last of the fleet.

Anyway, I got him on the radio phone. He come back to say:

"Old man, nothing we can do for you. We got our hands full ourselves. Don't know what we're going to do ourselves. Too rough for any lifeboat to live now. You can't come to we and we can't go to you."

"Yiss, old son," I tells him. "I knows that right enough."

We could just get a glimpse of her now and again, half-mile abeam of us, and she was making terrible heavy weather of it, but not so bad as us, for she wasn't leaking and her engine was still working.

"Yiss. That's it then, bye," I told him. "We're finished anyway, Charlie. Too bad . . . too bad, but that's it now."

The wind got worse, close to a hurricane, a living gale, with snow and rain until there was nothing to be seen. The *Terra Nova* was gone, and we didn't know but what she'd sunk. There was no sight nor sound of Sid Hill and the *Eagle*. We was driving broadside for land now with all sails blown out, every scrap of canvas blown clean out of the bolt ropes. No steerage way at all, and the vessel full of water and lying like a log. If she'd been an iron ship she'd have gone under long before, but there was so much wood into her she somehow kept afloat all that day.

Towards evening she began to drive across the mess of sunkers and shoal water lying off Fogo Island. It was a hard sight, I'll tell you! Some of those sunkers was breaking and spouting fifty feet into the air. We couldn't do a thing for ourselves. All hands was crowded onto the bridge and into the bridgeway waiting for her to strike. As she was driving over one shoal patch, a sea broke clean over the whole ship and washed most of the Marconi shack overboard, putting us out of commission entirely; but the old *Ranger* never touched the bottom.

Finally we drove clear of the shoal ground, though our chances didn't look much brighter for that. It was coming on for night and we were driving down on a weather shore with no chance to make a harbour. We could see the cliffs of Change Islands to the south'ard and the water was flying up over the rocks as high as the heavens. No ship nor man could have lived a minute on a shore like that.

Just before dark we saw an edge of ice between us and the land. It was a field of ice the gale had packed into the channel between Change Islands and Baccalhoa Island. It was all broke up and slobby, but it was ice, and that was some better than black rock! And that's where we fetched up.

The *Ranger* rolled into the ice broadside. She rolled and she rolled, and all the time she hove in, and she hove in until she was a half-mile from the edge of the pack and into ice heavy enough to hold her steady. There was still a big surge under her but for all of that she was as sheltered as if she'd been alongside Bowrings wharf.

Well now, that put a different look on things. All hands turned to again and that crowd of old fellers and young lads worked until they got every drop of water out of her! They used hand pumps and buckets and barrels and whatever in hell they could find, and early in the morning of the next day they had her dry. And she stayed that way. Never leaked when she was in the ice – never had before and wasn't going to change her ways.

The next job was to get steam up. The engines had to be dried and cleaned. Whatever there was to burn, coal and wood, was soaked with salt water and the devil if it would burn. Then I remembered something the old skippers used to do. I told the chief to stoke her up with seal fat.

While all the men was working I was on deck looking at the mess. My, my, my and wasn't she a hard-looking sight? But when I looked seaward I was some glad we was where we was to. The seas coming into the edge of the ice was running mountains high. Nothing could have lived out there. If it hadn't been for the ice, we'd have been all penned up and gone in the breach!

Sparkie managed to get his set going again good enough to send out a call, and who did he raise but Skipper Sid in the *Eagle*. Sid had drove up into Cobb's Arm a few miles to the west'ard of us and found a harbour, but he said he only *just* done it.

We held on all day, fixing her up, tightening her up, trying to do something with her; but towards evening the wind shifted southerly and the ice started to go abroad, sagging down on Baccalhoa. That was a poor business because the seas were still going right over that island, a hundred feet into the air.

I asked the chief if there was any chance to get a bit of steam and he went below and tried to turn her over but there still wasn't enough pressure in the boilers. The ice had all gone slack by then and we were beginning to drive towards open water, and it breaking white as milk. I told the chief to give her another try.

"If you can't do nothing with her now," I said, "get ready to leave her. Two hours from now there won't be a man left alive if we stays on board."

Well, he tried her again, and again it was no use.

"All right, byes," I told the crowd. "That's it now. Get out of her the quickest way you know!"

We had two smashed-up dories left and we put them over the side. The ice was all broke up, and heaving up and down, and surging in and out, and men couldn't live on it without they had something to hold onto. We put a line on each dory and a bunch of men would grab the gunwales and half-walk and half-swim through the slob till they got to safer ice, then we'd haul the dories back and send off another crowd.

It was time now for me to leave her, but I couldn't find the heart to do it. She'd been a good old thing, you know. Never killed a man, so far as I ever heard. Skipper John Dominie and Eli Kean wouldn't go without I went. I could see now she was bound to drive onto Baccalhoa and not God Almighty could save her, so at last I give the word.

By that time the dories was finished – swamped and useless – so each of us took a plank and over we went. When the sea hove in and the ice tightened we'd pick up our planks and copy like youngsters as far as we could get before it hove out and the ice went apart. Then we'd throw ourselves down on the planks till the ice hove in again. When we reached the safe ice there was a crowd of Sid's men had come overland to give us a hand. Our fellows went off with them to the *Eagle* for a warm bunk and some hot grub, but I hung on a while to watch her go.

She drove straight down on that island like a bird. When she was right under it, a great big sea took her and hove her stern clear out of the water. Spars, funnel and everything else went out of her like she was shaking herself clear of everything she had; and then she rolled down under and was gone. It was as quick as that; she went as quick as that . . .

V

Other Lives

Human life comprised a very small part of the fabric of living beings which originally enlivened Newfoundland and its surrounding waters. Until the coming of western man there was a harmonious interweaving of mankind and the others. The European invasion forever disrupted that harmony. It did so on such a massive scale that many life forms, including the Beothuk Indians, were utterly destroyed. Those which were not exterminated were, almost without exception, massively reduced in numbers.

Having become the dominant animals, and having made all of the others subservient to our desires, we conveniently forget how things were before our coming. We have put out of mind the atrocities we inflicted on both the human and non-human aboriginal inhabitants. But any truthful account of life on the Rock would indeed be wanting if this bloody aspect of the story was completely neglected. Here, then, are a few – a very few – echoes of the many voices we have stilled in Newfoundland.

Spearbird

The 12th day of April, having then been 27 days from England, we came on soundings and knew it to be the Bank of Newfoundland. We would have understood this well enough from other indications for it seemed as if all the Fowles of Air were gathered thereunto. They so bemused the eye with their perpetual comings and goings that their numbers quite defied description. There can be but few places on Earth where is to be seen such a manifestation of the fecundity of His Creation.

This eighteenth-century commentary reflects the astonishment of early European visitors on their first encounters with the astronomical congregations of birds inhabiting the northeastern approaches to America. This was truly a world of wings. Elfin dovekies, swallow-like storm petrels, deep-diving murres, puffins, and auks, soaring kittiwakes, aerobatic shearwaters, fulmars and skuas, and great-winged gannets all contributed to the multitudes. In storm and calm, by day and night, in winter and summer, the oceanic birds formed spreading islands of life upon the surface of the sea and filled the air above with seemingly endless skeins and clouds of flickering pinions.

All were able fishermen, spending the greater part of their lives on, over and under salt water, going ashore only briefly to "propagate their kind." All were at home with ocean; but there was one amongst them which was uniquely so, for it had entirely abandoned the world of air.

A large and elegant creature, boldly patterned in glossy black above and gleaming white below, it was totally flightless, its wings having metamorphosed into stubby, powerful, feathered fins more suitable to a fish than to a bird. It could cleave a passage through the deeps with speed and manoeuvrability surpassing that of most fishes. A sleek undersea projectile torpedoing into the dark depths to 300 feet or more, it could remain submerged a quarter of an hour. On the surface, it floated high and proud, flamboyantly visible, having no need to hide itself since it had no airborne enemies.

Paired couples lived dispersed over the endless reaches of the North Atlantic; but, on occasion, uncountable numbers would congregate to form vast flotillas in especially food-rich regions. Once a year the couples climbed up on some isolated rock or desolate islet to rear their single chicks. Ashore, they were impressive figures, standing so tall that their heads reached halfway to a man's midriff. They walked bolt upright with shambling little steps and the rolling gait of all true sailors. Intensely social during the breeding season, they crowded into rookeries that held hundreds of thousands of rudimentary nests so closely packed that it was difficult for the adult birds to move about.

Through the long course of time this exceptional creature bore many names. The ancient Norse called it *geirfugel* – spearbird; while the even more ancient Basques knew it as *arponaz*–spearbill. Both names paid tribute to the great bird's massive, fluted mandibles. Spanish and Portuguese voyagers called it *pinguin* – the fat one–a reference to the thick layer of blubber that encased it. By the beginning of the sixteenth century most deep-water men of whatever nation had adopted some version of this later name, as *pennegouin* in French, and *pingwen* in English. Indeed, it was the first and the *true* penguin. But before the nineteenth century ended, all of its original names had been stripped from it and it passed out of time carrying a tag attached to dusty museum specimens by modern science . . . *great auk*. I shall refer to it by the names bestowed on it by those who knew it in life.

Look now at Newfoundland before Europe began to cast its engulfing shadow over the New World.

A little cluster of men gathers in darkness beside two bark canoes drawn up on a stony beach on the west coast of the great island. They peer earnestly into the pre-dawn sky. Slowly the light strengthens, revealing a few tendrils of high cloud in the western dome. There is no threat of wind. The men smile their satisfaction at one another and at the tall, tawny one who leads them on this June day.

As they wade into the landwash, carefully holding their fragile craft clear of the kelp-slimed rocks, the sun explodes over the hills behind them. On the sea horizon, a string of looming shadows begins to take on the contours of a low-lying archipelago. Aimless cat's paws riffle the water as the canoes drive out from land towards distant islands, leaving the scattered tents of the people to dwindle into insignificance against a sombre wall of forest.

In the full glare of morning, the offshore islands become haloed with a glittering haze of flashing wings as their inhabitants depart to begin the day's fishing. Phalanx after phalanx of arrow-swift murres and puffins fill the air with their rush and rustle. Above them, massed echelons of snowy gannets row steadily on black-tipped wings. Terns, kittiwakes and larger gulls fly arabesques betwixt and between until the sky seems everywhere alive with flight.

The sea through which the canoes ease is living too. Endless flotillas of the big black-and-white divers that fly in water, instead of air, stream outward from the low-lying islands. The first flock comes porpoising past the canoes. The men cease paddling and their leader touches a bone amulet hanging around his neck, upon which is carved an image of the spear-billed bird.

The morning is half-spent before the paddlers close with the island of their choice. Now the multitudes of birds that have remained on it to incubate their eggs or brood their young begin to take alarm. Soon they are rising in such numbers that the sky is obscured as by a blizzard. So vast is this airborne armada that the sun's light is dimmed and the surface of the sea hisses from the rain of droppings falling into it.

As the canoes approach the island, winged masses descend on them like the funnel of a tornado. The rush of air through stiffened pinions and the harsh clangour of bird cries make it hard for the men to hear each other's shouts as they leap overside and carry the canoes to safety on the sloping rocks of the foreshore.

They move with hunched shoulders, as if cringing under the weight of furious life above and around them. Not twenty feet from the landing place, rank after serried rank of spearbills stand, so closely packed that they seem almost shoulder to shoulder. An army of occupation hundreds of thousands strong covers almost the entire surface of the mile-long island. Each individual bird is incubating a single enormous egg in a shallow depression in the stinking mass of guano that everywhere overlies the ancient rock. The birds nearest the intruders turn as one to face the threat, bodies erect and fearsome beaks thrust out.

The men move warily, each holding his long, pointed paddle before him like a lance. The leader pauses, fingers his amulet again and, in a voice hardly audible above the shrieking hubbub, shouts an apology for what he and his companions are about to do.

Abruptly the paddles become flails. At the first thud of wood on bone and flesh, the foremost ranks of spearbills begin to break and fall back, each bird stumbling clumsily into those behind. Confused by the crush, those in the rear strike angrily at neighbours who are being pushed across the invisible boundaries of each one's tiny territory. Defence of territory becomes a more pressing issue than defence against the human intruders and chaos ripples through the massed battalions.

While some of the men continue flailing at the nearest birds until they have killed three or four dozen, the rest hurriedly fill sealskin shoulder bags with eggs. Not ten minutes after landing they begin their retreat, dragging the slain birds by their necks and humping the heavy bags of eggs to the beached canoes. Loading and launching are done with the urgency of thieves. Each man seizes his paddle and, half-deafened by the noise, half-choked by the almost palpable stench, he flees as if pursued by devils. None looks back at the pandemonium still sweeping the Island of Birds.

This vignette is set at the Port au Choix peninsula which juts out from the west coast of Newfoundland into the Gulf of St. Lawrence. Here archaeologists have been sifting through the rich remains of a series of aboriginal cultures, Eskimoan and Archaic Indian, that drew heavily upon the sea for sustenance over a stretch of several thousand years.

The reliance of these ancient peoples on the spearbill in particular is revealed by the great quantities of spearbill bones uncovered in middens, living sites, and even in graves. One Indian grave alone yielded more than 200 mandibles, while another contained the image of a spearbill incised on bone.

Nevertheless, those early peoples were never in danger of eating themselves out of house and home by levying too heavy a toll. They took no more than they needed, with the result that when Europeans arrived on the scene, they found spearbill rookeries thriving all along the eastern coasts of North America from Labrador to Cape Cod, but nowhere were they more numerous and densely populated than off the coasts of Newfoundland.

One April day in 1534 two Breton smacks of the sort usually employed in the cod fisheries at *Terre Neuve* put to sea from the port of Saint Malo. They were not, however, going fishing. They were under charter to a hawk-visaged, 42-year-old entrepreneur named Jacques Cartier outbound to make a commercial reconnaissance of the inland sea the French called *La Grande Baie*, now the Gulf of St. Lawrence.

The two little sixty-tonners crossed the Western Ocean and made their landfall at Cape Bonavista in northeastern Newfoundland. Here they encountered the tongue of Arctic pack ice driven south by the Labrador Current and were forced to seek shelter in the busy fishermen's harbour at Santa Catalina. While they waited for the ice to release them, the seamen assembled and rigged two *barcques*, thirty-foot fishing cutters brought across the ocean broken down in sections. Eventually, as Cartier's chronicler recorded, the wind veered offshore, blowing the ice seaward and opening a passage along the Newfoundland coast to the northward.

On the 21st of the month of May we set forth from harbour . . . and sailed as far as the Isle of Birds, which island was completely surrounded and encompassed by the barrier of ice, broken and split into cakes. In spite of this, our two barcques were sent off to the island to procure some of the birds, whose numbers were so great as to be incredible, unless one has seen them for himself, for although the island is scarcely a league in circumference, it is so exceeding full of birds that one would think they had been stowed there [as tightly as one would stow the hold of a ship].

In the air and round about on the water are a hundred times as many as on the island itself. Some of these birds are as large as geese, being black and white with a beak like a raven. These stay always in the water, not being able to fly in the air because they have only small wings, about half the size of a man's hand, with which, however, they move as quickly through the water as the other birds fly through the air. And these birds are so fat it is a marvel to behold. We call them *Apponatz*, and in less than half an hour our two barcques were laden with them as if laden with stones. Of these birds each of our ships salted four or five casks, not counting those we were able to eat fresh.

In the spring of the following year Cartier undertook a second expedition to determine the commercial potential of the New World and again stopped at the Isle of Birds where another, but equally astonished, chronicler had this to say:

This island is so exceedingly full of birds that all the ships of France might load a cargo of them without anyone noticing that any had been removed. We took away two barcque loads to add to our stores.

So reads the earliest surviving record of an encounter between Europeans and spearbills in North America; but it was assuredly not the first encounter. The course Cartier's Bretons steered had been established well before 1505, and his Isle of Birds was already a well-known sea mark. Now called Funk Island, it is a 35-foot-high slab of granite, half a mile long by a quarter wide, lying some thirty miles off the northeast Newfoundland coast. Its name is archaic English signifying an atrocious stench.

Funk Island lay well clear of the dangerous reefs that fringe the adjacent mainland coast and inshore islands, and for these reasons it was the preferred rookery at which inbound ships could call to fill their casks with salted spearbill carcasses. But it was by no means the only such rookery in the region. Forty miles to the east, in the mouth of Bonavista Bay, are two islands, each of which also once bore the name Funk and are still called Stinking Islands. At about the same distance southwest lie the twin Penguin Islands. On the nearby Wadham group, local fishermen found a veritable charnel house of partly burned bones they identified as the remains of "pinwins" slaughtered and boiled to make oil.

Spearbill rookeries flourished along the whole 5,000-mile coast of Newfoundland wherever suitable offshore islets existed. In 1536 an English expedition visited the south coast. An abridged account of it comes from Richard Hakluyt's *Principal Voyages . . . of the English Nation.*

One, Master Hore of London, encouraged divers gentlemen to accompany him on a voyage of discovery upon the northeast parts of America: wherein his persuasions took such effect that many gentlemen very willingly entered into the action with him.

From the time of their setting out, they were at sea above two months until they came to [the region] about Cape Breton. Shaping their course from thence northeastward, they came to the Island of Penguin, whereon they went and found it full of great fowls, white and grey and as big as geese, and they saw infinite numbers of their eggs. They drove a great number of the fowls into their boats and took many of their eggs. They dressed [the birds] and ate them and found them to be very good and nourishing meat.

Hore's island lies fifteen miles off Cape La Hune in the middle of Newfoundland's south coast. The first Europeans to discover it were Portuguese who gave it the name it still bears. As was the case with the Funks on the northwest coast, this Penguin Island provided a convenient place for vessels inbound from Europe to the Gulf via the southern route, to fill their salt-meat casks.

The south coast of Newfoundland was well-endowed with spearbill colonies, including Green Island near St. Pierre et Miquelon, which, according to local tradition, may still have harboured a few *pengouins* until the beginning of the eighteenth century; and the Ramea group where, so I was told by an old man of mixed European and Indian blood from nearby Burgeo, the last *penwins* were killed on Offer Rock soon after his Micmac ancestors emigrated to Newfoundland from Cape Breton about 1750.

The importance of seabird rookeries to European seamen was enormous. These men were expected to survive, and work like dogs, on a diet consisting principally of salt meat and ship's biscuit. The meat was mainly lean and stringy beef or horse, and the biscuit was baked to the consistency of concrete, and usually shot through with weevils. Even these almost inedible staples were frequently in short supply due to the miserliness of ship-owners who seemed to believe that "wind and water" were enough to feed a sailor. Indeed, it was usual to supply the ships with only enough salt meat for the outward voyage, leaving the hard-driven, half-starved men to forage for themselves upon arrival. Apart from fish (most kinds of which, if eaten as a steady diet in cold latitudes, can result in chronic malnutrition because of a low fat content), the most convenient single source of food in season was what could be had from the bird rookeries.

Initially, seabirds of a dozen or more species crowded the offshore islands and islets. However, most were good fliers who often nested on ledges and cliff faces where their young and eggs were difficult or impossible to reach. Adults mostly took to wing at the approach of intruders and so could seldom be killed in quantity except with a profligate expenditure of shot and powder. Consequently, the main weight of European predation fell on the flightless spearbill, which was especially attractive because of its large, fat and well-muscled carcass. Its eggs too were preferred above all others, not only because of their great size (as long and broad as a human hand) but because they were so easily collected. There was no question about it: so long as it lasted, the spearbill was the best buy in the shop.

In the 1570s Captain Anthony Parkhurst wrote about the spearbill in Newfoundland:

At an island named Pengwin we may drive them on a plank [directly] into our ship, as many as will lade her . . . There is more meat on one of them than on a goose. The Frenchmen that fish near the grand bay do bring but small store of meat with them, but victual themselves always with these birds.

Around 1600 Richard Whitbourne noted:

These Penguins are as big as geese and . . . they multiply so infinitely upon a certain flat island that men drive them from hence upon a board, into their boats by the hundreds at a time, as if God had made the innocency of so poor a creature to become such an admirable instrument for the sustenation of man.

The idea that God created all living creatures to serve man's needs was not, of course, unique with Whitbourne. It is deeply ingrained in Judeo-Christian philosophy and continues to provide one of the major rationalizations with which we justify the wholesale destruction of other animals.

Justifiable or not, the mass destruction of seabird rookeries in the New World proceeded apace. The birds were a staple of fishermen and settlers alike. Writing of the French presence in the region around 1615, Lescarbot tells us:

The greatest abundance [the people have] comes from certain islands where are such quantity of ducks, gannets, puffins, seagulls, cormorants and others that it is a wonderful thing to see [and] will seem to some almost incredible . . . we passed some of those islands where in a quarter of an hour we loaded our longboat with them. We had only to strike them down with staves until we were weary of striking.

Courtemanche, writing in 1705 about the north shore of the Gulf, describes the rookeries there and adds: "for a whole month they slaughter them with iron-tipped clubs in such quantity that it is an incredible thing."

In the early eighteenth century, as guns and powder became cheaper and more available, the seabird slaughter took on a new dimension. "The birds fly by in swarms to go to their laying in spring on the bird islands . . . At this time there is such prodigious carnage that we shot up to 1,000 gunshots every day."

The carnage resulting from the "gunning" of adult birds in passage to, from and at the rookeries grew with the passing centuries. As late as 1900, punt-gunners were shooting, in a single day, "half-a-boat load, which would be about four or five hundred eiders, scoters, puffins, murres, gulls, etc."

As if the destruction of adults and partly grown young was not horrendous enough, the seabirds had also to endure a mounting wastage of their eggs. Egging began in a relatively small way with casual raids on rookeries by ships' crews and fishermen seeking food for themselves. As John Mason, writing about life in Newfoundland around 1620, put it:

The sea fowles are Gulls white and grey, Penguins, Sea Pigeons, Ice Birds, Bottlenoses and other sorts . . . [and] all are bountiful to us with their eggs, as good as our Turkie or Hens, with which the Islands are well replenished.

This began to change after the beginning of the eighteenth century, by which time the rapid growth of human populations along the Atlantic seaboard was creating a commercial market for many "products" of land and sea . . . amongst them seabird eggs. Egging now became a profitable business and professional eggers began to ransack the coasts, denuding every rookery they could find. By about 1780 American eggers had so savaged the bird islands along the eastern coasts of the United States that they could no longer supply the burgeoning demand from cities such as Boston and New York. Consequently, the export of seabird eggs became a profitable business for the British colonies to the north.

As was to be expected, the spearbill was a foremost victim in early times. Aaron Thomas wrote this description of penguin egging in Newfoundland.

If you go to the Funks for eggs, to be certain of getting them fresh you pursue the following rule: you drive, knock and Shove the poor Penguins into heaps. You then scrape all their Eggs in Tumps in the same manner you would a heap of Apples in an Orchard

. . . these Eggs, from being dropped some time, are stale and useless, but you having cleared a space of ground . . . retire for a day or two . . . at the end of which time you will find plenty of [new-laid] Eggs – fresh for certain!

A British naval captain investigating commercial egging in Newfoundland reported:

Parties repair [to the Funks] to collect eggs and feathers. At one time a very considerable profit could be gained but lately, owing to the war of extermination, it has greatly diminished. One vessel nevertheless is said to have cleared 200 Pounds currency in a single trip.

William Palmer, who visited Funk Island in 1887, added this postscript:

What must have been the multitudes of birds in former years on this lonely island. Great auks, murres, razorbills, puffins, Arctic terns, gannets undoubtedly swarmed, and were never molested except by an occasional visit from the now-extinct Newfoundland red man; but now since the white fisherman began to plunder it, how changed. Today but for the Arctic terns and the puffins the island may be said to be deserted. [Although] sixteen barrels of murres and razorbill eggs have been known to be gathered at a time and taken to St. John's, we did not see a dozen eggs.

By the latter part of the sixteenth century the demand for oil had become insatiable. Mineral oil was as yet effectively unknown, and vegetable oils were scarce and unduly expensive. In consequence, most commercial oil was made from animal fats. One of the chief sources of this was oil derived from sea animals which was generally known as trayne, or train oil. Unfortunately for the spearbills, the blanket of fat that served to insulate them from the frigid North Atlantic could be rendered into an excellent grade of oil. The Basques were probably the first to exploit this source as an adjunct to their massive whaling enterprises in New World waters; but it soon became a profitable sideline to the fisheries pursued by other nations.

Crude tryworks were commonplace in most fishing harbours by 1600. They were fired up whenever the fishermen had the time and opportunity to make an incidental haul of some local form of life which would make train. Thus seals, walrus, whales, porpoises . . . and seabirds all served their turn. Because of its great size, high fat content and abundance on its breeding rookeries, the spearbill was the prime target for as long as it lasted. Round about 1630, so Nicolas Denys tells us, French ships fishing for cod often loaded ten to twelve puncheons of penguin oil as well. Since thousands of spearbill carcasses were needed to produce such a quantity of train, it is apparent that this was no petty enterprise. Nor was it limited to the French. English, Spanish and Portuguese cod fishers were also butchering the birds for oil on a similar scale, and some were even making special voyages to isolated rookeries where they would set up portable tryworks during the spearbill breeding season. They were able to boil oil on even the most barren rocks by feeding the fires with spearbill skins and carcasses after the layer of fat had been removed. Some of the more profligate and ruthless of the oilers used the entire bird, as Aaron Thomas, writing about Funk Island as it was near the end of the eighteenth century, confirms.

While you abide on this Island you are in the constant practize of horrid crueltys, for you not only Skin [the Penguins] *Alive*, but you burn them *Alive* also . . . You take a Kettle with you and kindle the fire under it, and this fire is absolutely made from the unfortunate Penguins themselves.

Boiling the corpses for train did not exhaust the opportunities to profit from the destruction of seabird populations. Although immense summer runs of herring, capelin, mackerel and squid normally provided fishermen with bait in any required quantity, there was sometimes a hiatus between the runs, or before the school-fish "struck in" to the coast. Shore-based fishermen soon found a solution to such temporary bait shortages – particularly during June and July. Raiding parties would sweep the seabird islands, massacring adults and young alike. The corpses would then be torn into fragments with which to bait the hand lines that were the principal form of cod-fishing gear.

In the days of their abundance, penguins made up a major part of the seabird bait, and this destruction, added to the kill for food and oil, had its inevitable result. No single species, no matter how numerous in the beginning, could have withstood such carnage indefinitely. By the mid-1700s only a handful of shrunken and beleaguered rookeries still existed. Then a new scourge was visited upon them.

During the latter part of that century, "wide-awake" entrepreneurs, mostly from New England, began exploiting a growing demand for feathers and down to be used in bedding and for upholstery both in America and in Europe. Each spring droves of schooners from as far south as Chesapeake Bay appeared on the coasts of Newfoundland and the Gulf seeking the islands where colonial seabirds nested. At first they concentrated on eider ducks, taking not only the down with which the nests were lined, but also shooting and netting countless thousands of adults. So ruthless were they that the once seemingly inexhaustible eider flocks were soon diminished to "worthless remnants." The pillagers then turned on the seabird rookeries, including the last remaining spearbill colonies.

In 1775 Newfoundland authorities petitioned Britain to stop the massacre.

Contiguous to the North part of the Island are a great many islands where birds breed in abundance and which were of great service to the inhabitants for food in winter and for bait for catching fish during summer. [These inhabitants are] now almost deprived, as a great part of the birds have been destroyed within a few years by crews of men who kill them in their breeding season for feathers, of which they make a traffic . . . we pray an entire stop except for food or bait.

A decade later, colonist and diarist George Cartwright made this prophetic journal entry:

A boat came in from Funk Island laden with birds, chiefly penguins . . . innumerable flocks of sea fowl breed [there] every summer, which are of great service to the poor inhabitants who make voyages there to load with birds and eggs . . . but it has been customary in late years for several crews of men to live all summer on that island for the sole purpose of killing the birds for the sake of their feathers; the destruction they have made is incredible. If a stop is not soon put to that practice, the whole breed will be diminished to nothing, particularly the penguins, for this is now the only island they have left to breed upon; all other lying so near the shores of Newfoundland, they are continually robbed.

The indignation of the merchant aristocracy of Newfoundland was not exactly selfless. Before 1800, the Reverend Philip Tocque wrote:

The penguin was plentiful on Funk Island [where] incredible numbers were killed . . . Heaps of them were burnt as fuel . . . there being no fuel on the island. [Before the destruction wrought by the feather trade] the merchants of Bonavista used to sell these birds to the poor people by the hundred-weight, instead of salt pork.

The most grimly graphic description of what was taking place comes from Aaron Thomas.

At some Leagues distant from the Northern Shore are the islands of Fogo, Stinking Island and Funk Island. They are generally called the Funks from the stinking Smell which salutes your Nose on landing on them. I shall be particular on Funk Island. My observations on that place will apply to other Islands.

Funk Island is a barren spot inhabited only by Penguins and other Birds. The astonishing quantity which resort to this Island is beyond . . . belief. As soon as you put your foot on shore you meet with such Thousands of them that you cannot find a place for your feet and they are so lazy that they will not attempt to move out of your way.

If you come for their Feathers you do not give yourself the trouble of killing them, but lay hold of one and pluck off the best of the Feathers. You then turn the poor Penguin adrift, with his Skin half naked and torn off, to perish at his leasure. This is not a very humane method, but it is the common Practize.

I had the following information from a person in St. John's . . . "About twenty years ago when this kind of Traffick was Lawfull, I made two Trips to the Funks. In these Trips I gathered, with one person with me, half a Ton of Feathers and as many Eggs as sold in St. John's for Thirty Pounds!"

This skinning and taking the Eggs from the Funks is now prohibited and they are allowed to take the Birds only for Bait to catch Fish with. [But] about three years ago some fellows were detected in this kind of Plunder. They were brought to St. John's and flogged at a Cart's Tail. But I am told there is a quantity of Feathers [still] purloined from these Islands every year.

Complaints about the destruction of the penguins were now being heard from another quarter as well. Through almost three centuries the strikingly patterned birds had served inbound seamen as infallible indicators that they had arrived over the Grand Banks and so were approaching a land whose dangerous coasts were often hidden by impenetrable fogs. From earliest times Rutters and Pilots [books of sailing directions] used by the westfaring nations contained some variant of the following excerpt from the 1774 edition of *The English Pilot*.

You may know you are on the Bank by the great quantities of fowles but none are to be minded so much as the Pengwin, for these never go without the Bank as the others do, for they are always on it.

By 1792, Sir Richard Bonnycastle was reporting to the English authorities that "this sure sea mark on the Grand Banks has now totally disappeared, from the ruthless trade in eggs and skins." Two years later the Colonial Secretary in London finally forbade the destruction of penguins for the feather trade because "they afford a supply of food and bait, and are useful in warning vessels that they are nearing land."

This prohibition not only came too late, it was virtually ignored in Newfoundland where some merchants had decided that if they could not make the Yankees desist from a good thing, then they had best join them. The consequence was that, by 1802, the last penguin rookery in North America, on that lonely rock called Funk, had been destroyed.

Whereas it had taken our forebears a thousand and more years to extirpate the spearbill from European waters, it took modern man a mere three centuries to exterminate it in the New World. Although this was an undoubted victory in our ongoing war against the rest of animate creation, the perpetrators of it, and we their inheritors, have been reluctant to claim the credit.

White Ghosts

At a weight of 1,200 pounds or more and a length of up to eleven feet, the white or, as it is now usually known, the polar bear is one of the largest terrestrial carnivores extant. It is unmatched in agility and strength. Ernest Thompson Seton describes one capturing a 100-pound seal in the water, then leaping up onto the edge of an ice floe "with his prey in his teeth, like a Mink landing a trout." It has been seen to kill a beluga, weighing about two tons, in the whale's own element, then drag the carcass above tide line.

A long-lived animal, it can attain an age of forty years. It is equally at home on solid land or floating ice and its flowing, loose-limbed gait can carry it along at thirty miles an hour. It can leap ten-foot crevasses and scale nearly sheer cliff faces and ice pinnacles. Its performance is equally astounding in the water. Layered with fat that not only provides it with insulation and flotation but can also sustain it for weeks during a time of food shortage, it is equipped with a thick coat of water-repellent hair enabling it to withstand prolonged immersion in icy seas that would kill other members of the bear family. Its enormous paddle paws, up to a foot in diameter, can propel its sleekly streamlined body through the water at six knots. Ships have encountered white bears swimming strongly 300 miles from the nearest land and showing no signs of distress.

In times past, the white bear was not restricted to polar regions. In fact, the animal most often singled out for notice by early voyagers to the northeastern coasts of the New World was the white bear. As the historic record clearly shows, this was not due to its novelty but to the fact that it was one of the commonest large mammals present.

Sagas of the Norse adventurers who sailed the Labrador and Newfoundland coasts around A.D. 1000 all mention the white bear, and *only* that species. Thorfinn Karlsefni even named an island off southeastern Labrador in honour of it.

Although almost everything else relevant to John Cabot's 1497 voyage to Newfoundland and beyond has been lost, a map from that period showing Cabot's *Prima Terra Vista* – probably New-foundland – still exists. It carried this legend: "[Here] *there are many white bears.*" Another reference comes from the results of a later voyage by Cabot's son, Sebastian. "He [Sebastian] says there are great numbers of bears there, which eat codfishes . . . the bears plunge into the midst of a shoal of these codfishes and . . . draw them to shore . . . this is thought to be the reason why such large numbers of bears do not trouble the people of the country."

The earliest accounts of encounters with white bears are found in Jacques Cartier's voyage of 1534. A white bear was met with on Funk Island, where it had presumably been living the life of Riley on a diet of spearbills. The following day, Cartier's ship overtook a white bear swimming in the open sea and his men killed it.

Two years later the English expedition of Master Hore was wrecked in a fiord on the south coast of Newfoundland. Richard Hakluyt, who interviewed some of the survivors, tells us that they saw "stores of bears, both black and white, of whom they killed some and took them for no bad food." It is notable that this is the first mention in the early annals of *black* bears, which, being forest animals, were only occasionally to be encountered on the coasts. Hore's people, however, seem to have penetrated rather deeply into the country, up a fiord that may well have been the one that to this day is called White Bear Bay.

The name is by no means unique. At least twenty White Bear bays, lakes, rivers, coves and islands still dot the map of Newfoundland. Together with a good many more in Labrador, they testify to the one-time widespread distribution and abundance of their majestic namesake.

Anthony Parkhurst reported from Newfoundland in 1574-78 that the plethora of white bears had its advantages. There was, he said, such a "plentie of bears everywhere . . . that you may kill them as oft as you list: their flesh is as good as young beef." However, he added, "The Beares also be as bold [as the local foxes and] will not spare at midday to take your fish before your face, and I believe would not hurt anybody unless they be forced." That Parkhurst was referring to the white bear is evident not only from his description of their behaviour, but also from the testimony of Stephen Parmenius, who briefly visited eastern Newfoundland in 1583 and noted: "Beares also appear about the fishers' stages of the Country, and are sometimes killed, but they seem to be white as I conjectured from their skins."

Boldness has always been one of the white bear's most notable and, as far as Europeans are concerned, disturbing characteristics. Yet its audacity seems to be based not on brute arrogance so much as on the calm belief that it has no enemies and therefore can go where it pleases with impunity. In the days when contact with it was restricted to native peoples, this confidence was usually well placed. Although primitive man could and did kill white bears, he usually chose to avoid conflict, partly because discretion was the better part of valour and partly due to an admiration for the animal that amounted to something close to veneration. For their part, the bears reciprocated by adopting a live-and-let-live attitude towards mankind. This lack of aggressiveness seems to have surprised early explorers but they did not reciprocate it.

It was *de rigeur* in Judeo-Christian-dominated cultures to believe that all large carnivores were inherently savage and ferocious animals that should be treated as inimical, and destroyed whenever possible. The white bear was no exception. From as early as the sixteenth century it bore a horrid reputation as a man-eater that much preferred crunching human skulls to seal skulls. Such canards were legion, although the stark truth is that only a handful of authentic records attest to unprovoked attacks by white bears on human beings – and some of these are suspect.

Although the bears had co-existed successfully with aboriginal mankind, they were unable to do so with the new human interlopers. Fed up (quite literally) with eating fish, whether salt or fresh, European fishermen summering on New World coasts lusted after red meat; and one of the most readily accessible sources of such was the white or water bear, as they sometimes called it. Abundant on the fishing coasts, it flaunted its presence not just by reason of its colour but because it had so little fear of man that it would neither hide nor flee when he appeared. To the contrary, it deliberately sought out fishermen's shore establishments, which its perceptive nose could detect from many miles away, and felt free to help itself from flakes and drying racks, thereby infuriating the human owners. For these several reasons, together with the fact that its shaggy pelt was a valuable curiosity in Europe, it early became a target for destruction.

The wonder is that it lasted as long as it did. Nevertheless, towards the end of the seventeenth century its numbers had been so sadly reduced that it was a rarity in southern Newfoundland, where it had by then acquired a mythical reputation. Baron Lahontan wrote of it in 1680:

The White Bears are monstrous Animals . . . they are so fierce that they will come and attack a Sloop in the Sea with seven or eight men in it . . . I never saw but one of them . . . which had certainly tore me to pieces if I had not spy'd it at a distance and so had time to run back to shelter to Fort Louis at Placentia [on Newfoundland's southeast coast].

Although becoming scarce in Newfoundland, the bears were still holding their own on the Atlantic coast of Labrador, which had not yet been infested by Europeans. In 1775 the Moravian missionary Jens Munk coasted north along that shore as far as Davis Inlet and recorded that "This land abounds with Deer, Foxes, White and Black Bears." However, it was Captain George Cartwright, first European to establish a "plantation" (a trading post-cum-seal-fishery-cum-anything-else that could be turned to profit) in southeastern Labrador, who left us one of the best accounts of the life and times of the great white bear on the Atlantic seaboard of America.

Cartwright operated several salmon fisheries, one of which was in Sandwich Bay on White Bear River–so called by him because it was also fished, and heavily so, by white bears. What follows is condensed from his account of a visit to nearby Eagle River on July 22, 1778.

About half a mile upriver, I came to a very strong shoot of water, from thence I saw several white bears fishing in the stream above. I waited for them, and in a short time, a bitch with a small cub swam close to the other shore, and landed a little below. The bitch immediately went into the woods, but the cub sat down upon a rock, when I sent a ball through it, at the distance of a hundred and twenty yards at the least, and knocked it over; but getting up again it crawled into the woods, where I heard it crying mournfully, and concluded that it could not long survive.

The report of my gun brought some others down, and another she bear, with a cub of eighteen months old came swimming close under me. I shot the bitch through the head and killed her dead. The cub perceiving this and getting sight of me made at me with great ferocity; but just as the creature was about to revenge the death of his dam, I saluted him with a load of large shot in his right eye, which not only knocked that out, but also made him close the other. He no sooner was able to keep his left eye open, than he made at me again, quite mad with rage and pain; but when he came to the foot of the bank, I gave him another salute with the other barrel, and blinded him most completely; his whole head was then entirely covered with blood. He blundered into the woods, knocking his head against every rock and tree that he met with.

I now perceived that two others had just landed about sixty yards above me, and were fiercely looking round them. The bears advanced a few yards to the edge of the woods, and the old one was looking sternly at me. The danger of firing at her I knew was great, as she was seconded by a cub of eighteen months; but I could not resist the temptation. I fortunately sent my ball through her heart, and dropped her; but getting up again, she ran some yards into the woods, where I soon found her dead, without her cub.

The captain and Jack coming up, I was informed that Jack had shot one of those white ones which first passed me; that the beast had gone up on a small barren hill, some little distance within the woods, and there died.

Leaving them to skin this bear, I advanced higher up the river, until I came opposite a beautiful cataract. There I sat down upon some bare rocks, to contemplate the scene before me, and to observe the manoeuvres of the bears, numbers of which were then in sight.

I had not sat there long, ere my attention was diverted to an enormous, old, dog bear, which came out of some alder bushes on my right and was walking towards me, with his eyes fixed on the ground, and his nose not far from it. I rested my elbows, and in that position suffered him to come within five yards of me before I drew the trigger, when I placed my ball in the centre of his skull, and killed him dead: but as the shore was a flat reclining rock, he rolled round until he fell into the river.

On casting my eyes around, I perceived another beast of equal size, raised half out of the water. He no sooner discovered me, than he made towards me as fast as he could swim. As I was not then prepared to receive him, I ran into the wood to make ready my unerring rifle. Whilst I was employed in that operation, he dived and brought up a salmon; which he repeatedly tossed up a yard or two in the air, and letting fall into the water, would dive and bring it up again. Being now ready, I advanced to the attack, and presently perceived him, standing in the water with his fore paws upon a rock, devouring the salmon. I crept through the bushes until I came opposite to him, and interrupted his repast, by sending a ball through his head; it entered a little above his left eye, went out at the root of his right ear, and knocked him over, he then appeared to be in the agonies of death for some time; but at last recovered sufficiently to land on my side of the river, and to stagger into the woods.

Never in my life did I regret the want of ammunition so much as on this day; as I was by the failure interrupted in the finest sport that man ever had. I am certain that I could with great ease have killed four or five brace more. They were in such plenty that I counted thirty-two white bears but there were certainly many more, as they generally retire into the woods to sleep after making a hearty meal.

Having now only two balls left beside that in my rifle, I thought it was most prudent to return to the boat and wait the return of the other people. It was not long before they came down; for they were not able to skin the second bear. Although his body was afloat in the water and nothing but his head rested upon a flat rock, yet they could not lift even that up. We judged him to be as much as twelve hundred pounds weight; nor could he well be less than that, as he stood six feet high, as his carcass was as big as the largest ox I ever saw. Thus ended in disappointment, the noblest day's sport I ever saw: for we got only one skin, although we had killed six bears.

Cartwright encountered white bears at all seasons. In late April of 1776 one of his men "saw the tracks of near a hundred white bears which had lately crossed Sandwich Bay." He also recorded the species as still to be found in Newfoundland. It clearly whelped in south Labrador since he not only correctly gives the whelping time but refers to females with young cubs. In discussing the farming possibilities of southern Labrador, he concluded it would be too difficult and expensive "to fence against the white bears and wolves," which were clearly *the* major predators of the region. It is also of interest that in Cartwright's time not only were a great many white bears still living on the Labrador, they were co-existing with at least 600 Inuit and an even larger number of Nascopie Indians.

But, as elsewhere, co-existence with Europeans proved to be a different proposition. What had been one of the commonest large mammals in Newfoundland became one of the rarest and by the end of the nineteenth century had become little more than a fast-fading wraith. Since 1960 perhaps two dozen have come south on the pack ice, but at least fifteen of these have been intercepted by Norwegian sealers off Newfoundland and killed "in self-defence." In the spring of 1962 one that escaped the sealers walked into the outport village of Rose Blanche on Newfoundland's southwest coast. First seen emerging from the village cemetery, its appearance caused such panic that all hands fled for the safety of their houses. The bear paid them no heed. Making its way to the water, it swam off towards the harbour entrance where it encountered two men in a dory. They deflected it with yells and by banging their oars against the gunwales. The bear thereupon changed course towards the opposite shore of the harbour. By dint of frantic rowing, the men reached their fishing store, snatched up their guns, and were in time to shoot it dead as it stood, perplexed, in the landwash, unsure which way to go.

A more recent visitation took place in eastern Newfoundland on May 9, 1973, when a young bear, already wounded, walked into the outskirts of the village of New Chelsea, near Heart's Content. It threatened no one and no thing but, like all of its kind over the long years, it was met with gunfire.

"Comin' down the road there, he looked like a bloody big ghost," remembers one of those who saw it die.

Indeed. A great White Ghost.

Joey and the Potheads

About 1592 cartographer Petrius Plancius drew a map of the New World. Like many maps of that era it was illustrated with vignettes of life. One such is a lively and detailed image imprinted on the east coast of Newfoundland.

The scene is the foot of a deep bay. The foreground is filled with rowboats, each carrying two men. This flotilla has just completed driving a school of small whales onto a gently sloping beach and, while some of the boatmen attack the stranded animals with lance-like darts, others on shore are already at work stripping off blubber. In the distance, a tryworks sends a great coil of black smoke into the sky. The whales, not much larger than the boats, have bulbous, protruding foreheads. They are clearly pilot whales. And this picture could, with some minor variations, equally well represent a scene from Newfoundland in the 1950s.

The sleek, black pilot is gregarious, living in schools or clans containing up to several hundreds of individuals of all ages and both sexes. Growing to twenty feet in length and weighing two to three tons, they sport elegant dove-grey throat patches, long and flexible front flippers, and watermelon-sized, oil-filled bulges on their foreheads. This peculiar but not unattractive feature, which serves as part of the animal's echo-location equipment, gives rise to the inelegant name of pothead, especially in vogue in Newfoundland.

Its chief food is a small species of squid that schools in almost unimaginable numbers. Throughout most of the year, these squid live in the deeps well away from shore and there the pilots pursue them, diving into darkness to enormous depths. However, during the summer the squid strike in to shore to mate and lay their eggs, coming right up to the landwash and sometimes even entering brackish lagoons and fresh-water streams. The pilots fearlessly venture after them and accidental strandings sometimes take place when the whales chase squid into shallow, murky waters.

In European waters in prehistoric times such accidents must have been spectacularly rewarding to shoreside scavengers, including man. Eventually our ancestors realized that they had no need to wait passively for such gifts from the gods but could make them happen. So the whale drive was born, perhaps in north British or Scandinavian waters.

When a clan of pilots swept into a fiord or dead-end bay following the squid, a rabble of boats would put out from shore and attempt to bar the whales' avenue of escape. Men beat on hollow logs, howled and shrieked, pounded the gunwales with paddles, and churned the water into foam. Later generations added trumpets, horns and bells.

The purpose of this din was to panic the whales into heedless flight towards shore. The noise also tended to disrupt their delicate sonar sense, thus masking the dangers posed by the shoals ahead until it was too late to turn back. Once the driven whales were wallowing helplessly in the shallows, the boats would push in amongst them; hunters stabbing ferociously with spears, lances, even swords, attempting to immobilize as many of the creatures as they could.

Exploitation of North American pilot whales by Europeans must have begun early in the sixteenth century since by the time of Petrius Plancius it had become sufficiently important to warrant its advertisement on his map. By the eighteenth century it had become a traditional seasonal occupation for fishermen living in the deep bays of the northeast coast of Newfoundland and at other suitable drive sites as far south as Cape Cod. Some Newfoundlanders found a way to profit from it by substituting pothead oil for the more valuable seal oil and selling it to the rapacious St. John's merchants – a classic case of the biter being bit.

So long as it remained localized and small in scale, this fishery posed no major threat to the continued existence of a species that is believed to have mustered on the order of 60,000 individuals in Newfoundland waters alone.

In the 1950s that all changed.

Newfoundland, it will be remembered, joined Canada in 1949. The man who claims personal credit for this confederation and who became the first Premier of Canada's tenth province is Joseph Smallwood, a one-time socialist who, by 1950, had been transformed into a born-again believer in entrepreneurial capitalism. Joey, as he was generally known, was determined to industrialize Newfoundland and, to this end, sent emissaries to scour the western world with offers of financial assistance, free land, tax benefits and any manner of other inducements that might persuade new enterprises to come to Newfoundland. Perhaps the most seductive inducement was the offer of a free hand to "develop" Newfoundland's natural resources.

Amongst those who descended on the island with schemes ranging from building a machine-gun arsenal to a condom factory was one representing mainland mink ranchers. He explained to Smallwood that the mink industry, then largely based in Canada's western provinces where a combination of the right climate and access to the cheap meat of wild horses had made it immensely profitable, was facing difficulties. The wild horses had almost all been converted into mink feed. The proposal was that the mink industry relocate in Newfoundland and thereby make that province a world centre for the production of luxury furs.

Smallwood was much enamoured of the idea, which certainly had more glamour attached to it than did the condom plant. When he inquired what would be wanted from the province, he was told it would suffice if Newfoundland paid the costs of moving the ranchers east, provided free land, subsidized the construction of new ranches, and provided an unlimited supply of meat for mink feed. Although Smallwood was only too happy to acquiesce, he was uncertain about the meat supply. Where would that come from? Ah, said the representative, from a source that is presently doing nobody any good, not earning a penny for Canada: namely, the pilot whale.

Since Newfoundland's marine resources now came under the jurisdiction of the federal government, Ottawa had to be consulted. The federal Department of Fisheries enthusiastically embraced the proposal. It instructed its scientific experts to assess pilot whale "stocks" and draw up a management program for "harvesting" them on the basis of "maximum sustained yield."

Everything was going swimmingly. The only problem was *how* to "harvest" the whales. Happily, the owners of Arctic Fisheries, a Norwegian whale processing plant at Dildo, in Trinity Bay, proved co-operative.

The chosen method of "harvesting" the pilots proved to be an innovative combination of old and new. During slack intervals when the three big, diesel whale killers which supplied Arctic Fisheries were not harpooning humpbacks, finners, seis and Minke whales, they carried out sweeps of Trinity Bay, locating clans of pilot whales at distances of as much as thirty miles from Dildo. Through the skilful use of ultrasonic underwater transmitters, combined with deafening engine and propeller noises to confuse and terrorize the small whales, the killer boats herded the pilots towards the foot of Trinity Bay.

Three killing beaches were selected, adjacent to the outports of New Harbour, Chapel Arm and Old Shop. Having been alerted that a drive was starting, fishermen from these places who had been hired for the purpose would stand by at sea in a variegated collection of trap skiffs, power dories, long-liners and outboard-engined "sporting" boats. Radio contact kept everyone informed of what was happening, and when the knife-edged bows of the big whalers foamed into view, boatmen and shoremen alike were ready to receive the driven pilot clans, which by then had disintegrated into a disoriented mob fleeing in panic.

About a mile off the chosen beach, the killer ships "delivered" the results of the round-up to the fishermen, whose boats now formed a curved line of "beaters" to seaward of the whales. In the words of a journalist hired to write a publicity hand-out for the federal Department of Fisheries:

This is perhaps the most thrilling phase of the hunt, certainly the most noisy. Coursing back and forth behind the potheads the boatriders create a cacophonous din – beating on drums, slapping oars in the water, throwing stones, yelling and halooing – with the staccato noise of the open exhaust motors overriding all . . .

the drive continues into the shallow water at the edge of the beach where the struggling whales stir up blinding mud and silt . . . the whales are then killed by lancing.

The killing was not quite as clean and easy as this suggests. Individual whales might be stabbed scores of times, sometimes by boys ten years of age and under using knives lashed to sticks. It was no surprise to the blood-drenched butchers on the beach to discover that some of the whales they were cutting up were still alive. Almost completely immobilized by their own weight, such unfortunate victims could only flex their flukes in agony as cutting spades sliced through their flesh.

What was even worse was the practice of holding live whales on the beach. When so many had been stranded that the flensers could not deal with them, the surplus animals were sometimes "preserved alive" by hauling them clear of high-tide mark with tractors or teams of horses. During cool and cloudy weather they might endure for as much as three or four days, dying by inches, before the butchers finally got around to them.

The first season of this new fishery – the summer of 1951 – was a smashing success. The fact that only two mink farms had yet been established in Newfoundland, and no freezing or meat-storage facilities had been built, did not detract from that success. By summer's end at least 3,100 pilot whales had been slaughtered on the beaches near Dildo – and mostly left to rot. Meat was removed from less than a hundred corpses, and much of even this went bad before it could be used by the mink ranchers.

All that was salvageable from this colossal shambles were several hundred gallons of the light and viscous oil found in the melon on the pilot's head. This oil is very stable at a wide range of temperatures and, like that of the sperm whale, commands a premium price for use as a lubricant in fine instruments and in guided and ballistic missiles.

By 1955 the situation had improved somewhat. Construction of a freezing plant in which whale meat could be stored, together with the installation of a "corral" of buoyed netting in which the surplus animals from a drive could be held alive until "taken to the beaches for processing on an assembly line basis," at least reduced the wastage. It did not reduce the scale of the destruction. This had increased with each passing year until, in 1956, it reached the astounding total of *10,000 pilot whales in that single season.*

The mink industry was now flourishing and had become so lucrative that Joey himself became part-owner of a ranch. Women of fashion and wealth all over the civilized world were wearing the latest pastel shades of mutant mink from Newfoundland. Unfortunately, even though the fur farms had expanded by leaps and bounds, they could not begin to use anything like the quantity of pilot whales that were now being slaughtered. Nevertheless, the overkill was considered justifiable because of the increased production of melon oil.

It seemed that the pilot whale had found its place and purpose in the human scheme of life. Then things began to go askew. In 1957 the killers were only able to butcher 7,800 whales; and thereafter the size of the pilot herd mysteriously declined until, by 1964, only 3,000 could be landed. According to experts of the Department of Fisheries, the decrease was apparent rather than real. It was probably due, they explained, not to "over-harvesting," but to temporary alterations in the migratory patterns of the pilot whales' chief prey, the squid, brought about by "changed hydrographic factors." The experts predicted that the squid would soon return and bring the whales. Meantime, it was suggested, why not feed the mink on Minke whales? This play on words was considered amusing enough to warrant its publication in a staid research bulletin devoted to population dynamics.

In due course, the squid (which tend to be cyclic) did return. But the great clans of pilot whales did not. They could not – because they had been destroyed. In a single decade, *more than 48,000 of them had died on the beaches of Trinity Bay.* One would have thought that, with this figure in hand, even Fisheries management experts and their scientific advisers might have reached the obvious conclusion, and called a halt to the massacre before it was too late. That they did not do so may seem inexplicable; nevertheless, it is a fact.

In 1967 the hunters were only able to kill 739 pilots. In 1971 they only succeeded in killing *six*!

By then the pilot whale clans that had once enlivened the waters of Newfoundland and, in migration, the seas as far south as Cape Cod, had been virtually exterminated – not by accident or by miscalculation, but with cold deliberation, in the name of that most holy of modern icons, the gross god Profit.

No one was even taken to task for this horrendous bloodletting, this massive act of biocide, perhaps because it took place in one of the world's more "advanced" nations where such crimes can readily be rationalized on the basis of economic determinism. Yet if an emergent African country was to slaughter some 60,000 elephants simply to supply the luxury trade with ivory, we can be sure such an act would be loudly denounced by us as a barbarous outrage.

There is an epilogue. Having been responsible for the depletion of wild horse herds in Alberta, beluga whales at Churchill in northern Manitoba, and the near extinction of pilot whales in Newfoundland, the mink ranchers again began to experience difficulties maintaining an adequate level of profit. For a while they fed their animals on Minke meat, but when that whale too was reduced to near the vanishing point, they were forced by lack of any other available mammalian substitutes to switch to fish. Such a diet proved incapable of producing the quality of fur demanded by discerning women, and so the Great Newfoundland Mink Bubble burst – pricked, as it were, by the phallus of unbridled greed.

More Fish in the Sea?

Early voyagers to the northeastern approaches of America discovered two kinds of land. One was high and dry, and they called it the Main. The other lay submerged beneath 30 to 150 fathoms of green waters, and they called it the Banks. The waters of the several banks off Newfoundland form an aqueous pasture of unparalleled size and fecundity – a three-dimensional one with a volume sufficient to inundate much of North America to a depth of a yard or more. In 1500 the life forms inhabiting these waters had a sheer mass unmatched anywhere in the world. This was the realm where cod was king.

The name that John Cabot used for Newfoundland in 1497 was *Baccalaos*, that being the one bestowed on it by Portuguese who had led the way. The word means, simply, land of cod. And Peter Martyr (circa 1516) tells us that "in the sea adjacent [to Newfoundland, Cabot] found so great a quantity . . . of great fish . . . called baccalaos . . . that at times they even stayed the passage of his ships."

The Grand Banks lying to the eastward of Newfoundland were a cod fisher's version of the Promised Land. By 1575, more than 300 French, Portuguese and English fishing vessels were annually reaping a rich harvest there. Members of Sir Humphrey Gilbert's colonizing venture fairly babbled at the abundance of baccalaos. Cod, wrote one of the visitors, were present "in incredible abundance, whereby great gains grow to them that travel to these parts: the hook is no sooner thrown out but it is eftsoons drawn up with some goodly fish." To which one of his companions added: "We were becalmed a small time during which we laid out hook and lines to take Cod, and drew in, in less than two hours, fish so large and in such abundance that for many days after we fed on no other provision." A third summed it up: "Incredible quantity and no less variety of fishes in the seas [especially] Cod, which alone draweth many nations thither and is become the most famous fishing of the world."

Each new arrival on these fabulous fishing grounds found the same thing and had much the same reaction. When the *Grace* of Bristol sheltered at the island of St. Pierre in 1594, her people "laid the ship upon the lee, and in 2 houres space we tooke with our hooks 3 or 4 hundred great Cod for the provision of our ship." Charles Leigh in 1597 noted: "About this Island there is as great an abundance of cods as is any place to be found. In a little more than an houre we caught with hookes 250 of them."

At the turn of the sixteenth century as many as 650 vessels were catching thousands of tons of cod in New World waters, using only baited hooks and handlines. As John Mason, an English fishing skipper working out of a Newfoundland shore station, noted: "Cods are so thick by the shore that we hardly have been able to row a boat through them. I have killed [many] of them with a Pike . . . Three men going to Sea in a boat, with some on shore to dress and dry them, in 30 days will commonly kill between 25 and thirty thousand, worth with the oyle arising from [their livers], 100 or 200 Pounds."

The slaughter was equally enormous elsewhere in the region. In Cape Breton and the Gulf, according to Nicolas Denys: "Scarcely an harbour [exists] where there are not several fishing vessels . . . taking every day 15,000 [to] 30,000 fish . . . this fish constitutes a kind of inexhaustible manna."

Near the end of the sixteenth century Richard Whitbourne, another fishing skipper, wrote that the average lading for any ship fishing Newfoundland waters tallied 125,000 cod. These were from virgin cod populations producing fish up to six or seven feet in length and weighing as much as 200 pounds, in sharp contrast with today's average weight of about six pounds. In Whitbourne's time the annual cod fishery in the northeastern approaches yielded about 368,000 quintals of "made" (dried or salted) cod, representing well over one hundred thousand tons "live weight."

By 1620 the cod fleet exceeded 1,000 vessels, many making two voyages annually: a summer one for dry cod and a winter trip from which the cod were carried back to Europe in pickle as "green fish." Yet, despite the enormous destruction, there was no indication that cod stocks were diminishing. As the seventeenth century neared its end, travellers such as Baron Lahontan were still writing about the cod as if its population had no bounds.

You can scarce imagine what quantities of Cod fish were catched by our Seamen in the space of a quarter of an hour . . . the Hook was no sooner at the bottom than a Fish was catched . . . [the men] had nothing to do but to throw in, and take up without interruption . . . However, as we were so plentifully entertained at the cost of these Fishes, so such of them as continued in the Sea made sufficient reprisals upon the Corps of a Captain and several Soldiers, who dy'd of the Scurvy, and were thrown overboard.

The first hint that the destruction might be excessive (and it is a veiled hint) comes from Charlevoix in the 1720s. After first telling us that "the number of the cod seems to equal that of the grains of sand," he adds:

For more than two centuries there have been loaded with them [at the Grand Banks] from two to three hundred [French] ships annually, notwithstanding [which] the diminution is not perceivable. It might not, however, be amiss to discontinue this fishery from time to time [on the Grand Bank], the more so as the gulph of St. Lawrence [together with] the River for more than sixty leagues, the coasts of Acadia, those of Cape Breton and of Newfoundland, are no less replenished with this fish than the great bank. These are true mines, which are more valuable, and require much less expense than those of Peru and Mexico.

That Charlevoix was not exaggerating the value of the cod fishery is confirmed by the fact that, in 1747, 564 French vessels manned by 27,500 fishermen brought home codfish worth a million pounds sterling – a gigantic sum for those days.

At about this same time New Englanders, who had by now depleted the lesser stocks of cod available on the southern banks, began moving into the northern fishery. They did so with such energy that, by 1783, over 600 American vessels were fishing the Gulf of St. Lawrence, mostly for cod, although they also caught immense quantities of herring. In that year, at least 1,500 ships of all nations were working the North American "cod mines" for all they were worth.

By 1800 English- and French-based vessels had become notably fewer, but Newfoundlanders, Canadians and Americans more than made up the loss. In 1812, 1,600 fishing vessels, largely American, were in the Gulf, with as many more Newfoundland and Nova Scotia ships fishing the outer banks and the Atlantic coast of Labrador.

Those were the days of the great fleets of "white wings," when the sails of fishing schooners seemed to stretch from horizon to horizon. In addition to this vessel fishery, thousands of inshore men fished cod in small boats from every little cove and harbour. Vesselmen and shoremen alike still mostly fished in the old way with hooks and lines because "the glut of cod" was still so great that nothing more sophisticated was needed.

In 1876 John Rowan went aboard "a schooner cod-fishing close to shore . . . They were fishing in about three fathoms of water and we could see the bottom actually paved with codfish. I caught a dozen in about fifteen minutes; my next neighbour [a crewman] on the deck of the schooner caught three times as many, grumbling all the time that it was the worst fishing season he had ever known."

Between 1899 and 1904 Newfoundland alone annually exported about 1,200,000 quintals of dry fish, representing about 400,000 tons of cod, live weight. By 1907 the Newfoundland catch had risen to nearly 430,000 tons; and there were then some 1,600 vessels of other nationalities, fishing the Grand Banks.

But then a chill began spreading over the Banks—one that did not come from the almost perpetual fog. Cod started to become harder to catch, and every year it seemed to take a little longer to fill a ship. At this juncture, nobody so much as breathed the possibility that the Banks were being over-fished. Instead, one of the age-old fisherman's explanations for a shortage was invoked: the cod had changed their ways and, temporarily, had gone somewhere else.

The history of nineteenth-century discovery of immense schools of cod along the Labrador coast, even as far north as Cape Chidley, was quoted as confirmation that cod change their grounds. In actual fact the Labrador cod had comprised a distinct and virgin population. They had not stayed that way for long. By 1845, 200 Newfoundland vessels were fishing "down north," and by 1880, up to 1,200. In 1880 as many as 30,000 Newfoundlanders ("floaters" if they fished from anchored vessels, and "stationers" if they fished from shore bases) were making almost 400,000 quintals of salt cod on the Labrador coast alone.

The Labrador cod soon went the way of all flesh. The catch steadily declined thereafter until, by mid-twentieth century, the once far-famed Labrador fishery collapsed. Attempts were again made to ascribe the disappearance of the Labrador fish to one of those mythical migrations. This time it did not wash. The fact was that King Cod was becoming scarce throughout the whole of his wide North Atlantic realm. In 1956 cod landings for Grand Banks, Newfoundland waters were down to 80,000 metric tonnes live weight, about a fifth of what they had been only half a century earlier.

When a prey animal becomes scarce in nature, its predators normally decline in numbers too, thereby giving the prey an opportunity to recover. Industrial man works in the opposite way. As cod became scarcer, pressure on the remaining stocks mounted. Scarcity brought ever-rising prices, which in turn attracted more and more fishermen, willing to spend more and more money on gear. New, bigger, more destructive ships came into service and the bottom trawl, which scours the bed of the ocean like a gigantic harrow, destroying spawn and other life, almost totally replaced older fishing methods. During the 1960s fleets of big draggers and factory ships were coming to the Banks from a dozen European and Asian countries to engage in an uncontrolled killing frenzy over what remained of the cod populations. The result was that, between 1962 and 1967, cod landings *increased* until, in 1968, the catch topped two million tons. Soon thereafter, the whole northwest Atlantic cod fishery began to collapse for want of fish to catch.

The Canadian government has made some bumbling and half-hearted attempts to conserve what remains of the cod stocks, but other nations – such as France – fishing the banks off Newfoundland have proved uncooperative – as indeed have the larger Canadian fishing companies, which were unhappy with the catch quotas allotted to them.

In truth they were being treated very generously. In the spring of 1989 federal fisheries experts allowed that they had somehow been overestimating the size of the remaining cod stocks – by as much as 50 per cent! They now proposed that unless quotas were cut by at least that much, the remaining stocks (a mere 2 per cent of the aboriginal population) would be "at risk." However, such a draconian measure was not to be considered by Prime Minister Brian Mulroney's government – which reluctantly reduced the

Canadian cod catch quotas by about 20 per cent but allowed the French an *increased* quota.

Politicians are mostly purblind, but the people they represent are not always so. Skipper Arthur Jackman summed up things in Newfoundland in these prophetic words:

Take a good look about ye now, for 'tis all going out afore long. This old island fed we people so long as we took no more'n we had to have. That's how it was when I was a youngster. Now 'tis all changed and gone abroad. The seals has gone under, and the whales, and the codfish'll not be long behind. 'Tis only the gold they be after, these times, and I don't say they'll give up on it until there's nothing more to take. Then the people will have to get out of our old Rock. The way she's pointing, they'll have to haul their boats, bar up their houses, and take to their heels. I believes 'twill be a bad lookout, me son.

VI

Deep-water Men

Before confederation with Canada the outports of Newfoundland did much more than rear a race of superlative fishermen – they produced some of the world's finest ocean-going mariners. In sail and in steam, serving in every capacity from deckhand and stoker to master mariner and chief engineer, they manned vessels which flew the British red ensign in every ocean of the world, but especially in the Atlantic. They were recognized everywhere as a breed apart – seamen of indomitable courage and uncanny ability, bred of and from the sea.

The measure of their worth is well illustrated by their accomplishments aboard the deep-sea salvage and rescue tugs which sailed mostly out of Halifax, Nova Scotia, or St. John's, Newfoundland, but which – regardless of their home ports – were largely manned by Newfoundlanders.

During the 1930s and on through the war years, the salvage and rescue business in the western approaches of the North Atlantic was dominated by a Canadian company called Foundation Maritime – and the pillar of that company was a 650-ton, 165-foot, coal-fired, steam-powered, iron tug built in 1918. Her name was *Foundation Franklin*, and she became a legend. One of her masters became a legend too.

The Man from Burin

Captain Harry Brushett was born in the year 1898, in the town of Burin on Placentia Bay. There he grew to manhood, and at the age of twelve he went out to the Grand Banks under sail and learned to fish. He had five years of the Banking schooners before he became mate of a two-masted Burin schooner called the *Vanessa*. At the age of eighteen Harry Brushett became master of the *Vanessa*, "going foreign" to Alicante in Spain with cargoes of Newfoundland salt fish.

On his nineteenth birthday he was storm-taken in mid-Atlantic and, after thirty-six days of struggling to stay afloat, the *Vanessa* sank under the young skipper, leaving him and his crew of six adrift in a broken dory. Ten days later they were picked up by a Norwegian tramp steamer, and eventually returned to their home port.

Two *days* after his homecoming, Harry Brushett put to sea as master of the schooner *Mary II*. Her destination—Alicante.

He sailed her until 1920, when he became skipper of the new, three-masted *George A. Wood* and, at the same time, bosun to a slight and lively Burin girl called Eva. Burin wives do not stay at home when the captains go to sea, and so for the next five years Eva sailed in the *George A. Wood*, from Burin to Cadiz, Portugal, Jamaica and Italy, carrying fish outbound, and bringing home cargoes of rum, salt, sugar and general trade.

When, in 1925, the Burin merchant who owned the *Wood* went bankrupt, Harry Brushett turned to steam. He spent the last years of the decade skippering freighters creeping from port to port all over the North Atlantic.

The depression of 1929 was the beginning of the dark time. Newfoundland sank into an abyss of suffering that was medieval. Good skippers could be had for seaman's wages, and there were too few ships to go around. Harry was lucky to get a mate's berth in the little tramps in the Newfoundland and Nova Scotian coastal trade.

He did not enjoy that life. Ship-owners are seldom generous, and in those years they were particularly penurious and grasping. The coasters worked twenty-four hours a day; they were under-manned, badly found, and their people grossly underpaid. It was barely a living.

In 1938 Brushett was on the beach when he was offered a mate's berth for a voyage in *Foundation Franklin*. It was no permanent job and the pay was not even as good as on the coastal steamers; but that single voyage left an indelible imprint on Brushett. What he saw of salvage and rescue work was enough to convince him that here was a life well suited to his independent nature. He went back to the coast tramps after that voyage, but he kept his eyes on the salvage tugs thereafter.

When the manager of Foundation Maritime met him on the street one day in early 1941 and inquired whether Harry would care to take command of *Foundation Franklin*, there was no hesitation. So it was that in April of that year a most remarkable vessel and a most remarkable man became an entity.

Brushett was then forty-three years of age and in that particular prime which relative youth and thirty years at sea alone can give a man. His appearance betrayed few indications of his character. His face might well have been that of a scholarly pedagogue in some small outport village. He was long and thin, "a tall, lean drink of water," as one of his men called him; using the word "water" quite advisedly, for Brushett never drank hard liquor. This abstinence (which was not a matter of principle but simply of distaste) made him somewhat incomprehensible to the salvage crews, most of whom tended to the other extreme. Brushett's incisive quality of command and his aura of almost Victorian rectitude also tended to set him apart from the men who served under him. Outwardly and in casual conversation he seemed the antithesis of the roaring, hell-for-leather tugboat man. But he *could* be roused – if there was good reason – to the kind of fearsomeness for which Newfoundland skippers have a wide renown.

When he took command of *Franklin*, Brushett found a motley crowd. There was an unpredictable genius named Neil McLeod as chief engineer, with steady, indomitable Reginald Poirier as second. On deck was Tom Paisley from Fogo as first officer, and Emile Forgeron, one of a huge family of boys, most of whom were in the tugboat business, as second. Cyril Marryat from Conception Bay occupied the radio shack.

The balance of the 24-man crew included a hard core of Newfoundland stokers, oilers and deckhands. By 1941 the Navy and the Merchant Marine had taken the pick of east coast sailors – nevertheless, the men who signed on for salvage work were often the most experienced seamen, even if they did have idiosyncrasies which made them unappreciated aboard naval and merchant ships.

"The first day out," Chief Engineer McLeod recalled, "my gang was always useless. Then they'd begin to sober up. But before that awful moment of pure sobriety disabled them completely, they would get into the vanilla extract. Then we'd have steam!"

Not all the hands were old shellbacks. There was one poor Jewish lad, out of a St. John's clothing shop, who had got into a small spot of trouble ashore, and hurriedly shipped out in *Franklin*. He made an adequate stoker once he overcame his aversion to eating fat sowbelly. Then there was a six-foot "jack-a-tar" (of French and Micmac lineage) from Cornerbrook, wanted by the police on a manslaughter charge. There was also an ex-sealer from Wesleyville in Bonavista Bay who was afflicted with hallucinations. He would hold long conversations with *Franklin*'s boilers, or with her bilge pumps, but he became an excellent oiler nonetheless.

They were not a dull crowd. To the last man they were individualists, from unorthodox moulds. And they were probably the only kind of men who could have survived the years which lay ahead and who could have accomplished the impossible with such monotonous regularity.

When *Franklin* put to sea under her new master, the shape of the war had changed. The early months of confusion were largely past. The Canadian Navy had shown a heartening growth; and just in time, for the U-boats had crossed the Atlantic and were about to begin a sustained assault upon the western end of the great convoy bridge. For months to come the Navy was to be outmatched and even outnumbered by its adversaries, and during this period scores of ships were to go down off the Canadian seaboard, while others barely floated, their bellies ripped by torpedo blasts, waiting in hopes of rescue.

Most ships from eastern North America (with the exception of vessels of sixteen knots or better) bound for allied ports in Europe came first to Halifax, where they were assigned to convoys.

Bedford Basin a day or so before a major convoy sailed was wonderful. On occasion more than a hundred freighters of every size and nationality lay so thickly clustered that from the heights of the old citadel they appeared as an unbroken expanse of spars and superstructures. Halifax had become the most important port in the western world, for through it passed more than three-quarters of the total tonnage which was sustaining Britain in her darkest hour.

This mighty concentration of ships, and the circumstances which surrounded them, made for a steady increase in the number of maritime accidents. During 1941 Foundation's tugs and salvage vessels rescued twenty-seven ships, almost all of which would have been lost but for their efforts.

Spectacular as this record was, it represented only part of the salvage tugs' activities. When a ship was in distress a tug went out to her. When there were no SOS calls, the tugs worked just as hard at a myriad other tasks. *Franklin*'s log for this period is a frenzied record.

On April 11 Brushett took her to sea for the first time. Her destination was Boston, towing the torpedoed freighter *Polar Chief*. On April 20 *Franklin* arrived in Halifax, and on the twenty-first sailed for Shelburne to assist in the launching of a big new schooner which had become stuck on the ways. She sailed the following day for Argentia, Newfoundland, with two leaky wooden scows in tow. The scows almost sank off Canso, so Brushett had to put into Louisburg. While the scows were being repaired, *Franklin* sailed for Janvrin Island to haul the freighter *Mana* off the rocks. When that job was completed she was diverted into the Bras d'Or Lakes to rescue the motor vessel *Dixie Sword*, which had also run aground. After releasing this ship, *Franklin* sailed for Inhabitants Bay to pick up the derrick-scow *Foundation Masson* and deliver her to Sydney. From Sydney she sailed for Halifax, where she had half a day in port before setting off to salvage the SS *Ceres*, which was ashore in Sea Coal Bay. That job was completed on the twenty-eighth of May, and on the twenty-ninth *Franklin* sailed for Rockland, Maine, towing the damaged freighter *Frances Dawson* . . . and so the record goes until the reader examining that log becomes incredulous, for surely, he tells himself, no ship and no men either could maintain such a pace month in, month out, year in, year out.

However, a ship's log speaks nothing but the truth. From April 1941 till April 1942, *Foundation Franklin* steamed more than fifty thousand miles – a double circumnavigation of the globe. It was seldom that she was in any port for longer than it took to fill her bunkers, take on stores, and clear again. For her men life was an endless sequence of days and nights in stinking and miserable quarters on a small and most uncomfortable vessel. For her engineer officers it was an endless battle to keep the worn old machinery turning out a steady eleven knots. For the deck officers it was worst of all. As any merchant officer well knows, the hardest moments of a voyage are the beginning and the end, the departure and the ultimate landfall. Once well at sea, life settles into a routine that is only occasionally disrupted by storms or accident. But the approach to land, in thick weather, at night, or even in the clear light of day, is always hard.

Franklin spent most of her time entering or leaving ports, or working close inshore upon dangerous coasts. In blinding blizzards, in black fog, in every sort of weather, this was her fate: to be continually at the beginning or the end. And her officers had more to worry them than the safety of their ship alone, since more often than not they had an unwieldy tow, a crippled ship, a derrick, a dredge, or a string of barges hanging on behind.

For Brushett, there was the added strain of learning a new and difficult trade – not from an instructor versed in its intricacies, but solely from experience and observation. As master he could not ask advice from his underlings, nor could he admit to knowing less than they. His method was to allow the salvage foreman and other specialists in his crew to carry on without any interference from the bridge while Brushett ran his ship – and watched. He watched to good effect. Before the summer ended he was as conversant with salvage techniques as many a man who had spent years in that complicated trade.

Biafra

On July 8, 1941, *Franklin* again sailed for Argentia with the two scows which had almost sunk during the first attempt in May. The scows continued to prove intractable and during a hard breeze on the night of July 10 the tow-lines broke and both went off on their own. Finding them in darkness and in a blow was an ugly business, but before dawn the wanderers had been rounded up, volunteers had boarded them from a dory, and they were again safely tethered.

It was with considerable relief that Brushett delivered them to Argentia, and then set sail for Louisburg, where a derrick lay waiting to be towed to Halifax.

That derrick was destined to wait a long time.

Early on July 12 a fast convoy of nearly fifty freighters had put out from Halifax bound for the British Isles. Escorted by three Canadian warships, the convoy first made its way up the Nova Scotian coast past Scatari, then swung east along the southern coast of Newfoundland. Its three columns of merchantmen steamed close on one another's tails in unaccustomed and uneasy proximity – for no merchant skipper ever enjoyed having *one* other ship, let alone fifty of them in such intimate propinquity.

That night, while the convoy was entering a bank of fog, one of the escorts got a submarine contact. The warships swung back to drop depth charges while the commodore of the convoy gave the dispersal order.

Only those who have lived through it can comprehend the fearful confusion which can result when fifty ponderous vessels crowded into a square mile or so of ocean suddenly proceed each its own separate way, and at full speed. Blanket the sea with fog and darkness, and the scene takes on the qualities of a gargantuan nightmare. On this occasion there were three collisions; but a single vessel took the brunt of them, for she was hit twice within three minutes.

She was the *Biafra*, a 7,000-tonner fully laden with war cargo. When the dispersal order was received, *Biafra* turned hard to starboard out of the middle line of the convoy and almost at once was struck fair amidships by another vessel. The shock rolled her down until her port rails were under; but she staggered to her feet and, while the water rushed into her engine room, started to turn back to her original course. The turn was never completed, for she was struck again by a vessel from her own column.

There was panic aboard *Biafra*. The first collison had damaged her enough so that her chances of survival seemed remote; the second seemed to seal her doom. Her engine room, stokehold and number three cargo hold filled up to sea level within a few minutes and she lay helpless, with water pouring steadily into all her after-holds. Half an hour later she lay quite alone, and sinking fast, while the rest of the convoy stampeded blindly off into the night like a herd of frightened steers.

Despite the possibility that the submarine might also hear it, she radioed a general SOS. The submarine had now become the lesser of two evils.

Marryat, on listening-watch on *Franklin*'s radio, heard the call at 2 a.m., July 13, and moments later Brushett was giving a new course to the helmsman, while Neil McLeod was working *Franklin*'s engine up to speed.

Franklin was then one hundred and twenty miles from the scene of the collision, or about ten hours' steaming time. But when Marryat received the following message from *Biafra*: HURRY, I AM MAKING WATER FAST, McLeod waved his magic wand and *Franklin* was soon logging almost fourteen knots; as fast as she had ever gone in her life.

With a great foaming bone in her teeth and hot black clouds of smoke panting from both her funnels, she came bearing down through the fog. At 11 a.m. she raised *Biafra*. The lookout kept a wary eye open for submarines, but everyone else was staring at the crippled ship which had loomed suddenly out of the murk ahead.

Listing fourteen degrees, and so far down by the stern that her after well-deck was almost awash, she seemed to be hanging on in complete defiance of the laws of buoyancy.

This was not a job where Brushett could stand aside and watch his salvage men do the work. This was *his* job, and his alone. He acted with assurance and without a moment's hesitation.

He had immediately recognized that the only hope of saving the big vessel lay in getting one of *Franklin*'s big, motor-driven salvage pumps aboard her. Simply taking her in tow would have been so much waste effort, for she would have sunk before she was halfway to the nearest port. But swinging a three-ton pump out of the tug's hold and hoisting it up and onto the deck of a merchantman while there is a heavy beam sea running is no casual procedure. There were those aboard *Franklin* who thought it could not be done.

Brushett was not one of them. While he was still running down on *Biafra*, the hatch covers were coming off the after-hold, and slings were being made fast to a gasoline-driven, six-inch centrifugal pump. The two pumpmen, Buck Dassylva and his assistant Bob Cooper, were standing by. *Franklin* came sweeping in under *Biafra*'s counter, rounded-to, and in a moment had a heaving line aboard. Within three minutes the heaving line had been replaced by a spring line, and as soon as the two ships had been joined by this slender umbilicus, Brushett ordered the pump to be hoisted away. For a long minute it swung at the end of *Franklin*'s boom. The tug rose on a wave and at the crucial instant the boom was swung inboard of *Biafra*; the pump dropped to her decks as lightly as a bird; the slings were cast off; and before *Franklin* had begun to drop away into the trough, she had swung her boom into the clear again.

It was a masterful piece of ship-handling; but Dassylva and Cooper equalled it. At the instant when *Franklin*'s boat-deck was level with *Biafra*'s well-deck, both men leaped across the intervening space. The fact that they were jumping to a sinking ship did not bother them. They, with their pump, would see to it that she did *not* sink.

Brushett would have liked to put a second pump on board, but he had no more six-inchers and it would have invited almost certain disaster to have tried to swing one of the huge eight-inch pumps across the gap.

While the transfer had been taking place, another tug, almost unnoticed in the excitement, had come out of the murk on *Biafra*'s bow and had quietly put a towing line aboard the ship. She was the competing *Cruizer* out of Sydney. For a while it looked as if she would take this salvage job right out from under Brushett's nose.

When he saw what had happened, the side of Brushett that his crew had not yet seen came to the fore.

He raised his megaphone and in a cold, controlled voice called to *Biafra*'s skipper.

"I see you've taken *Cruizer's* wire. With half our power she has half our chances of getting you into port. You've two minutes to decide if you intend to keep her on – before we leave."

Confronted by this ultimatum, *Biafra's* skipper hurriedly bellowed an order to his crew, and *Cruizer* found herself towing nothing more substantial than a hundred-fathom length of steel cable. Discomfited, she drew off, while *Franklin* put her own wire aboard *Biafra* and began to work up speed.

Meanwhile Cooper and Dassylva had got a suction line down into *Biafra's* after-holds, and the pump was running. Seen from aboard the crippled ship, *Biafra's* plight looked even more desperate than it had done from *Franklin's* decks. Her already dangerous list was steadily increasing. She had no power of any sort and all of her own pumps were therefore out of action. She had been torn open amidships, and the great V-shaped gash was twenty feet wide at the top and extended far down below the water-line. Apart from the completely flooded engine room, stoke-hold and numbers three, four and five holds, the two remaining after-holds were already better than half flooded. Dassylva and Cooper knew that at all costs they must hold the levels in these two, for if the water gained much more, the ship would go down by the stern. With only one pump, they engaged the sea in battle.

Franklin was now towing full out. At 6:30 p.m. *Biafra's* master signalled Brushett to stop immediately. His ship was going down, he said, and he wanted to disembark his crew. Brushett stopped and most of *Biafra's* people quickly clambered into the lifeboats and rowed across to *Cruizer*, which was still standing by. *Biafra* was now abandoned except for her senior officers and the two pump men from *Franklin*. These two did not share in the general alarm. They were almost holding their own against the inflowing water, and believed they could keep *Biafra* floating for another hour or two.

At 7:30 p.m. Brushett heard the outer bell buoy of Louisburg harbour ahead of him. The fog was impenetrable and an onshore wind with a growing sea was making up. Nevertheless, he had no choice but to go in. *Franklin* almost ran down the pilot boat which had been summoned by radio, and which had come out most reluctantly. The pilot came on board, but flatly refused to try to take either *Franklin* or *Biafra* through the narrow gut of the harbour entrance.

"Lie out here till dawn," he said, "and then I'll take you in."

Once again the mild-mannered skipper of the *Franklin* showed his mettle. "That ship astern of me," Brushett said quietly, "is sinking. She will not last an hour more. She is going to be beached in Louisburg before that hour's up – if I have to pilot her inside myself."

Given no alternative, the pilot reluctantly agreed to help. By then it was almost pitch-dark. With *Cruizer* on a wire from *Biafra*'s stern to help steer her, *Franklin* began nosing forward, smelling her way through the black shroud.

The little convoy safely passed through the outer arm and approached an abrupt turn in the channel which leads to the inner harbour. *Franklin* made the turn, but *Biafra* failed to follow. There was a muffled grating sound as she went aground on Battery Shoal.

Biafra was temporarily safe, but not yet saved.

Franklin reeled in her wire then went alongside the casualty to swing five more pumps aboard. When these were all working, an attempt was made to haul the vessel off the shoal. It failed, but Brushett was not distressed. He had hoped to be able to take the ship to the foot of the inner harbour and beach her on the mud bottom there, but since she preferred Battery Shoal, there she should stay until she had been repaired.

The patching took three days and was done by *Franklin*'s diver, a St. John's man. He made a wooden patch for her gaping wound, building it plank by plank, while working at depths of twenty feet in water that was too murky to allow him any visibility. So the patch grew, plank by plank, until it was well above water level. It was then covered from top to bottom with heavy canvas to seal the cracks between the planks – and the job was done.

Now Cooper and Dassylva took over. The rumble of their pumps and the roar of water pouring over *Biafra*'s side echoed across the harbour for half a day until, at high tide, *Franklin* took a strain on the tow wire and the big ship slid off the shoal and idled contentedly along behind the tug to a berth beside a wharf.

There remained the task of making her seaworthy for the long tow to the nearest dry-dock. This consisted largely of fitting a "hard patch" of cement (as opposed to a "soft patch" of wood or canvas) inside *Biafra*'s hull. While this work was being done the tug lay alongside, supplying steam and power to the damaged ship and, in the process, using up most of her coal. Then, on the sixth day, Marryat came into *Franklin*'s wheelhouse with a new SOS.

The message was from the Imperial Oil tanker *Icoma*, which had struck the coast rocks while in thick fog some twelve miles east of the port and had smashed her rudder. Her call was urgent. She was holding herself off a weather shore with her anchor alone, but the sea was heavy and she was beginning to drag. Her operator told Marryat that if help did not reach her within an hour or two, she would be forced in over reefs and become a total loss.

Incredibly, *Biafra*'s people tried to prevent *Franklin* from answering this call, by refusing to let go her mooring lines. Brushett abandoned the lines and was under way in fifteen minutes.

The fog was still impenetrable when *Franklin* got outside, and Brushett took her down the coast by ear alone, listening first to the sound of the breakers on the reefs, and then to the mournful hoot of *Icoma*'s whistle. The sea was running strongly and the same onshore wind which had caused trouble during the *Biafra* rescue was still blowing hard.

Brushett never saw *Icoma* until he was a ship's length from her. He had gone in by the leadline, between and around the same rocks that had smashed *Icoma*'s rudder, and in a fog so dense that he could barely see the surface of the water from his bridge. *Icoma* had drifted so far in by then that her starboard side was scraping up and down on the first ledge.

It took just seventeen minutes to connect up to her. Three hours later she was safely anchored in Louisburg. It had been as coldly daring a rescue as *Franklin* ever made; but it had gone so smoothly that it was soon forgotten even by the men who helped her do the job.

War at Sea

Foundation Franklin and her motley crew were seldom idle during the winter of 1941-42, and when spring approached it brought no respite. March gales began working up to their annual paroxysm. The worst season of the year for shipping in the North Atlantic had come again; but in the spring of 1942 the gales and seas took second place to the murderous assaults of men against other men.

Grand Admiral Doenitz had convinced Hitler that the place to cut the arteries of the western allies lay at their beginnings in the coastal waters off the American continent. So in the early spring the U-boats sailed westward, not in ones and twos, but in packs; until there were as many as twenty of them operating in Canadian and Newfoundland coastal waters at any one time.

Convoy after convoy, inbound or outbound, was attacked. In St. John's and Halifax merchant seamen who had survived the unheralded explosions and the perishing waters of the winter sea appeared in pathetic little groups at Seamen's Homes and in the hospitals. They were few in numbers, but they represented many ships.

Franklin's people saw them and heard their tales, and the fear which no seaman can escape grew in their hearts. They knew that a single torpedo in Franklin's belly would send her to the bottom so swiftly that there would be no time to launch a boat. There would be only time to die.

And they blamed the Navy for placing them in jeopardy.

Their hostility towards the Navy was not without justification. Naval escort vessels which put into port after convoy voyages sometimes lay at dock for days on end allowing their crews to recover from their ordeals, while the salvage and rescue tugs, which suffered the same grievous treatment under gale and sea, knew no rest at all. The salvage crews watched green hands and green officers in spanking naval uniforms do foolish things that jeopardized not only the escort vessels but the merchant-men they were supposed to guard. They lived in the shadow of the Navy's overweening pride, and of its condescending attitude towards the dirty, disreputable vessels of the salvage fleet.

"Maybe we had no business to feel the way we did," Harry Brushett remembered. "But every time I came ashore and saw the papers, I'd read that the Navy had the war at sea damn near won. And I'd wonder about the ten or a dozen distress calls that

Sparks had picked up during our last voyage – calls from ships that went down before anyone could reach them. I'd see the merchant seamen being treated like something not quite human, with nowhere to go but the cat houses and the dirtiest dives. The streets would be full of the Navy, strutting about as if they owned the place.

"Probably we'd have taken it all with just the usual amount of bitching, except for one thing. When *Franklin* went to sea, the Navy wasn't there. Maybe they had too much to do and no ships to spare. But we used to see the escort vessels – frigates, corvettes and destroyers – lying in St. John's and Halifax so thick you couldn't have sculled a dory between them – while we were going out alone to try and haul in some torpedoed merchantman. The Navy may have had good reasons for the way it acted. We never heard them. They wouldn't bother to explain things to chaps like us. So we had to go by appearances, and the appearances were bad."

Right or wrong, this was the way the men who sailed the salvage tugs had begun to feel – and it was an unhealthy state of mind. One of the results was that it became increasingly difficult to obtain hands to man the tugs, and almost impossible to keep any except Newfoundlanders for more than one or two voyages. It was a situation that could not go on, and it was Harry Brushett who put a stop to it.

On Sunday, March 22, *Franklin* was berthed at St. John's after rescuing a disabled freighter, when the Navy ordered her out to the assistance of the torpedoed British tanker *Athelviscount* at a point six hundred miles southeast of Newfoundland.

Brushett countered with an ultimatum that was tantamount to mutiny. Unless an escort was forthcoming, he said, the tug would lie at Bowring's wharf until doomsday.

It is doubtful if any other merchant skipper could have made that ultimatum stick – but Brushett did. Two hours later a corvette came dashing towards the harbour mouth, signalling *Franklin* to fall in astern.

The weather outside was thick. Snow squalls and fog patches whipped across the Banks in the grip of a rising westerly that was blowing the disabled tanker farther eastward with every hour.

She was already near *Franklin*'s extreme range, and Brushett was driving his ship hard in an effort to reach her quickly – but *Franklin*'s best in that weather was only about twelve knots. That must have seemed like a tedious crawl to the commander of the corvette. Or perhaps he was annoyed at having been sent to sea for such a trivial matter. At any rate, the escort made no attempt to stay close to its charge, but went haring away at full speed in a series of gigantic circles.

Brushett watched this performance with a jaundiced eye until just before dusk when the corvette happened to come in sight again. Then he ordered Marryat to send an Aldis lamp signal:

> . . . SUGGEST YOU SLOW DOWN AND SAVE FUEL BY HOLDING STATION ON ME WE HAVE A LONG WAY TO GO.

The corvette did not even deign to reply, but went whooping off into the murk again and vanished.

That night the weather thickened even more, and by midnight the storm, the snow squalls and the scud had reduced visibility to the point where *Franklin*'s people were only able to catch occasional glimpses of the corvette as she cut in across their bows at more and more infrequent intervals. At dawn they glimpsed her heeling hard over in a turn. They did not see her again until four days had passed.

The weather cleared but the gale continued unabated until March 26, when *Franklin* arrived at the pinpoint in grey nothingness where the *Athelviscount* should have been. The tanker was not there, and nothing in the heaving expanse of foam-flecked sea gave any clue to her whereabouts. As usual, *Franklin*'s transmitter had been sealed by the Navy for security reasons before the voyage began, but Marryat maintained a listening watch while *Franklin* began a search pattern along the *Athelviscount*'s presumed line of drift.

She was still searching some hours later when a United States destroyer came on the air to announce that she was standing by the torpedoed tanker. Marryat hastily took a direction finding bearing on this transmission, and *Franklin* began to run it down. The sea was singularly violent and it was not until dusk that the lookout raised a smudge on the horizon.

The smudge soon resolved itself into the lean profile of a destroyer, and the American knifed down on *Franklin*, saluted, then turned to lead the way.

The 10,000-ton *Athelviscount* loomed up out of the turmoil of the sea like a water-borne Gibraltar. She had been westbound in ballast when an acoustic torpedo took her in the stern, and now her bows were thrust up to the dark skies in a ponderous wedge of steel, while her counter lay almost at a level with the sea.

Brushett's attention was fixed so intently on her that he hardly noticed a third ship standing by. It was the escort corvette which, having lost *Franklin* after the first night out, had come straight on to the casualty, getting new positions as she came, but not bothering to relay these to the rescue tug. As *Franklin* turned towards the tanker, the corvette shot out busily to meet her–her lamp blinking briskly as she came. This time it was her turn to be ignored. Brushett was far too busy to even waste a glance on her.

Under almost any other circumstances he would have lain off until dawn before trying to connect. However, Brushett had concluded that another twelve hours' drift towards the east would spell the difference between success or failure in his attempts to save this ship. It was vital that a line be put aboard the casualty before darkness came, but the seas were so immense, and the tanker's bows reared up so high, and fell so far, that not even Brushett dared take *Franklin* in close enough to put a heaving-line aboard.

Coming up to windward of the tanker he signalled that he would fire a rocket-line over her bows but, as the tube flamed over the big ship, dragging the light messenger line behind it, he saw that only three or four men were running forward to retrieve it. There were not nearly enough of them to be able to haul in more than a few yards of the two-inch, steel towing cable which would follow the messenger line. Brushett now had no alternative but to ease his tug in to such close quarters that her destruction beneath the plunging forefoot of the tanker seemed certain. Nevertheless, he somehow managed to keep *Franklin* from being sliced open until the twin bridles had been hauled up the steel cliff, and the wire was secured.

At 8 p.m. of a black winter night *Franklin* took up the strain and the tow began. It was only then that there was time for communication with the casualty. As the *Athelviscount*'s lamp flickered through the darkness, Brushett learned why there were so few men upon her decks.

When the torpedo struck – full in the engine room – almost the entire engineer staff together with some of the deckhands had been working amongst the machinery on an emergency repair. The blast had killed every man inside the engine room and had wounded most of those in the accommodations aft. The entire stern section of the ship had flooded until only the empty cargo tanks forward were left to hold her up. When *Franklin* took her in tow she was literally floating on her midship bulkheads.

The message to the tug concluded with these words:

WE LIKE YOUR LOOKS AND THINK YOU WILL GET US IN. It was signed, as if in confirmation of a hopeful omen: Captain Franklin.

As the tow got under way, the American destroyer foamed up alongside and her lamp began to wink:

GOOD LUCK TO YOU WE HAVE TO GO BUT LEAVE YOU IN GOOD HANDS.

By "good hands" she presumably meant the corvette. If so, she meant well, but she was not very accurate. Hardly had she passed out of sight when the corvette again began to signal to the *Franklin*:

AM RUNNING SHORT OF FUEL, she flashed, NOW RETURNING TO ST. JOHN'S.

Five minutes later she was gone.

So *Franklin* and the tanker were left alone seven hundred and fifty miles from the nearest land, in a force 8 gale and in submarine-infested waters, to sink or swim as best they could.

They were not as much alone as they might have wished. During the next few days Marryat received three warnings of U-boats along the route which *Franklin* would have had to follow to reach Halifax. In addition he intercepted four SOS calls from ships which had been attacked between *Franklin* and the Nova Scotian coast. The sea looked empty, but it was not.

When the Homeric struggle began, *Franklin* was almost equidistant from St. John's and Halifax. Before sailing, Brushett had been instructed to make for Halifax; but the Western Ocean seemed bent on seeing to it that *Franklin* did not go to either port. An excerpt from the ship's log sets the tone.

"March 27. *Day commences with west-south-west wind rapidly increasing to gale force with rough sea. 6:56 a.m. Tow-line parts due to chafing across casualty's bows. Too rough to reconnect. Standing by for moderating weather . . .* "

Franklin's log gives no more than an intimation of the kind of weather which was being brewed that day; but any man who knew Harry Brushett would also know that a storm which could prevent his even putting a rocket line aboard the casualty must have been fearsome indeed.

During that morning the two ships drifted at such a pace that by noon they were twenty-five miles farther east than they had been at dawn. Plotting the drift, Brushett saw failure facing him and he could not stand the prospect. He rang down for half-speed on the engine, eased around out of the tremendous head-seas, and then blew—rather than ran—down on the tanker like a Mother Carey's chicken.

Reversing the usual order of things, he shot up under the *Athelviscount's* lee (a position normally to be avoided because a big ship, with more surface to the wind, always drifts off faster than a small one, and may well overrun a little vessel which is to leeward of her). The first mate, clinging to the wing of the bridge, fired the rocket pistol. The line blew out almost parallel to the tanker, dragging the rocket off its course; but before it was quite lost, the projectile snagged in the tanker's foremast rigging.

Desperate hands grasped for and seized it, and at once the messenger line began to pay out. Handling the engine room telegraph with the precision of an organist, Brushett meanwhile kept his little vessel from being overrun by the massive bulk of the tanker until the wire had again gone across the narrow gap. This time it was shackled to one of *Athelviscount's* anchor chains hung over the bow, so that there would be no further danger of its chafing.

Franklin forged ahead and took the strain. It took her two hours to even bring *Athelviscount's* head into the wind again, and more than this she could not do. Although labouring valiantly, she was unable to even hold her own. More slowly now, but just as implacably, tug and tow were still being blown to the east.

Struggling like a beast upon a treadmill, *Franklin* kept at her task as if unconscious of the uselessness of her attempt to defeat the imponderable forces of the sea. The wind howled somberly in her rigging. The grey seas flung their spume high over her mastheads. And she lay down to it and pulled with a strangely insistent stubbornness that is the property of life itself.

There was no improvement throughout the four days which followed. Those days bore no relation to time as we know it. They were, rather, a cessation in time–an absence of it. Nothing changed, except that men and ships grew four aeons older.

On the morning of the fifth day Brushett looked at the dead-reckoning position on his chart (it had been six days since he had been able to get a fix from the heavens) and then he turned to his mate.

"Grandy," he said, "we'll give it another twenty-four hours, and if the storm hasn't fallen light by then we'll turn around and run for Ireland."

He meant it too; but they did not have to make that choice. Towards evening on the fifth day the wind began to fall off. Although *Franklin*'s churning screw never changed its beat, the tow began almost imperceptibly to make some westing. By daybreak on the sixth day *Franklin* had regained the distance she had lost in the preceding five. She was back where she had started when the tow began.

As the wind dropped out *Franklin* was able to lay a course. Halifax was now out of the question as a destination, because of the depleted condition of *Franklin*'s bunkers and the prevailing westerly winds. St. John's it had to be.

The new course put the two ships into a gigantic beam sea and both proceeded to try to roll themselves to death. The tanker, huge and heavy in the water, was rolling viciously enough–but *Franklin* was rolling like a barrel on a demented teeter-totter. Early in the morning of April 1 she took a sea that laid her over until her starboard rails went under. That roll caught able-seaman Walter Wilson in the act of descending a companion ladder, and

Franklin's recovery was so violent that he was jerked off the ladder with such force that his right arm was sprung out of its socket. It flailed limply from his shoulder like a length of rope end.

Brushett and Grandy tried to slip the bone back into place, but they could do nothing with it. Brushett then told Marryat to call the *Athelviscount* on the lamp, to see if by any chance she had a doctor aboard. The tanker's reply came winking back:

MY STEWARD KNOWS FIRST AID BUT NO ONE CAN LAUNCH A BOAT IN SUCH A SEA.

To which Brushett replied:

WILL YOU TAKE A CHANCE IF WE COME AND FETCH YOU?

YES, came the instant answer, IF YOU CAN CHANCE IT SO CAN WE.

Franklin eased down to dead-slow while Grandy and three other Newfoundland seamen went aft and cast the lashings off the dory. Waiting their moment they threw the little boat over the taffrail and leaped aboard, all in one motion; then they were madly rowing to get clear as *Franklin's* stern heaved up and came crashing down.

What Captain Franklin's thoughts were as he beheld that little cockleshell bouncing towards him over the great swells, he never did reveal. But he was a brave man, and he kept his word. He and his steward hung down from *Athelviscount's* lee side on a Jacob's ladder that swung out then in against the ship like a pendulum; and as the dory lifted beneath them, they jumped for it.

Captain Franklin was the kind of seaman the salvage crew could understand. As he crouched in the bottom of the fragile bit of flotsam to which he had committed his life, his glance was caught by a wooden plug shoved rather haphazardly into a hole in the floorboards. Pointing to it, he raised his voice and yelled a question over the skirling wind:

"Is that the plug we pull out to drain her – when she fills?"

The Newfoundlanders grinned and rowed a little harder.

Captain Franklin and his steward were heaved aboard the tug by the boat's crew. Then they descended with Brushett into the forepeak where Wilson had been lashed down in his bunk. For the next three hours they worked over him with slings, with purchases, with every aid their knowledge and ingenuity could command; but without success. They had no anaesthetics either; but Wilson, a man fifty-six years of age, did not utter one cry of pain. Despite the decades of sea service behind them, the three sweating men were all violently seasick. They were not ashamed of it.

"The motion in that fo'castle would have made a stone god lose his biscuits," was Captain Franklin's comment.

They had done their best, but in the end they were forced to leave Wilson lashed to his bunk, his arm still dislocated, to endure until the voyage was ended.

Franklin had now been at sea ten days and nothing had been heard of her ashore since the departure of the corvette. Her owners and the Navy grew increasingly pessimistic as the days slid by. In fact, the Navy broadcast several messages giving permission to Brushett to break radio silence, if he was still afloat; but Brushett ordered Marryat to keep the transmitter sealed.

"The only hope we've got is silence," he said. "If we open up we can count on a sub finding us – but we cannot count on anyone else."

Marryat remained on listening watch. The days dragged on.

By April 4 *Franklin's* bunkers were nearly empty, making her so light that, in the terrible roll and heave of the sea, her propeller was being constantly thrust out of water. The engineers had to stand by the throttle every instant. As the propeller lifted and began to race, they would cut off the steam; as it buried itself again, they would give steam back to the cylinders.

Exhaustion had passed the point where it was felt by those whom it had engulfed. Stokers and deckhands alike shovelled coal, hauled ashes, and did not know what they were doing.

Brushett himself was at the limits of his endurance, for he had hardly been off his bridge since the voyage began. He would not rest. "There were seventeen men aboard that casualty," he remembered later. "There was the ship herself. And there was *Franklin* and her crew. I wasn't tired."

By April 5 the Navy had concluded that *Franklin* and her tow had gone down. Then, late that afternoon, an aircraft returning to its base at Argentia, after an anti-submarine patrol over the

Grand Banks, suddenly went on the air with a coded signal. An hour later those who had been tensely waiting in Foundation Maritime's harbour-side office received this message:

AIRCRAFT REPORTS BRIEF SIGHTING TWIN STACK TUG TOWING WHAT APPEARS TO BE A SINKING SHIP 100 MILES S.E. ST. JOHNS.

In St. John's there was a great bustle. An escort vessel was warned to prepare for sea, and aircraft were ordered to fly over the area at dawn next morning. The first of the planes located *Franklin* at 10 a.m. on April 6 – just ten minutes after Harry Brushett had sighted the land mass of Cape Race.

The wind was moderate that morning but showing ominous signs of shifting to sou'east. *Franklin* had been towing for ten days, and had been at sea fourteen. She had less than a day's coal left. Brushett knew that if her fuel failed, or if the wind did go into the sou'east, both she and *Athelviscount* would probably drive ashore. He signalled Captain Franklin, suggesting that he and his remaining crew come aboard the tug. If the worst came to the worst, *Franklin* could slip the tow and try to claw off the lee shore before her fuel ran out.

Both ships were stopped while the survivors from the tanker came aboard the *Franklin*. As they got under way again the two masters stood on *Franklin*'s bridge together and watched the sky with eyes in which perpetual strain would leave a mark which would still be there when both lay dying.

They watched the sky. Down in the engine room McLeod and Poirier watched the steam gauges. There was nothing in the bunkers now but dust.

Night came down. The glass began to drop. The wind was rising and slowly shifting, but it had not yet begun to really blow. It seemed to prolong its indecision from hour to hour with a cruelty that was almost human. Then at dawn, for no good reason and contrary to all precedent, it simply dropped away, leaving a great bank of fog settling across the approaches to St. John's harbour.

Out of that fog came a corvette, steaming as if the hounds of hell were on her tail. She circled *Franklin* and the tow, jauntily kicked her heels and signalled: I AM YOUR ESCORT FOLLOW ME.

Franklin did not follow. *Athelviscount* was now drawing forty-one feet of water and there was a depth of only forty-two feet in the entrance passage to the harbour at low tide. *Franklin* stopped her engines and waited for the rising tide. It came at last, but with it came wind and a blinding snow squall. Brushett dared not wait for visibility to clear. Inching her way silently (she could not waste steam blowing fog warnings with her horn), *Franklin* came blind into the narrow entrance and there was greeted by three harbour tugs who quickly put their lines aboard *Athelviscount* and guided her the last few hundred yards towards an anchorage.

The story should have ended then, but there was an epilogue.

Once safely arrived in the harbour *Athelviscount* was boarded by a party of naval officers who took command of the last few minutes of the tow. One of them stationed himself on the tanker's bridge and, having signalled for the three harbour tugs to pull ahead, he turned to watch something happening astern. The tugs pulled. The mooring wire, which *Franklin* had already made fast to a buoy, snapped like a string and *Athelviscount* went charging across the harbour and fetched up hard against the opposite side.

Burning a mixture of coal dust and berserk rage, *Franklin* came bursting up alongside the tanker and Brushett stepped to the wing of the bridge. For a pregnant moment he stared up at the gold-braided officers above him, and then he bellowed in a voice that all St. John's could hear:

"Why in the hell don't you brass monkeys stay up in the trees where you belong?"

The brass monkeys hurriedly vanished from his sight.

Having freed the *Athelviscount* and then re-moored her, *Franklin* made fast to Bowring's dock, with just enough coal left, as McLeod put it, "to cook a pot of beans."

Almost before the lines were fast, a sub-lieutenant, R.C.N., stepped aboard. Captain Brushett was under orders to report at once to the senior naval officer.

"Now what?" asked Brushett, and the messenger replied stiffly, "There have been alleged infringements of regulations by your vessel."

Captain Franklin was standing close enough to overhear.

"Mind if I come with you, Cap?" he asked, and grinned.

Brushett grinned in reply – but the grin was thin and wolfish. They went off together.

Fortunately, the senior naval officer in St. John's had once been a working seaman himself. Therefore, he did not order either Brushett or Captain Franklin to be clapped in jail at the conclusion of that memorable interview, as a lesser man might well have done. When the two masters had left his office, he wiped his brow and turned to his chief of staff.

"The last time I got a strip torn off me as wide as that," he said nostalgically, "was when I was a midshipman with the China Fleet. You'd better see that *Franklin* gets an escort from now on!"

Sometimes the Navy kept that promise – more often it did not. But with or without an escort, Brushett and *Foundation Franklin* and her crew of mainly Newfoundlanders rescued some twenty-four more ships, their valuable cargoes together with several hundred men, before the war came to an end.

"The Old Girl seemed to have a charmed life," Brushett remembers. "But there were times when she ran it kind of close."

One such took place early in 1945 when *Franklin* was bound for Sydney after delivering a dredge to St. John's.

The pack was especially bad that year and as twilight fell, Brushett found his ship beset by ice. For an hour he worked her along the leads but as darkness became complete he gave up the attempt to reach the open sea and elected to spend the hours till dawn in a polyna – an ice-free lake within the pack.

It was a pleasant place to lie, for there was no sea running within the protection of the ice, and *Franklin*'s people were able to make her fast to the edge of the pack, stop her engines and relax.

The third mate was on watch until midnight and he made himself comfortable on the bridge. This snug harbour reminded him of certain cosy ports he had known along the Labrador coast during his fishing days, and the flicker of the northern lights across the polyna's expanse of black water aided the illusion. He was admiring the lights when his reverie was brought to an abrupt end by the realization that he was looking at something which had no business to be where it was. He snatched the night-glasses from their hook, stared for a moment, and then in a horrified voice muttered down the voice pipe to Brushett's cabin.

"Cap," he said. "You'd best get up here quick!"

Brushett was awake, which was fortunate, for otherwise he would never have heard his subordinate's subdued call to action. He pulled on his boots, went out on deck and climbed the bridge ladder.

The mate handed him the glasses and wordlessly pointed to the northern shore of the lake.

Brushett stared.

There could be no doubt about it. The outline of a submarine's conning tower, silhouetted against white ice under the swishing yellow of the northern lights, was not something about which a man could easily be mistaken.

Brushett and his mate looked into each other's eyes, and when they spoke it was – by unspoken agreement – in the most muted of whispers. "Go below," Brushett said, "and tell the men that if any of them so much as clears his throat or scratches a match I'll have his hide – if the fish don't get it first."

It was an awful night – and endless. There were some aboard the *Franklin* who later claimed that they did not even breathe until the dawn – but that is probably an exaggeration. Not even a Newfoundlander can go that long without oxygen.

"*We* tried to sound and look like a small black piece of darkness," Brushett recalled, "and we must have succeeded – or maybe he saw us all right but thought we were just a little fishing trawler and didn't want to give away his position by wasting a shell on anything so insignificant. Anyhow, he submerged an hour before dawn and we never saw hide nor hair of him again."

Fort Boise

With war's end, *Franklin* returned to the traditional conflict between the Western Ocean and the ships that sailed upon it. While those Newfoundlanders (and they were legion) who had served in naval ships and in the merchant marine were returning to their peace-time lives, *Franklin*'s men continued to sail their doughty old champion over the unquiet waters.

During the spring and summer of 1946, they were mainly employed in towing decommissioned destroyers up the St. Lawrence to Quebec. This was routine labour, but not dull. Towing dead destroyers through the narrow and congested shipping lanes was taut and exhausting work but, as Brushett remarked: "It was what the old ship was designed and built to do some thirty years ago."

That was true enough, for as H.M.S. *Frisky*, *Franklin* had originally been intended for just this kind of task in World War I. The wheel had now come full cycle.

Her people were restive and uneasy all that summer. They had reason to worry, for her owners had weighed her up – and found her wanting.

"The day of the coal-burners is gone," they said. "She costs too much to run."

"Too old," another added. "She's an antique now. Have to do everything the hard way on her. We need the kind of tug where everything is automatic."

Not everyone agreed. There were those who remembered that *Foundation Franklin* had made the fortunes of the company. These few came to her defence, and the upshot was that it was decided to obtain cost estimates for her conversion from coal to oil. A stay of execution had been granted and *Franklin* and Brushett made the most of it when, on August 23, a vessel named *Fort Boise* went ashore amongst the numberless rocks and ledges off St. Pierre, only a few score miles west of Captain Brushett's home port of Burin.

The *Fort Boise* was a 7,100-ton Britisher loaded with a part cargo of zinc concentrate and inbound for the Gulf. Her course should have carried her well south of the treacherous waters near the St. Pierre et Miquelon archipelago, but someone erred and the error was compounded by a dense fog. Shortly before midnight *Fort Boise* drove in amongst the reefs of the Great Bank, past the doleful beat of the surf on Lost Children Shoal, and struck the rocks.

Foundation Maritime first heard of the disaster at dawn on August 23, via a radio message from a shipping agent on St. Pierre. According to his report, the *Boise* was not seriously damaged; the weather was good; and salvage prospects seemed excellent.

Franklin was at that time undergoing her annual inspection and refit. Hurriedly she was put in order; bunkers were taken in and her salvage gear was loaded. At noon on the twenty-third Brushett took her to sea.

She arrived off the casualty during mid-morning of August 25 and Brushett dropped his anchor half a mile outside the shoals while diver Tom Nolan, acting as salvage foreman, took a dory in to inspect the wreck. Nolan found the vessel hard aground from her bridge forward, and surrounded by such a nest of rocks and reefs that even his dory had to wiggle like a fish to make its way through them.

These sunkers lie scattered off St. Pierre in such profusion that it is as if the contents of a celestial stone-boat had been dumped into a shallow sea. A prevalence of heavy fogs, sharp squalls and onshore gales does nothing to make the place more attractive. There is also a very swift and unpredictable current which sets at four knots in among the sunkers. In the background is the brooding loom of the almost barren cliffs of St. Pierre itself.

Nolan's report on the condition of the *Fort Boise* was not optimistic. The ship was completely flooded in her number two and number three holds, while number one was filling fast. Her cargo of zinc concentrate had turned into a kind of glutinous mud which boded ill for the salvage pumps. Her main structure had been badly strained and there were signs that she was already beginning to break apart below the water line.

Brushett and Nolan concluded that, given fair weather, they stood a chance of saving her.

Work began at once. *Franklin* eased in between the sunkers, sometimes with only half a dozen feet between her sides and the black rocks; but she kept coming until she lay alongside the wreck. Her boom was swung out and pumps and self-closing clam buckets were hoisted aboard *Fort Boise*. With almost all of *Franklin*'s crew to help him, Nolan set about installing the pump intakes in the flooded holds, while the ship's crew rigged the clam buckets to their own derricks and began jettisoning the heavy zinc concentrate into the sea. Once these operations were under way *Franklin* backed delicately out of that mouthful of granite teeth and laid two sets of ground tackle – enormous anchors with attached cables running two thousand feet to seaward. By dusk the pumps and clams were operating and the inner ends of the ground tackle wires had been made fast to winches on the wreck's stern.

The preliminary work had been done expeditiously. Now it but remained to clam the remaining cargo out and pump the holds before the attempt to free the *Fort Boise* could be made. Brushett estimated that forty-eight hours of calm weather would see the job completed.

August 26th was calm. All day the clams grappled with the thick slime in the wreck's holds. All day the pumps – three four-inchers and two eight-inchers – bellowed and belched under the guiding hand of Bob Cooper. By dusk the water in number one hold was under control and its level was slowly falling; by dusk five hundred tons of concentrate had gone into the sea.

That was the good news. The day brought bad news as well. That morning the salvage vessel *Traverse*, carrying additonal pumps, had put out from Sydney to join *Franklin*. At noon Brushett received a message from her master to the effect that a sou'easter had made up so fast and strong that *Traverse* had been forced to heave-to. Two hours later the news came that she had been driven back to port.

Brushett waited for that wind to reach St. Pierre.

He spent the night on deck while the pumps and derricks on *Fort Boise* worked at a desperate pace. An hour before dawn the fog began to thin and Brushett felt the first, warning touch of the easterly upon his cheek.

Nolan came up on *Franklin*'s bridge.

"Give us just six hours more," he begged, "and you can haul her off on the evening tide."

He knew full well what he was asking. *Franklin* now had only a skeleton crew aboard, for all but three or four of her people were needed on the *Fort Boise* if there was to be any hope of saving that vessel. This meant that Brushett did not have enough hands to take his tug into safe waters off shore, but would be forced to remain tied to the wreck, in the middle of a murderous shoal, while a rising sou'east wind beat the sea into a weapon of destruction. The temptation for Brushett to recall his crew and put to sea at once must have been nearly irresistible.

Franklin remained fast alongside the *Fort Boise*.

Brushett gave them their six hours, and several more for good measure. Then at 6 p.m. he took some of his crew back aboard, connected his tow wire to *Fort Boise*'s stern, cast off his lines, and began jockeying his way out of that deathtrap against a stiff sou'easter and a mounting sea that was baring the teeth of a hundred rocks not seen before.

Franklin sailed with only four men on deck and four below. Both Brushett on the tug and Nolan on the wreck were taking a calculated risk – the one that he might lose his men; the other that he might lose his life. Both knew that there was no chance of success unless Nolan and his gang remained upon the freighter to work the pumps and the winches attached to the ground tackle. It was a risk to which they had not wished to expose *Fort Boise*'s crew and, before he cast off, Brushett had tried to persuade *Boise*'s master to send his people on board *Franklin*. That suggestion had been met with a sharp rebuff, perhaps because of the unfounded suspicion that Brushett might be hoping to increase the salvage award by rescuing a ship abandoned by her crew.

High tide was due at 9 p.m. At 8 p.m. *Franklin* began to work up power, and Nolan's gang began to winch in on the ground tackle. *Fort Boise* was lifting and pounding heavily as the seas rolled in under her. From *Franklin*'s bridge Brushett could see her only as a formless bulk picked out with yellow lights and outlined by the faint phosphorescence of the breaking seas that dashed against her stern and broke upon the rocks to either side. Darkness was now almost total.

Marryat was listening intently for the voice of the radio operator on *Fort Boise* – waiting for the one phrase which would release him and all of *Franklin*'s people from the growing tension. But the phrase "She's moving" was never spoken. At 8:27 *Boise*'s operator began to shout into his radio telephone:

"Something's gone wrong . . . she's starting to break up . . . I can hear the plates begin to . . . "

At that instant the voice cut off and every light aboard *Fort Boise* went out.

"One minute I could see her outline plain enough – the next she seemed to vanish," Brushett remembered. "Marryat came running to the bridge to tell me all he knew–which wasn't much. We had no idea if she had bust in two and sunk, or what. We only knew the tow wire was still fast to something that wouldn't move."

The five minutes of waiting which followed seemed interminable. Although Brushett knew that disaster had struck in the darkness astern of him, he did not know what form it had taken and, until he knew, he could make no move to counter it. Clinging to the bridge rail he waited for some sign, and as he waited the fog swept in from the sounding sea and began to turn the darkness into an impenetrable shroud.

Through that as yet imperfect veil, a faint light flickered. Marryat and Brushett reached out their minds towards it.

"Aldis lamp," Marryat muttered. "Wait . . . "

Letter by letter he read the message from the wreck.

Fort Boise's number two bulkhead had suddenly fractured right across. The seas had rushed into her engine room and stokehold. She was holding together only by a thread of steel and might break apart at any instant. Her master was asking *Franklin* to go down to leeward (which was to say inshore, through the whole depth of the shoals) and stand by to pick up the lifeboats as they were blown through the white foam of the breakers.

Brushett sent a signal ordering *Fort Boise* to case off the towline. There was no answer to this message, and Brushett could not wait; he ordered the steel cable cut free aboard the *Franklin* and then, ringing for half speed, he prepared to do a thing that almost turned the St. Pierre pilot who was with him in the wheelhouse into an old man.

In darkness, in thickening fog, in half a gale of wind, and with a big sea breaking, he turned *Franklin* straight into the heart of the Great Shoal.

Cecil Bellfountain was first mate that trip. He stood by the fathometer, an awkward mechanical device on the after part of the boat-deck, and called out the soundings.

"I called them until we reached four fathoms. After that the machine was no good anyway, so I just stood there and watched him take her in. We had the searchlight on, but the fog muffled it pretty much. I think he must have taken her in by ear alone. I could see a sunker right alongsides us to starboard, then there'd be one to port, then one dead ahead – and all of them breaking white. Once she rubbed her side against one of them. He kept on nosing her in, it seemed like for an hour, and then all of a sudden there was a faint hail. The searchlight swung to port and I could see a boat trying to work out to us, but not making any headway. It was right in a patch of breaking water–*Franklin* sidled over and headed right in there too."

The boat contained Cooper and Nolan and the fourteen men of *Franklin*'s crew who had been aboard the wreck. They had stayed with *Fort Boise* for some thirty minutes after she had been abandoned by her own crew, who had put out in a big, powered lifeboat which stood a reasonable chance of being able to angle off across the wind and so get clear, not only of the shoals, but of the dangerous weather shore of St. Pierre itself. Nolan had lingered in an attempt to persuade *Fort Boise*'s captain, radio operator, chief officer and chief engineer to abandon their vessel. He had been unsuccessful, and to ensure the safety of his own gang he had finally been forced to leave.

When they came to lower Nolan's boat from the wreck, she dropped full on a head of rock and stove in her bottom so that she was floating on her buoyancy chambers alone. Up to their waists in water, the men struggled to fight free of the surrounding reefs. There were four oars in the boat but only three oarlocks. So three men rowed, while the rest paddled with their hands.

They did not try to follow the track of the powered lifeboat. That would have been suicidal, for had they escaped the reefs they must inevitably have been cast up upon the island's shore, where neither men nor boats could have survived the pounding surf. They had only one hope of living – and that was to get to windward and work their way out to sea.

It was a pitifully slim chance, for the almost submerged boat was as lifeless as a log and their trivial efforts with three oars, and with their hands, could accomplish little more than to prevent her from sweeping backward onto the nearby reefs.

Although they were all aware of the imminence of death, only one man cracked. He began to scream against the whining wind: "Turn round and run for shore! For the love of God, turn round and run for shore!" The unrelieved fear in his voice froze fourteen of his companions into the immobility which precedes panic. The fifteenth man was Nolan. He seized an oar and brandished it like a battle-axe.

"Shut up!" he roared. "Shut up or else I'll kill you now!"

It was at this instant that the fog-diffused beam of Franklin's searchlight touched the boat.

"Although we could see where Franklin was, we hadn't a chance of reaching her," Tom Nolan remembered. "The lifeboat was as hard to move as one of the rocks, and it was all we could do to hold her where she was. I was sure that we were done. I never figured even Brushett would bring his ship any deeper into that stuff.

"But that's just what he did. He nosed her in until her stem wasn't twenty feet off of us; then someone threw a heaving line and we caught hold of it and made it fast. At the same time Cap began to back the Franklin out.

"I don't know how far it was he pulled us backward, but it must have been close to a thousand yards. He'd come that far into the reefs to pick us up . . . Well now, there may be other skippers who would have done as much, and other ships that could have done it, but I never met the one nor the other yet, and I don't think I ever will."

Once clear of the reefs the boat was hauled alongside and her crew taken on board the tug. The last of them was hardly over the rail when Brushett spotted the faint flicker of a tiny light from the direction of the wreck. It was accompanied by the prolonged and hideous clangour of tearing steel – Fort Boise was breaking up.

Marryat had joined Brushett on the bridge and he spelled out fragments of a message. The four officers were abandoning the wreck on a life-raft, and they were asking for *Franklin*'s aid.

"Tell them to stay put," Brushett said urgently to Marryat. "Tell them to put a line on what's left of the ship and hang on in her lee until we can slack a boat down to them on a line. If they cast off from her, they're done."

Marryat tapped the message out on the big signal lamp – but there was no acknowledgement. Again and again he repeated it. There was no further sign of life from the dead ship.

The severing of communications put Brushett in a frightful quandary. He could not tell if his message had been received; but he knew that, if it had not, the four officers were as good as dead. For a moment he considered whether to try to thread the shoals once more; but there could only have been one answer to that. He now had the lives of twenty-six men to think about, and he could not gamble these on the faint possibility that he might be able to save the other four.

Reluctantly he gave the order to swing *Franklin*'s head out to sea, and then he laid a course down into Fortune Bay in pursuit of *Fort Boise*'s other boat. It was his intention to return at dawn and, if the life-raft was still attached to the wreckage, to slack a boat down to it on the end of a long line.

It was just after dawn when *Franklin* came into St. Pierre with the balance of *Fort Boise*'s crew, whom she had plucked from their drifting boat some twenty miles nor'west of the island. Brushett proposed to land them before returning to the wreck.

But there was no need to return to her. The officers aboard *Fort Boise* had either failed to receive Brushett's message, or had ignored it. The life-raft, smashed into flotsam, had already come ashore, and the St. Pierraise had recovered the broken bodies of its four passengers.

In late December of 1946 Foundation Maritime acquired a spanking-new ocean-going salvage tug. She was a giant of her kind – a 1,200-ton, 3,500-horsepower, twin diesel equipped with the last word in nautical technology. It was now inevitable that *Franklin* would have to go. The days of the tough, hard-driving little steam tugs were coming to an end the wide seas over. Unfortunately, this was also true of the kind of men who had made *Franklin* great. They were being supplanted by men of a new breed – able enough, but more and more technicians, and less and less seamen.

Captain Harry Brushett was one of the first to see which way the wind was blowing, and he was not prepared to make himself over according to a new pattern. Almost brusquely he turned his back upon the sea and upon all the long years he had lived thereon. In January of 1947 the Man from Burin went ashore and, as they used to say, swallowed the anchor for good and all.

VII

Come from Away

Canadians arriving on Newfoundland's shores are warmly welcomed but are only granted adoptive entry into the tribe. They remain stigmatized as people "come from away."

I was such a one when, in 1958, I bought myself a small fishing schooner at Muddy Hole, a tiny outport on the eastern coast of the island – a coast which, quite inexplicably, is known as the Southern Shore. During the succeeding winter my schooner was refitted (more or less) by Enos Coffin, her original builder. In the spring of 1959 I drove my jeep east from Ontario, ready to take command of my new vessel.

But things grew complicated, and there were many obstacles to be overcome before my publisher, Jack McClelland, and I were ready to set sail in Happy Adventure, as I had hopefully christened the little ship. Troubles we had; but the treatment we two "come from aways" received at the hands of the outport people more than compensated us for all our difficulties.

Ferryland

My presence at Muddy Hole and the problems I was having as I tried to make my vessel fit for sea soon became known in nearby Ferryland. One day my jeep took a fainting spell outside the white-painted picket fence enclosing a sprawling old house on Ferryland's outskirts.

I went up to the house to ask for help and was met at the door by a big, heavy-set man smiling broadly. Before I could open my mouth he forestalled me.

"Come you in, Skipper Mowat," he boomed. "Come you in and have a cup of tay and tell we your troubles."

Howard Morry was then in his eightieth year, though he looked no more than fifty. Tall and firmly joined, with a rubicund and unlined face, he was the epitome of a farmer-fisherman from Drake's time. A widower, he lived with his rangy and laconic son Bill and voluble daughter-in-law Pat. Bill and Pat ran a general store and a small salt fish drying plant. They had two charming children, a boy and a girl.

From that first encounter until I sailed away from the Southern Shore the Morry home was mine. Pat fed me fantastic meals, bullied the hell out of me and saw to it that I seldom went to bed sober. Bill made me part of the ancient fishing pattern of the harbour, sending me out with the trap boat crews; showing me the art of making salt-fish, and subjecting me to his own fierce, unyielding belief in the importance of continuity. Young Peter Morry, age ten, took me on long, secret walks into the "country" over trails made by the Masterless Men, and up to high places like the Gaze, a long hillcrest from which, for centuries, women watched for the returning ships, or men stood guard to cry the alarm when pirate sails hove over the horizon.

However, it was Howard Morry who truly took me into the heart and soul of Newfoundland and Newfoundlanders. Howard was one of those rare people whose feeling for the past amounted to an intense and loving intimacy. His Devonshire great-great-grandfather had been the first Morry to reach the Southern Shore, and all the tales that had come down the long ladder of the generations had finished up in Howard's head – and in his heart.

During his middle years he suffered a severe accident and had to lie a-bed for twenty months. He used this time to transcribe every memory of Ferryland he had ever heard into thirty school scribblers. When he was well again, and back at sea and at his trade, he negligently tossed this priceless treasure into a corner where some children found it and used the books to make a bonfire. When Howard told me about this incident, I was appalled. He only chucked. "'Twas of no account. I still have every word of it written in me head."

Howard not only knew the story of Ferryland during his own family's time but he knew it, and felt part of it, as far back as history can go. That was a long way back since Ferryland is one of the places in Newfoundland where the patina of human occupation is thick enough to really soften the bony face of the old Rock.

The broad and well-protected harbour lying at the foot of low, swelling hills, fringed by a wide foreshore of grassy meadows, welcomed some of the earliest European visitors to North America. Basque cod fishers sheltered in Ferryland harbour well before the end of the fifteenth century. During the first decades of the sixteenth century, Bretons and Normans had fishing stations along its beaches. It appears on a French chart of 1537 as *Farillon*. Yet the French must have come late upon the scene for this name was not of their bestowal. Even then it was a corruption of an earlier name.

The French held Farillon as a permanent settlement until it was seized from them by English pirates about 1600. In 1621 Lord Baltimore chose it as the site of a grandiose plantation scheme he had proposed for Newfoundland. However, the Lord was hag-ridden. His wife, Mary, could not stand Firiland, as it was then called, and two years later persuaded her master to shift south to what became the State of Maryland.

Over the succeeding centuries other overlords usurped nominal control of the place, and sweated the inhabitants. But its people, of mixed French, West Country English, Jersey and Irish stock, went on about their business with the sea, paying very little heed to those who rode upon their backs. Tough, stubborn, infinitely enduring, they survived the black years of the Fishing Admirals when English kings bowed to the demands of powerful fishing interests in the Motherland and decreed that no one could settle in the New Land; that it should be kept free of permanent inhabitants, to be used only as a seasonal fishing station by the crews of English ships.

The people of Ferryland held to their home. They held to it through an interminable series of raids by French, New Englanders, Portuguese and just plain buccaneers. They held on with the tenaciousness of barnacles. Several times Ferryland had to fight for its life against full-scale naval and military attacks. It survived. It and its people *have* survived through more than four centuries. Howard had innumerable tales to tell that illustrated the nature of the crucible that had formed his people. There was the story of the Masterless Men, for example.

During the eighteenth century the English fishing fleet was largely manned by men who had been driven to sea by starvation, or who had been tricked by "recruiters" into making the long, hard voyage across the seas. Having reached Newfoundland, many of these men refused to return home again. Treated like slaves by the local "planters," they reacted like Spartan slaves and fled from the little harbours into the desolate interior. Here they formed a society of their own, one that endured for a hundred years. They became veritable outlaws in the romantic tradition of Robin Hood, living the forest life and robbing the rich to succour not only themselves but also oppressed inhabitants of the coast.

The interior of the Avalon peninsula became the Country of the Masterless Men. Only the best-armed bands of King's men dared enter their domain. Secret trails ran everywhere, and the villages of the Masterless Men were hidden in a score of deep vales, one of which was within five miles of Ferryland under the loom of a massive hill known as the Butter Pot.

The Masterless Men were never conquered and never subdued; they gradually melded with the coastal settlers and their blood still runs in the veins of the people of the Southern Shore.

Howard Morry brought these men to life again, and others like them, as he took me on little trips along the coast to outports like Bear Cove, La Manche, Admiral's Cove, Cappahayden, Renews, Fermeuse, Aquaforte, Bauline and other places with equally strange names. Yet Ferryland remained at the heart of his love.

One afternoon he took me out to Bois Island which lies in the broad mouth of Ferryland harbour. Once it was well wooded, but that was in distant days. Now no trees grow on it and it is a place of fantasy.

Forgotten or ignored by official historians, familiar only to a handful of men like Howard, it was once a great fortress. Around its almost sheer perimeter is an earthwork circumvallation. At least five heavy gun batteries still lie emplaced at intervals, the muzzles of the guns showing black and stark through a guanoed growth of mosses. Powder magazines, the ruins of dwelling houses, and even an ancient well can still be traced. According to Howard, it was first fortified before 1600 by the French. By 1610 it had been taken by the English super-pirate Peter Easton and was gradually improved until it became an almost impregnable structure and the key to Ferryland's long survival.

In shoal water at the foot of a great crevice lay four corroding, twenty-pound, long guns of the seventeenth century, just as they had been left when an eighteenth-century privateer attempted to steal them from the temporarily abandoned fort. Nothing else appeared to have been disturbed since the fort last lived. Here were no guides, no gravel paths, no fanciful recontructions. Here was the true reality of the past, dimmed only and not obliterated by the flickering centuries.

With the passing of men like Howard Morry, most of the rich and vital human past of Newfoundland will have gone beyond recall. I count myself lucky I had a chance to taste that way of life – the way of the cod fisher. One morning at four o'clock Howard woke me from a down-filled bed, fed me a whopping breakfast, and took me through the darkness to the stage head where I was to join the four-man crew of a trap boat.

She was a big, broad-beamed skiff powered by a five-horsepower, "jump spark," single-cylinder engine. It was calm and cold as we puttered out of the harbour accompanied in darkness by the muted reverberations from a score of other "one-lungers" pushing unseen boats towards the open sea.

Our crew had two cod traps to examine. Essentially these traps are great boxes of netting as much as fifty feet on a side. They have a bottom but no top. Stretching out from a "door" on one side is a long, vertically hung leader-net to guide the slow-moving cod into the trap. The whole affair is moored to the sea floor with huge wrought-iron anchors which are the last surviving artifacts of ancient and forgotten ships.

Our first trap was set in nine fathoms off Bois Island and we reached it just at dawn. While the rest of us leaned over the side of the skiff, staring into the dark waters, our skipper tested the trap with a jigger—a six-inch leaden fish equipped with two great hooks, hung on the end of a heavy line. He lowered the jigger into the trap and hauled sharply back. On the first try he hooked a fine fat cod and pulled it, shimmering, aboard.

"Good enough!" he said. "Let's haul her, byes."

So haul we did. Closing the trap mouth and then manhandling the tremendous weight of twine and rope took the best efforts of the five of us and it was half an hour before the trap began to "bag," with its floats upon the surface. As we passed armloads of tar-reeking, icy twine across the gunwales, the bag grew smaller and the water within it began to roil. We had a good haul. The trap held twenty or thirty quintals (the ancient and traditional measure) of prime cod seething helplessly against the meshes.

One of our number, a young man just entering his twenties, was working alongside the skiff from a pitching dory. He was having a hard time holding his position because of a big swell running in from seaward. An unexpected heave on the twine threw him off balance and his right arm slipped between the dory and the skiff just as they rolled together. The crack of breaking bones was clearly audible. He sat back heavily on the thwart of his dory and held his arm up for inspection. It was streaming with blood. A wrist-watch, just purchased and much treasured, had been completely crushed and driven into the flesh.

The injured youth lost hold of the net, and his dory began driving away on the tide rip. Our skipper cried out to us to let go of the trap while he started the engine, but the young man in the drifting dory stopped us.

"Don't ye be so foolish!" he shouted. "I'se able to care for myself! Don't ye free them fish!"

Using his good arm, he swung an oar over the side and hooked an end of the header rope with it, then with one hand and his teeth he pulled himself and the dory back to the skiff. We took him on board but he would not let us leave the trap until every last cod had been dip-netted out of it and the skiff was loaded down almost to her gunwales. During all this time, perhaps twenty minutes, he sat on the engine hatch watching us and grinning, as the blood soaked the sleeve of his heavy sweater and ran down his oilskin trousers.

It was ten o'clock when we got back to the stage, and the sun was high and hot. Pat Morry met us with a truck and we took the lad away to the doctor who set the bones and took sixteen stitches to close the wound. I went along and as we left the doctor's little office the young man apologized to me. "Skipper, I hopes I never spiled yer marnin!"

No, he had not "spiled" my morning. And how was I to find words to tell him what kind of a man I knew him to be? He would have been dreadfully embarrassed if I had tried.

Whenever I stayed at the Morrys' overnight I would go to the stage head the following morning to welcome the trap boats home. Invariably I would be joined there by Uncle Jim Welch and Uncle John Hawkins. They were eighty-eight and ninety years old respectively. Both had been fishermen all their lives but, as Uncle John put it, "We'm just a mite too old for that game now, bye. No good fer it no more." They were still good enough to check each boat as it arrived, to make acid comments on the quality and quantity of the fish, and to keep the "young fellers" (men of forty and fifty) up to the mark. Uncle John first went to sea in a dory, jigging fish with his father, at the age of eight. He was a late starter. Uncle Jim had begun *his* fishing career at the age of six.

The stories Howard Morry had to tell were a blend of the comic and the tragic, for that is the blend of ordinary life. One evening we were talking about the priests along the coast (the Southern Shore is almost exclusively Roman Catholic) and Howard told me the tale of Billard and the goat.

Everybody on the Southern Shore grew potatoes, and Billard was particularly proud of his patch. Unfortunately, one of his neighbours kept goats, and goats like potatoes too. One morning Billard was harvesting his spuds, bent down, eyes on the peaty ground, when the priest happened by. The Father paused, leaned on the fence and asked:

"Are ye diggin' 'em, Billard?"

Billard glanced out under his bushy eyebrows, failed to see the priest and met, instead, the amber stare of a particularly outrageous billy goat peering through another section of the fence.

"Yiss, ye whore!" answered Billard fiercely. "And if 'twasn't fer you, there'd be a lot more of 'em!"

The same evening Howard told me a different kind of tale. A hundred and seventy years ago a middle-aged man appeared in Ferryland. He was a runaway from a fishing ship, an "Irish Youngster" – the name given to the men and boys of any age who, fleeing starvation in Ireland, indentured themselves to the English fishing fleet and the Newfoundland planters.

Ferryland people took him in and made him welcome but he was a "afeard." He was convinced he would be recaptured and returned to servitude. He took a young girl for wife and began fishing on his own, but fear never left him. One autumn he took his wife and two babies and rowed away down the coast to a hidden cove which no large ship and few boats would dare to enter. Here he built a tilt (a tiny wooden cabin) and began living an exile's life.

Once or twice each year he would row into Ferryland to trade his salt fish for essential goods. Then he would disappear again. Apart from these rare trips, he, his wife and his two young sons lived as if they were the only people in the world. They lived from the sea and off the land, catching fish, killing caribou and ducks for meat, and growing a few potatoes in a tiny patch scrabbled out of the moss at the foot of the sea cliffs that guarded them.

One February morning the man was stricken with paralysis. For two weeks his wife nursed him, but he grew worse. Finally she decided she must go for help. She left the boys, aged nine and ten, to care for their father and set out single-handed in a skiff to row the forty miles to Ferryland. It was wicked, winter weather and the pack ice was particularly bad that year.

She had made fifteen miles when a gale came up and the ice set against the shore, nipping the skiff and crushing it. The woman made her way on foot ("copying," they call it) across the floe ice to the land. She then climbed the ice-sheathed cliffs, swam or waded several small rivers, and eventually fought her way through the snow-laden forest to Ferryland.

It was some time before she recovered strength enough to tell her story; and it was seven long days before the storm, a roaring nor'easter, fell light enough to allow a party of fishermen to make their long way along the landward edge of the ice to the distant, hidden cove.

They were met by the two boys, shy to the point of utter silence at this intrusion of strange faces. The men went up to the little house and found it snug and warm and tidy, but the bed was empty. They asked the two boys where their father was; and the eldest, the ten-year-old, silently led them off to a lean-to shack some distance from the cabin. They opened the door and there they found the missing man.

He was strung up to the roof beam by his feet and he had been neatly skinned and drawn.

"You see how it was," Howard explained. "The boys had never looked at human death before. But they had seen a good many deer killed and had watched their father draw and skin them, and so, poor little lads, they thought that must be the right way to treat anything that died, be it man or beast. They did the best they could . . . "

Shopping on the Southern Shore

One fine day Jack McClelland and I drove to St. John's, New-foundland's capital, in search of some of the myriad bits and pieces which we still needed to make *Happy Adventure* seawor-thy. When we reached the city we parted, each with his own list, agreeing to meet at six o'clock at a waterfront bar. I arrived at the bar a little before time. Jack appeared a few minutes later, and I hardly recognized him. His blond, usually impeccable hair was a tangled mop. His eyes glared wildly. There was a spasmodic twitch to his left cheek muscles and his breath was coming and going in sharp, hard whistles.

It required three double rums before he was able to describe his day, and then he only told me the highlights. He told of entering shop after shop, most of them empty of customers but full of sales clerks, and of seeing every clerk immediately vanish as if Jack was the carrier of bubonic plague.

"That's because," I explained sympathetically, "in St. John's it's considered socially demeaning for a clerk to wait on a cus-tomer. It isn't done if it can possibly be avoided."

Jack nodded grimly. "That was the least of it. I finally cornered a clerk in a hardware store just as he was making a break for the cellar. I backed him up against a rack of pitchforks and asked him, politely mind you, for five pounds of two-inch nails. And, my God, Farley, you know what he said?" Jack's voice rose to an almost falsetto register. "He said if I would care to leave my order they would try to fill it and I could pick it up next week!"

"You were lucky," I replied soothingly. "Usually they just tell you they don't have what you want, or they may have it next year, or the year after that, or the . . . "

"But that's not all," Jack interrupted, the twitch in his cheek growing more pronounced. "After searching for two bloody hours I finally found a liquor store and there was actually someone at the counter, and I asked him for a case of rum. You know what he did? He made me fill in an application for a special permit and then he sent me to the head office of the Liquor Control Board to get the permit. It took me an hour to find the place and when I got there everyone was gone for lunch, even though it was half-past three. I waited until half-past four and finally some scruffy little character came along and told me the goddamn place only processed permits on Wednesdays!"

"That's it, Jack. You see, in St. John's all the store and office people need a lot of rest. It's because they work so hard. But there's another problem too. Newfoundland merchants have so much money they don't *want* any more. Haven't got any *use* for it. It's an encumbrance to them. You can see how they must feel when a fellow like you comes along and shoves a pile of money at them. Anyway, what *did* you manage to get?"

Jack ground his teeth, thrust his hand into his jacket pocket, fished out a piece of paper and flung it on the table.

It was a parking ticket.

As for me, I had enjoyed a reasonably successful day by St. John's shopping standards. Out of the eighty-odd items on my list I had been able to purchase six. They were in a bag at my feet. Six bottles of rum. I had found a bootlegger who was not yet rich, and so didn't mind demeaning himself by dealing with the public. There were not many businessmen like him in St. John's.

Because most of what we needed for the boat was not to be had in St. John's or could not be pried loose from the merchants there, we learned to do what outport Newfoundlanders have done for centuries – we improvised. Enos Coffin was a master at this. When we needed chain plates for our rigging he got some scrap iron out of an ancient steamship wreck and *cold*-hammered the rusty metal on a rock until he produced four very serviceable sets of plates. Smaller items of hardware he improvised from whatever might be found in the innumerable greasy boxes that cluttered every fisherman's store in Muddy Hole, and into which, over the generations, every piece of scrap that had ever come to hand had been carefully put by against the hour of future need.

Occasionally we had to go further afield. Enos had built a cavernous coffin over the deck of the schooner, which was intended as a cabin but lacked any means of letting in the light so that the interior was as dark as the inside of a molasses barrel. After a long search, I did find a ship-chandler in St. John's who grudgingly admitted he could supply port lights – at seventy-five dollars each – *if* I was prepared to wait six months until they could be ordered from England. Since I was not prepared, Obie, Enos' assistant, came to the rescue.

Obie had relatives far down the Southern Shore on the Cape Pine peninsula. Cape Pine is a bleak, forbidding thumb of rock jutting out into the steamer lanes. It is rimmed with reefs and walled against the sea by sheer granite cliffs. It boasts two tiny clusters of humanity that somehow cling to the rock walls. How the people make a living seems, at first glance, to be a mystery, for they have no harbours and it is seldom they can launch their open boats off the tiny beaches because of the tremendous seas that rack those coasts. But the people of St. Shotts and St. Shores (originally St. Jacques and St. Georges) do have gainful employment, although they don't talk much about it to strangers.

The fact is that the people of St. Shotts and St. Shores have been professional wreckers for generations past. During less constrained times they practised the wrecker's art as a full-time occupation. Numbers of ships fell on their coasts, sometimes owing to a lamentable failure on the part of their captains to realize that the light they were steering by was *not* Cape Race (twenty miles to the eastward) but an excellent imitation thereof.

"In death there is life," a priest upon that shore used to intone as he stood on the cliffs, directing his parishioners in the salvage of cargo from some ship which had foundered on the wicked inshore reefs.

Nowadays the glorious free enterprise practice of using false lights has been curtailed. Nevertheless, occasional vessels still make their own fatal errors and end up against the Cape Pine cliffs. Such vessels and their cargo belong, by law, to the underwriters who have insured them, but the people of St. Shotts and St. Shores do not subscribe to this particular law, nor, I suspect, to any others.

Obie and I drove there in my jeep and we would never have reached the place in a lesser vehicle for there was no road at all most of the way. Our arrival created a sensation. Not only did people peer at us from behind the curtains of every house, but so did the round black eyes of a number of swile guns – long-barrelled, smooth-bore guns intended for killing seals but adaptable to any number of other uses.

Obie got out first, was identified, and immediately we were surrounded by masses of hulking great fellows who spoke a language that baffled me completely, even though by then I had developed some skill in dealing with Newfoundland dialects.

However, when we broke out a bottle of rum we soon found we were speaking a universal tongue. We stayed the night at St. Shotts, with a brief excursion to St. Shores, and it was all a dream; a magical transportation back through time to a rougher and wilder age. At one point an old woman showed me a small mahogany case crammed with gold coins, some of them of early Spanish vintage. I was told that almost everybody in the two settlements had a similar cache hidden away as insurance against the day when modern navigation aids finally deprive these people of their traditional means of making an honest living.

When we headed home the next morning, the jeep was deeply laden. We had eight port lights, one of which was twenty inches in diameter and, with its bronze setting, must have weighed close to a hundred pounds. We also had enough bronze and brass deck and cabin fittings to meet all our needs.

There are those who speak of the St. Shotts people as pirates. Maybe they are. However, if it comes to a choice between the pirates of St. Shotts and the pirates of St. John's, I know *my* choice.

Most of the residents of the Southern Shore were equally helpful. They and their ancestors had lived for centuries at the mercy of the merchants so they knew exactly what we were up against.

Foremost amongst them was Monty Windsor, a soft-spoken, thoughtful man who lived in a rambling house on a peninsula in Aquaforte Harbour. The house had been both imposing and handsome when the Windsors built it two hundred years earlier but it was now grown grey and sad. Monty Windsor was almost the last of his name in Aquaforte. He showed me the family Bible in which were recorded the births and the deaths of all the generations of Windsors dating back to 1774. Few of the men had died in bed. Most had perished at sea, some as fishermen, some as sailors, some as whalers, some as privateers. It was a strange old book whose margins had been used for a variety of non-religious but equally significant purposes.

Inked in a flowery and faded script at the end of Deuteronomy was a recipe for the cure of "throttles" (diphtheria). It called for the patient to smoke a clay pipe loaded with oakum (teased-out strands of tarred hemp rope) which had first been soaked in brimstone. After smoking this mixture he or she was to swallow a pint of black rum drawn straight from the keg.

Modern medical scientists may scoff, but it seemed self-evident to me that any bacillus or virus that could survive such a treatment would indeed have to be a super-bug. Again, any human being who could withstand the treatment probably had little to fear from germs.

Through the generations the Windsors had run a whaling factory, a salt-fish plant, and a number of big fishing schooners, but now all that remained was a warren of collapsing buildings on the harbour side. These structures held many memories of other ages but they also held treasures for such as we. Here we unearthed a great, two-bladed brass propeller that must have been made half a century earlier but which fitted the shaft of our engine perfectly. We found scores of blocks intended for three-masted schooners and enough smaller blocks to complete our own running rigging. Shackles, belaying pins, mast hoops, sister hooks – in fact, most of what we still needed – were to be found in the dusty corners of the Windsor buildings.

There remained one requirement that had us stymied. We needed two good spars, and such were not to be found. Old masts abounded on the beaches and in the rotting hulls of abandoned schooners but they were either too big or too old. After four centuries of ship building, wood gathering and forest fires, there was hardly any standing timber left on the Southern Shore – with one exception.

Across the narrow harbour from Monty's house was a stand of almost virgin spruce. It was, in a way, a sacred grove. It had belonged to the family since the arrival of the first Windsor and had been jealously guarded by each succeeding generation as a source of spars, gaffs and booms for the schooners of the Windsor fleet. Although that fleet had vanished many years earlier, the grove remained sacrosanct. While those trees still stood, undefiled and proud, something of the Windsor heritage remained intact. This, in any case, was how Monty felt about the grove. However, when he heard we were having trouble finding spars, he sent a message down to Muddy Hole inviting us to visit him.

We came, Jack and I, and Obie and Enos, and when we reached Monty's house he led us down to a scarred old dory lying on the shore. It was the last vessel of any kind the Windsors still owned. There were two axes and some rope lying on the dory's bottom.

"You fellows paddle across to the grove yonder," Monty told us in his quiet voice. "Climb up the slope a-ways to where you sees a big white rock, and just astern of it you'll find a stand of spruce as straight and true as any on this island. Take what you needs. And make good and sure you gets the best there is."

We did as we were told. Standing on the steep slope, in the odorous shadows of the trees, Enos marked the victims and we cut them down, limbed them, hauled them to the water's edge, and towed them back to the harbour side. I went up to pay Monty for them but he would have none of my money.

"Don't ye be talkin', Skipper. There'll never be need of another one of us cuttin' a stick out of that grove. Likely there'll never be another Windsor go to sea. I'll take it fine to know your little schooner's well spar'd with Windsor wood. It's what they trees was growed to be."

Maiden Voyage

One small difficulty still remained. We had no charts of the east coast of Newfoundland. The lack of charts, combined with a misleading compass and the dead certainty of running into fog, suggested we would do well to ship a pilot until we could make a port where charts could be bought and the compass adjusted.

The obvious choice for a pilot was Enos. He had sailed these waters all his life, often without a compass and usually without charts. We needed somebody like that. However, when we broached the matter to Enos he showed no enthusiasm. For a man who was usually as garrulous as an entire pack of politicians, his response was spectacularly succinct.

"No!" he grunted, and for emphasis spat a gob of tobacco juice on our newly painted cabin top.

There was no swaying him either. Persuasion got us nowhere. He kept on saying "No" and spitting until the cabin top developed a slippery brown sheen over most of its surface and we were prepared to give up. I was, at any rate, but Jack was made of sterner stuff.

"If the old bastard won't come willingly," Jack proclaimed, "we'll shanghai him."

"The hell with him, Jack. Forget it. We'll manage on our own."

"Forget him nothing! If this goddamn boat sinks I'm at least going to have the satisfaction of seeing him sink with it!"

There was no arguing with Jack in a mood like that.

He arranged a small farewell party on board *Happy Adventure* that night. Six or seven of our fishermen friends squeezed into the cabin and began ruminating at lugubrious length on the manifold perils of the sea. When they got tired of that, they began recalling the small schooners that had sailed out of Southern Shore ports and never been heard of again. The list went on and on until Enos began to grow restive.

"Well, byes," he interjected, "them was mostly poor-built boats, not fitten to go to sea. Not proper for it, you might say. Now you takes a boat like this 'un. Proper built and found. *She* won't be making ary widows on the shore."

This was the opening Jack had been waiting for.

"You're so right, Enos. In a boat as good as this a fellow could sail to hell and back."

Enos eyed Jack with sudden suspicion. "Aye," he replied cautiously. "She be good fer it!"

"*You* certainly wouldn't be afraid to sail in her, now would you, Enos?"

The trap was sprung.

"Well, now, me darlin' man, I don't say as I wouldn't, but a'course . . . "

"Good enough!" Jack shouted. "Farley, hand me the log. Enos, we'll sign you on as sailing master for the maiden voyage of the finest ship you ever built."

Enos struggled mightily but to no avail. He was under the eyes of six of his peers and one of them, without realizing it, became our ally.

"Sign on, sign on, Enos, me son. We knows you'm not afeard!"

So Enos signed his mark.

We sailed an hour after dawn. It was a fine morning, clear and warm, with a good draft of wind out of the nor'west to help us on our way and to keep the fog off shore. *Happy Adventure* made a brave sight as she rolled down the harbour towards the waiting sea. With all sails set and drawing, she lay over a little and snored sweetly through the water, actually overtaking and passing two or three belated trap skiffs bound out to the fishing grounds. Their crews grinned cheerfully at us, which is as close to a farewell as a Newfoundland seaman will allow himself. There is bad luck in farewells.

All that morning we sailed south on a long reach keeping a good offing from the grim sea cliffs. We came abeam of Cape Ballard and left it behind, then the wind began to fall light and fickle, ghosting for a change. The change came and the wind picked up from sou'east, a dead muzzler right on our bows, bringing the fog in towards us.

Enos began to grow agitated. We were approaching Cape Race, the southeast "corner" of Newfoundland and one of the most feared places in the Western Ocean. Its peculiar menace lies in the tidal currents that sweep past it. They are totally unpredictable and can carry an unwary vessel, or one blinded by fog, miles off her true course and so to destruction on the brooding cliffs.

In our innocence, Jack and I were not much worried and when Enos insisted that we down sail and start the engine we were inclined to mock him. He did not like this and withdrew into taciturnity, made worse by the fact that I had closed off the rum rations while we were at sea. Finally, to please him, we started the bullgine, or rather Jack did, after a blasphemous half-hour's struggle.

The joys of the day were now all behind us. Sombre clouds began closing off the sky; the air grew chill, presaging the coming of the fog; and the thunderous blatting of the single-cylinder engine deafened us, while the slow strokes of the great piston shook the little boat as an otter shakes a trout.

By four o'clock we still had reasonably good visibility and were abeam of Cape Race—and there we stuck. The engine thundered and the water boiled under our counter but we got no farther on our way. Hour after hour the massive highlands behind the cape refused to slip astern. Jack and I began to comprehend something of the power of the currents. Although we were making five knots through the water, a lee bow tide was running at almost the same speed against us.

The fog was slow in coming but the wall of grey slid inexorably nearer. At six-thirty Jack went below to rustle up some food. An instant later his head appeared in the companionway. The air of casual insouciance, which was as much a part of his seagoing gear as his jaunty yachting cap, had vanished.

"Christ!" he cried, and it was perhaps partly a prayer. "This bloody boat is sinking!"

I jumped to join him and found that he was undeniably right. Water was already sluicing across the floorboards in the main cabin. Spread-eagling the engine for better purchase, Jack began working the handle of the pump as if his life depended on it. It dawned on me his life *did* depend on it; and so did mine.

The next thing I knew, Enos had shouldered me aside. Taking one horrified look at the private swimming pool inside *Happy Adventure*, he shrieked:

"Lard Jasus, byes, she's gone!"

It was hardly the remark we needed to restore our faith in him or in his boat. Still yelling, he went on to diagnose the trouble.

He told us the stuffing box had fallen off. This meant that the ocean was free to enter the boat through the large hole in the sternpost that housed the vessel's shaft. And since we could not reach it, there was nothing we could do about it.

Enos now retreated into a mental room of his own, a dark hole filled with fatalistic thoughts. However, by giving him a bottle of rum to cherish, I managed to persuade him to take the tiller (the little boat had meanwhile been going in circles) and steer a course for Trepassey Bay, the nearest possible shelter, fifteen miles to the eastward, where I hoped we might manage to beach the vessel before she sank.

There was never any question of abandoning her. Our dory, so called, was a little plywood box barely capable of carrying one man. Life preservers would have been useless because we were in the Labrador Current where the waters are so cold that a man cannot survive immersion in them for more than a few minutes.

By dint of furious pumping, Jack and I found we could almost hold the water level where it was, although we could not gain upon the inflow. And so we pumped. The engine thundered on. We pumped. The minutes stretched into hours and we pumped.

Occasionally one of us crawled on deck to breathe and to rest our agonized muscles for a moment. At eight o'clock I stuck my head out of the companionway and saw the massive headland of Mistaken Point a mile or so to leeward. I glanced at Enos. He was staring straight ahead, his eyes half shut and his mouth pursed into a dark pit of despair. He had taken out his dentures, a thing he always did in moments of stress. When I called out to tell him we were nearly holding the leak, he gave no sign of hearing but continued staring over the bow as if he beheld some bleak and terrible vision from which he could not take his attention for a moment. Not at all cheered, I ducked back into the engine room.

And then the main pump jammed.

It was dark by this time so Jack held a flashlight while I unbolted the pump's face plate. The thing contained ten small coil springs and all of them leapt for freedom the instant the plate came off. They ricocheted off the cabin sides like a swarm of manic bees and fell, to sink below the surface of the water in the bilges.

It does not seem possible, but we found them all. It took twenty-five or thirty minutes of groping with numbed arms under oily, icy water, but we found them all, re-installed them, put back the face plate and again began to pump.

Meanwhile, the water had gained four inches. It was now over the lower part of the flywheel and less than two inches below the top of the carburetor. The flywheel spun a Niagara of spray onto the red-hot exhaust pipe, turning the dark and roaring engine room into a sauna bath. We pumped.

At about eleven o'clock I saw a flashing light ahead and we steered for it. Slightly cheered, Enos confirmed that it might be the buoy marking the entrance to Trepassey harbour. However, before we reached it the fog overtook us and the darkness became total. I took the tiller and we felt our way past the light buoy and across the surrounding shoals with only luck and the Old Man of the Sea to guide us.

As we entered the black gut which we hoped was the harbour entrance, I did not need Jack's warning shout to tell me that our time had about run out. The bullgine had begun to cough and splutter. The water level had reached her carburetor and, tough as she was, she could not remain alive for long on a mixture of gasoline and salt sea water.

Within Trepassey harbour all was inky black. No lights could be seen on the invisible shore. I steered blindly ahead, knowing that sooner or later we must strike the land. Then the engine coughed, stopped, picked up again, coughed and stopped for good. Silently, in that black night, the little ship ghosted forward.

Jack came tumbling out on deck for there was no point in remaining below while the vessel foundered. He had – and I remember this with great clarity–a flashlight in his mouth and a bottle of rum in each hand.

At that moment *Happy Adventure*'s forefoot hit something soft. She jarred a little, made a strange sucking sound, and the motion went out of her.

Jack believes *Happy Adventure* has a special kind of homing instinct. He may be right. Certainly she is never happier than when she is lying snuggled up against a working fish plant. Perhaps she identifies fish plants with the natal womb, which is not so strange when one remembers she was built in a fish-plant yard and that she spent the many months of her refit as a semi-permanent fixture in the fish-plant slip at Muddy Hole.

In any event, when she limped into Trepassey she unerringly found her way straight to her spiritual home. Even before we began playing flashlights on our surroundings, we knew this was so. The old familiar stench rose all around us like a dank miasma.

Jack and I cautiously went exploring, leaving Enos to celebrate his survival with what remained of the rum. The fog was so thick that our lights were nearly useless and we practically bumped into the first human being we encountered. He was the night watchman for Industrial Seafood Packers, a huge concern beside whose dock we had come to rest in a bed of primaeval ooze.

He seemed genuinely incredulous to find we did not have a radar set. How, he asked, had we found our way into the harbour? How had we missed striking the several draggers anchored in the fairway? And how, in hell's own name (his words), had we found the plant and managed to come alongside the wharf without hitting the L-shaped end where the cod-oil factory stood in lonely grandeur?

Since we could not answer these questions we evaded them, leaving him with the suspicion, which spread rapidly around Trepassey, that we possessed occult power. Witches and warlocks had not yet vanished from the outport scene in Newfoundland.

The watchman was a generous man and he told us we could stay at the wharf as long as we wished. He felt, however, that we might be happier if we moored a hundred feet farther to seaward.

" 'Tis the poipe, you know; the poipe what carries off the gurry from the plant. Ye've grounded right under she."

Happy Adventure had come home with a vengeance and, for all I know, it may have *been* vengeance at that.

Interlude in Burin Inlet

Enos jumped ship in Trepassey and when Jack and I set out on our next leg, which was to have taken us to the offshore French islands of *St. Pierre et Miquelon*, we were very much on our own. All went well until we were off Cape St. Mary and crossing the great maw of Placentia Bay, then all began to go wrong. Our little radio, which up to then had resolutely refused to function, came to life just long enough to warn us that a hurricane was on its way and all small vessels should seek shelter. We had little choice but to continue across the bay hoping to reach Burin Inlet, but then the fog came back and we spent a fearful night groping through an impenetrable murk, trying to home on the distant moaning of foghorns on the far shore.

Because we did not know any better, we pushed blindly landward and eventually entered sheltered waters without having seen man or boat, or any more than the looming shadows of the cliffs around us. Here, in Stygian darkness, and unaware of where we were, we dropped anchor and fell, exhausted, into our bunks.

I woke, and the cabin was streaming with sunlight. *Happy Adventure* was tugging at her anchor and a slop was banging against her bows, giving her life and motion. The wind was wheening through her rigging and a halyard was snapping sharply against the mast.

I got sleepily out of my bunk, went aft and pumped for an hour; then, duty done, crawled up on deck.

It was a stupendous day, brilliant and vibrant. A full gale was snorting over the surrounding hills, whipping torn clouds across an azure sky, but down in the long gleaming arm of what I could now recognize as Burin Inlet there was no more than a stiff breeze. Of fog, there was never a trace. Of life and people, there was evidence in plenty.

We were anchored on the edge of a fleet of trap skiffs, swamps (small rowboats), sea-going dories and two small coastal schooners. One big skiff was swinging at her moorings only twenty yards astern of us. A quarter of a mile to the eastward lay a little village of brightly painted houses, neat flakes and stages, and a tidy wooden church. Sitting in the white sunlight on the end of a small dock were five or six children patiently fishing for sculpins. A frieze of gaily dressed men and women moved along the shore road between their houses and the church. *And there was no fish plant anywhere in sight.*

Jack joined me, red-eyed, dirty-faced and tousle-headed (I do not know how *I* looked since we had no mirror on board), and together we welcomed our first visitor. He was an elderly man wearing his Sunday best and slowly rowing a dory towards us. When he came alongside he turned his head to take in the whole of our little vessel.

"Marnin', Skipper," he said finally. "Come in through the fog?"

I admitted that we had.

"Well now," he said and spat neatly into the water. "Come in through the fog, eh? Been up the inlet many times afore?"

I said we had never been in Burin Inlet before. And then he gave us our accolade.

"Don't know as I ever seed a thicker nor a blacker fog. Don't know as I'd a cared to bring a vessel in through it meself."

We acknowledged this high compliment by inviting him to come aboard but he refused. Instead he invited us to come ashore, assuring us that his Woman would be proud to give us Sunday dinner. When we tried to decline on the grounds that we were filthy dirty and had no clean clothing, he would have none of it. Telling us he would return for us in an hour's time, he rowed away without a backward glance.

Such was the beginning of one of the warmest and most enjoyable human associations I can recall. The people of Burin Inlet do not have many peers in this cold world of ours.

Unhappily, Jack could not remain to enjoy their hospitality. There was a telephone in Burin Cove and, foolishly, he used it to call Toronto. Instantly a flood of pressing business problems was unleashed upon him. The following morning he climbed aboard an ancient taxi for the long run back to St. John's over the almost non-existent Burin peninsula highway. Much depressed and considerably unmanned by his departure, I wanted to go with him but he would have none of that.

"You damn well stay aboard," he told me in his naval tone of voice. "I'll talk Mike Donovan into coming down to join you. Poor fellow, he won't know any better. And then the two of you take the boat to St. Pierre. You can leave her there if you want to, but you have to take her to St. Pierre where I can rejoin her later on. You hear?"

I heard and reluctantly agreed. When I rowed back aboard after saying good-bye, I found he had left something behind. Hanging in the fo'castle, like a modern version of a baronial coat-of-mail, was Jack's steel and elastic corset. Whatever damage *Happy Adventure* had inflicted on his spirit, she had at least made him forget about his aching back.

The days that followed were unbelievably peaceful and pleasant. I acquired a following of boys, almost all of them with the surname Moulton, and these were, in the vernacular, "right smart lads." Whenever I undertook a task, whether it was painting decks, reaving new rigging, or repacking the shaft housing, they were on hand to help. It frequently turned out they knew more about the work than I did, and not infrequently they turned me into a loafer with nothing to do but watch while they did my work.

When I encountered problems which neither the boys nor I could handle, the men of the inlet came to the rescue. One of them made a three-hour trip in his dory to find a welder and a welding outfit to repair the broken exhaust pipe. Another noticed I had no hawse pipe and that the anchor chain was cutting a deep groove in the rail. This man, also a Moulton, excavated a hawse pipe from someone's store, brought it to the ship, and installed it with consummate workmanship – without even being asked.

On my second day in Burin Cove the gale grew worse and swung around on shore so that *Happy Adventure* was in danger of dragging her anchor. Whereupon two men rowed out, came shyly aboard and volunteered to help me take the vessel across the inlet to the better protection afforded by Spoon Cove. That evening, after we had moved her, a ten-year-old boy rowed right across the inlet through a heavy chop to bring me my laundry which his mother had, out of the kindness of her heart, done for me at Burin Cove.

When she left Muddy Hole, *Happy Adventure* was in a disgraceful state of dirt, incomplete painting and general dishabille. Her arduous voyage had not improved her appearance but after a few days in Spoon Cove she began to look more like a ship. She glistened with fresh paint. Her cabin, scrubbed and polished, looked clean and ceased to smell like an abandoned abattoir.

Even the bullgine was painted, after first submitting to the cunning ministrations of old Uncle John Moulton, who knew more about make-and-break engines than their designer ever did. Uncle John made her go; and he sweet-talked her so she would even go for me, and go when she was asked.

I grew fat in Spoon Cove. Every family seemed anxious that I should have at least one meal with them, and when I grew bloated and invented excuses to stay aboard at mealtime, it did me little good. A timid knock on the cabin trunk would announce the arrival of a teen-age girl bearing a napkin-covered dish of hot fish-and-brewis, fresh baked cod, stewed bake-apples (the Newfoundland name for cloudberries), or some other equally delectable "scoff."

In the evenings the men would come aboard and yarn. Two or three of them would sit in the little cabin and talk, slowly, with long pauses, about their lives and their futures. They had lived good lives. Successful fishermen, they had built substantial houses which their wives kept immaculate; houses fitted with running water, bathrooms and other modern conveniences. They owned large, elaborate fish stores with big net lofts over them;

good sturdy stages, and fine sea-going boats which they built themselves from timber cut during the long winter months back "in the country."

However, there was an undercurrent of bewilderment and apprehension in their voices. The policies of the new (post-confederation) Newfoundland government, directed towards an attempt to convert the sea-girt island to a mainland-type industrial economy, were spelling the decline of the fisheries which had sustained the islanders through five centuries. It was becoming increasingly difficult to make a living from the sea. Grown men still stuck to it; but for the youngsters, including the lads who had adopted me, there now seemed little future except emigration to the mainland of Canada.

One of the men remembered how, shortly after Joseph Smallwood came to power, he told the people of the island to burn their stages, haul out their boats and throw away their gear because "you will never have to go fishing again. There will be jobs ashore for every one of you!"

"Ten year gone by since then," the fisherman mused, his face dark and intent in the dim light of my oil lamp. "Ten year, and the jobs he promised was all made of air and sea foam. 'Twas a good thing us never heeded what he said, else us'd have been in the same boat with t'ousands of outport fellers that has to live upon the dole. We'uns in Burin Inlet kept our boats and our gear and still catches fish as good as ever us did. But they's no price for fish these days."

"Aye," added one of his companions. "The fish is still there in plenty, byes. If Joey had spent all the millions he wasted on rubber boot plants and candy factories helpin' we fellers build deep-sea vessels like the Norwegians has, us'd be well found today."

"Jobs!" said a third man bitterly. "The only jobs he's found for we is diggin' our own graves!"

It was disturbing to listen to these men and to see them being herded towards defeat and despair. Nevertheless, the outport life was not yet dead in Spoon Cove. During my days there I tasted what, to me, seemed an almost idyllic existence and I savoured every moment of it.

There was the day we barked *Happy Adventure*'s canvas.

Barking is the ancient process whereby nets are soaked in a boiling-hot mixture of sea water, cod-liver oil, tar and natural resin. Barking stops the nets from rotting when under water, and prevents mildew when they are stored ashore; it was used in the past on schooner sails as well. When properly done, barking dyes the canvas a rich red-brown, and a man can leave his sails untended through weeks of rain and fog and never have them come to harm.

A few days before I arrived at Spoon Cove the fishermen had gathered together for a communal barking of their nets, and the barking kettle, an immense iron cauldron holding well over a hundred gallons, was still full of a malodorous mixture called "cutch." I was invited to make use of it, and two fourteen-year-olds, Alan and Gerald Moulton, volunteered to organize the job for me.

The next dawn I was awakened by a peculiarly pungent smell wafting into the cabin. When I came on deck the landwash was obscured under a pall of black smoke. The boys were busy on shore. They had lit a great fire under the barking pot and were feeding it with masses of "condemned" tarred netting. A few hundred feet above them on the slope two red-faced and indignant ladies were screeching. This was laundry day and their lines of clothing were rapidly turning a sooty grey. The boys paid not the slightest heed, and the ladies took in their laundry and vanished indoors to await a more propitious hour.

While the cutch heated up, a platoon of boys scrambled over the vessel unbending her sails. These were then carried to a vast flake, used in other times for drying fish, where they were spread out under the hot summer sun.

Then the fun began. Six boys armed with buckets commuted back and forth between the great pot and the flake. Pails of scalding cutch were poured on the canvas and the liquid vigorously scrubbed in with birch brooms. Within an hour everything in sight had turned dark red. The boys looked like the reincarnation of a tribe of Beothuk Indians. The very sea itself along the landwash turned a rusty brown. I sat apart in idleness and watched with awe as the boys scampered about in clouds of steam, yelling like banshees and working like red devils.

It was a very hot day and by the time they had emptied the pot the boys were ready for a break. One of them rather shyly asked if I would like to join them for a swim. I liked – so they led me off up the slope behind the harbour to their favourite pond. It was a long hike through stunted spruce groves, over bare rock outcrops and up stony draws to the very crest of the highest hill. The pond was shallow and had been warmed by the sun to a comfortable temperature. We all stripped off and splashed about for a while until Alan and one of the other lads produced willow rods from a hiding place in the grass and started fishing. I thought this must be wishful thinking on their part for a less fishy place I have seldom seen. However, they immediately began hauling in good-sized speckled trout. "Mud trout" they called them. By whatever name, they tasted sweet enough when I sat down to a mess of them for my supper late that night.

I had almost decided I would be content to spend the rest of the summer, if not the rest of my life, in Spoon Cove when Mike Donovan arrived, brimming wih energy and with enthusiasm. The idyll was at an end. Once more I had to face the prospect of continuing my voyage upon the grey, implacable seas.

Bay d'Espoir

Mike and I set sail from Burin and somehow found our way to the off-lying island of St. Pierre. It was no easy voyage. *Happy Adventure* resisted every league of the way, and when she arrived in French waters she proceeded to develop an antipathy towards everything Gallic that was just short of virulent. There followed an horrendous winter during which she sank to the bottom of St. Pierre harbour in what appeared to be a deliberate attempt to commit suicide, rather than linger in a foreign port.

The following spring I refloated and refurbished her, having promised that, if she would behave, I would take her back to her native land. In July she was ready to sail. My wife, Claire, joined me, and together we put to sea heading for Hermitage Bay on Newfoundland's south coast.

Probably because I had forgotten to pour the customary libation overboard for the Old Man of the Sea, the weather turned against us and a sou'west storm forced us to run for the shelter of Pushthrough, a little outport at the western mouth of the maze of great fiords called Bay d'Espoir. For the next several days blinding fog, gales and pouring rain kept us glued to the Pushthrough wharf. There we entertained and were entertained by many local residents, one of whom explained how the place had got its name.

The settlement is divided into two parts by a narrow channel or tickle. One night long, long ago, a whale made the mistake of trying to take a short-cut through the tickle and got stranded. *He* was in trouble, but so were the human residents. They knew that if he died and decomposed where he was, there would be no living in the place for years to come. Either he or the people would have to go. After some futile attempts to tow him out backwards with rowboats (there were no engines in those days) the entire population waded out into the tickle–and pushed him through.

Pushthrough gave Claire her first real experience of housekeeping on a small boat. Because *Happy Adventure*'s decks were almost as porous as her hull, the interior of the cabin quickly became saturated, and stayed that way through the next seven days of almost constant rain. An astounding variety of moulds and other fungi began to flourish in the cabin. Claire's *sotto voce* comments as she scraped green fuzz off the bacon, the bread or the butter suggested that her private school education had been much more catholic in content than I had previously suspected.

On the day she found a thick layer of gelatinous blue mould inside her slippers *after* she had put them on her bare feet, she surpassed herself. I lay on my soggy bunk and chortled, until she rounded on me.

"Go ahead," she snarled. "Laugh your fool head off! And when you get done, take a look at yourself in the mirror."

Intrigued, I wiped the moisture off the mirror and peered into it. There was no doubt about it: my reddish beard had developed a distinctly greenish cast.

For fear of becoming fungi-food before our time, we fled from Pushthrough into the fog-and-storm-free inner fiords of Bay d'Espoir, seeking warmth and sunshine. We found both, and as we penetrated deeper into the mysterious recesses of the great bay, we became deeply enamoured of its many inlets, hidden harbours, rock-walled runs and majestic scenery.

It is called Bay d'Espoir – Bay of Hope – only on modern maps; to the people who live in and near it, it is Bay Despair. But its *original* name was Bay d'Esprit, given to it perhaps four hundred years ago by French fishermen-settlers. This is its true name, for it is a haunted place – haunted by memories of the past when each of its innumerable coves held a handful of families of French, Jersey, English or Micmac Indian origin; and haunted too by the pathetic shades of the Red Indians, the Beothuks, who were slaughtered to the last man, woman and child by white settlers.

At the time we cruised its dark waters it was almost devoid of human life. Pass-My-Can Island, Harbour le Gallais, Great Jervais, Roti Bay, Goblin, Barasway de Cerf, the Locker, Snooks Cove, Jack Damp Cove, Lampidoes Passage – all, all were empty; an omen of the politically ordained future intended to concentrate most of Newfoundland's remaining people into a few score "growth centres" far removed from the sea.

Only at Head of the Bay, forty miles inland from the ocean that once gave them their life and sustenance, were there any people. This was truly Bay Despair. Here in the depressed villages of Milltown, St. Alban's and Morristown were the descendants of the sea dwellers, lured inland decades ago by the recruiters of an international pulp and paper company which needed cheap labour in the woods. When the cream of the pulpwood had been cut, the company pulled out without a thought for the dislocated lives it was leaving behind. It is an old story, told too many times – and still being told.

Still, there are worse fates than having to spend a summer in the seductive labyrinth of Bay d'Espoir. As we became increasingly familiar with its intricacies we reaped special rewards. One of these was when we penetrated into Conne River and encountered the last remaining settlement of Indians in Newfoundland – three score people of a Micmac tribe which had been brought to the Rock hundreds of years earlier by the French. One couple, Michael John and his blind wife, adopted us. Michael, then nearing eighty but still as tough as basalt, told us ageless tales of his own people and of the vanished Red Indians—tales no white man had heard before, perhaps. He gave us a vivid but heart-breaking glimpse into an older and, it may be, a better world than ours.

We also met a certain robust pair of brothers from Hermitage Bay who were the only men still actively fishing in Bay d'Espoir. Whenever we ran across them they would come alongside and load us up with redfish, lobsters, salmon, cod and big sea trout.

Bay d'Espoir fed us surpassingly well. In Harbour le Gallais we stripped off at low tide and waded about collecting blue mussels, horse mussels, soft-shelled clams and dainty scallops. In other coves we borrowed lobster pots to catch a meal of crabs.

On one particularly memorable occasion we were moored in a glorious little harbour at Raymond Point. It was late at night, and Claire I were lying cosily in our bunks reading by lamplight. Albert, our big black Newfoundland water dog, had gone ashore and was sniffing and snoofing at the water's edge. Then we heard a mighty splash and, a few moments later, his claws clattering on the deck. He dropped something squishy in the cockpit, then went ashore and again we heard a splash.

Curious, I climbed the companion ladder with a flashlight and was in time to meet him coming back aboard with a two-foot-long squid squirming in his mouth.

Great schools of squid were running up the bay and Albert, being a fishing dog without prejudices, had decided to catch a mess of them. His procedure was to sit on the end of a nearby abandoned wharf and wait for the phosphorescent flash as a squid surfaced. Then he leapt—a full-bodied dive that carried him far under the surface. He did not get every squid he tried for, but before I went to bed he had caught seven of the strange, big-eyed beasts.

It seemed a shame to waste them so the next day Claire cooked a Bay of Spirits dinner. It consisted of grilled trout followed by roast squid stuffed with minced clams, accompanied by tiny, sweet, wild peas. For dessert there were deep bowls of wild raspberries. That there was a shortage of supermarkets in Bay d'Espoir was a matter of no concern to us.

Leaving Bay d'Espoir we set course to the westward. With no particular destination in mind we made our cautious way along the iron-bound Sou'west Coast, taking time to enter and explore many of the great fiords which crack the towering coastal cliffs. We found them mostly devoid of people; but broken skeletons of fish stores, stages and flakes, together with clusters of abandoned houses, testified to the efficacy of Premier Smallwood's centralization program. It had already swept this part of the coast nearly clean of human life.

The fiords were magnificent but after a few weeks we had had our fill of ghosts and so began to hasten our progress westward. Then, off the Ramea Islands, *Happy Adventure* again began to leak like the proverbial sieve, forcing us to run hurriedly for the nearest port. This proved to be Burgeo, and we spent the subsequent several weeks in harbour there – moored to the fish plant wharf – while we tried unsuccessfully to staunch the schooner's leaks. One morning we awoke to frost on the decks and to the realization that the sailing season for small vessels was at an end. Our little ship was fated to remain in Burgeo until the following spring. And so we thought we might as well stay too.

Burgeo, or at any rate the eastern part of it where we lay moored, was not a thing of beauty. A new fish plant dominated the scene. The roar of its diesel generators deafened us, and the stench was an abomination under God. Nevertheless, the people seemed relatively uncontaminated by the arrival in their midst of the industrial age, and they were friendly and helpful. When we mentioned that we were thinking of wintering, we found ourselves being whisked off to the western end of the attenuated settlement to a little, semi-isolated community called Messers Cove.

Even at first glance Messers seemed like everything an outport should be, and nothing it should not be. It consisted of fourteen families of inshore fishermen whose gaily painted houses lined the shores of a snug little harbour. Perched high on a great granite boulder was a small, half-completed, white wooden bungalow whose windows looked south over the islands and beyond to the endless sweep of open ocean.

The little house was empty.

We offered to rent it but the owner, a young fisherman, would only sell. The season was late, and there was nowhere else in the world we particularly wanted to be. We liked Messers Cove and its people, and so we bought the place.

Before spring returned, that house had ceased to be simply a transients' haven. It was well on its way to becoming home. As the years slipped by, we who had "come from away" began to feel that this was where we belonged.

VIII

Messers Cove

Homecoming

A torment of sooty cloud scudded out of the mountainous barrens of southeastern Newfoundland. Harried by a furious nor'easter, eddies of sand-sharp snow beat against Port aux Basques – an unlovely cluster of wooden buildings sprawled across a bed of cold rock and colder muskeg. Frost-smoke swirled up from the waters of the harbour to marry the cloud wrack and go streaming out across Cabot Strait towards the looming cliffs of Cape Breton and the mainland of North America.

January can deal harshly with Newfoundland. It had dealt harshly enough with me and my wife, Claire, and the hundred or so other passengers who had endured the crossing of the Cabot Strait to Port aux Basques aboard the slab-sided, floating barn of a car ferry, *William Carson*. The passage from North Sydney, in Nova Scotia, normally takes six hours. This time the storm had extended it to twelve and the *Carson*, savaged by that surging sweep of wind and water, had meanly revenged herself on passengers and cargo alike. A ten-ton bulldozer, lashed to the deck with half-inch cables, had been pitched right through the steel bulwarks into the green depths. Grey-faced and desolate, most of the passengers lay helplessly asprawl in cabins reeking with the stench of vomit.

When the *Carson* eventually wallowed into Port aux Basques harbour and managed to get her lines ashore, there was a grateful if unsteady exodus down her gangplank. Most of the debarking passengers clambered aboard the antiquated coaches of a narrow-gauge railway which dawdled its way for six hundred miles to St. John's, on the eastern coast. However, for a score of men, women and children (Claire and I among them) Port aux Basques was not the end of the ordeal by sea. Our destinations were the scattering of sea-girt fishing villages thinly spread along the hundreds of miles of bold, bald headlands and canyoned fiords of the Sou'west Coast.

There was only one way to reach these places – the weekly coastal steamer. She was waiting for us: small, dowdy, dirty; in sharp contrast to the sham grandeur of the *Carson*. But, unprepossessing as she looked, the SS *Burgeo* was wise in the ways of the unforgiving world of water. She was a proper seaboat, not a floating motel. Day in, day out for more than twenty years, she had shuttled east and west, furnishing the physical link with the outside world for some forty outports which clung between wind and water to that formidable coast.

By 1967 more than half the outports originally served by the *Burgeo* had been "closed out," as their uprooted inhabitants described it. These age-old settlements had become victims of the cult of Progress even as the *Burgeo* herself was soon enough to become such a victim. In 1969 she was condemned, although still as sound as ever, and sold for scrap–an unwanted anachronism from an age now past and rejected. Left lying at a wharf in St. John's, she was stripped by souvenir hunters, and the coldness of a dead ship spread through her. But she was not quite dead. One dark winter's night, just before the cutting torches could start eating into her good Scots iron, she committed herself to her own element. So quietly that not even the watchman knew what she was about, she settled to the bottom of the harbour, there to become a monumental embarrassment to the authorities and a remembered heroine to the many thousands of outport people who had known and loved her during the long years of her service.

However, in mid-January of 1967 the *Burgeo* was still very much alive. Her Master, Captain Ro Penney, welcomed us aboard as we scrambled up the gangplank through a burst of driven sleet.

A small, neat, precise man, Skipper Ro was shy of women. He flushed and ducked his head as Claire came up to him.

"Well, me dear, back again," he muttered, apparently addressing his own feet. "Nip in out of the wet now. 'Tis dirty weather . . . dirty weather . . . "

He turned more familiarly to me.

"Come you up onto the bridge, Skipper Mowat. We'd best get under way afore this nor'easter busts its guts!"

During the years Claire and I had known the Sou'west Coast we had made at least a dozen voyages with Skipper Ro. We had met him first in the gloomy fiords of Bay Despair on a day when I brought my leaky little schooner alongside the *Burgeo*, looking for help in repairing my ancient engine. Not only did I get the assistance of the Chief Engineer, but Captain Ro himself came aboard, having first asked formal permission to do so. He paid me a high compliment then by addressing me as "Skipper," and he never failed to use the title whenever we met thereafter.

I wish I could still do him equal honour but, like the *Burgeo*, Captain Ro is gone. During a hurricane in Cabot Strait in the spring of 1970, he took the 10,000-ton Newfoundland train ferry *Patrick Morris* out in response to a distress call from a herring seiner. The seiner foundered before the *Morris* could reach her, and while Skipper Ro was trying to recover the body of one of the drowned fishermen, a forty-foot sea stove in the ferry's stern loading door swamping her. As the big ship began to go down, Captain Ro ordered the crew to the boats but three of the engine room crowd could not be found. Ro Penney refused to leave without them. He was steadfast to the end.

Skipper Ro tugged at the whistle lanyard and the *Burgeo*'s throaty voice rang deep and melancholy over the spume-whipped Port aux Basques harbour. The lines came in and we backed out into the stream. Once clear of the fairway buoy, the little ship bent to the gale and headed east, holding close in against the looming, snow-hazed land to find what lee there was.

I went below to the old-fashioned dining saloon with its Victorian, leaded glass windows, worn linen tablecloths, and battered but gleaming silverware. Most of the passengers were gathered there, having a mug-up of tea and bread and butter, and yarning companionably, for on the Sou'west Coast everyone knows everyone else, or is at least known to everyone else. Claire was sitting between the owner/skipper of a small dragger and his dumpy, jovial wife. I joined them. The nor'easter screamed in the top-hamper and the old reciprocating steam engine thumped its steady, heavy heartbeat underfoot as we listened to the gossip of the coast.

Had we heard that the government was going to close out the settlement of Grey River? The dragger owner snorted into his cup of tea. "Ha! By the Lard Jasus, they fellers in St. John's is goin' to find they needs a full cargo o' dynamite to shift Grey River. Aye, and I don't say as even that'll shift they people!"

Fish landings had been down. "Entirely too starmy all the fall months. Shore fishermen can't hardly git out at all. Even us fellers onto the draggers, we has to spend the best part of our sea time battened down or runnin' for shelter."

But there were compensations. "Niver did see such a toime for caribou. I tell ye, me son, they's thicker'n flies on a fish flake, and coming right down to the landwash to pick away at the kelp. Oh, yiss bye, they's lots o' country meat on the go!"

He smacked his lips and winked at his wife who promptly took up the tale.

"They got the new school open to Ramea, me dears. Yiss, an Lucy Fenelly got a new baby, and her man away working on the mainland these past ten months! That young student preacher, he only stayed long enough to christen the child and then he fair flew off the coast. I don't say 'twas his fault entirely. Lucy's got thirteen youngsters now, and they's none of 'em looks no more like her man than I does meself."

Over the third cup of tea, the dragger skipper, as an act of politeness, asked where we had been.

"Europe," I told him, "and Russia. Moscow first, then right through Siberia as far as the Pacific and the Arctic Coast."

"Roosia, eh? Yiss . . . well now, you'll be some glad to be getting home to Burgeo . . . Me dear man, they's some glut of herring on the coast this winter. Nothin's been seen the like of it for fifty year . . . "

Burgeo, our destination and the place from which the little steamer took her name, was the largest remaining settlement on the coast and, through the preceding five years, had been our home. Now, after six months of kaleidoscopic travel, we were yearning for this homecoming with its surcease from the grinding irritations of technological civilization.

Burgeo lies ninety miles to the east of Port aux Basques on a shore of such formidable aspect that it remains little known except to the scattering of fishermen and seamen who are its human inhabitants. The Sou'west Coast faces a vast sweep of waters rolling all the way up from the South Atlantic. It is a rare day when this oceanic plain lies quiet. Throughout most of the year onshore gales drive their thundering seas against granite cliffs which rise inland to a high, barren plateau, the home of caribou, arctic hares and ptarmigan.

Lying offshore from the fiord-riven cliffs are clusters of low islands, many of them sea-swept. Seeded among these, like dragon's teeth, lie innumerable reefs and rocks which the coast dwellers call—with chilling simplicity—"sunkers." The number of ships they have wrecked is legion and even in these days of electronic navigational magic, they remain a thing of terror on black and storm-swept nights, or when the corpse blanket of fog smothers land and sea alike.

The Burgeo Islands were officially "discovered" by western man in 1520 when a Portuguese explorer, Joaz Alvarez Fagundez, visited the archipelago. He named them *"Ilhas Dos Onze Mill Vierges"* in tribute to St. Ursula of Cologne who, in the fourteenth century, with a naiveté which must be unique in human annals, led 11,000 virgins against the heathens in the Holy Land. Fagundez may have had a sardonic sense of humour for if those windswept, rocky islands, surrounded by foaming reefs, were not precisely virginal, they most assuredly were barren.

However, the seas around the islands were anything *but* barren. They teemed with life. Seals, whales, even walrus, lived in multitudes in the plankton-rich waters along the abrupt coasts and over the off-lying banks. As for fish! Salmon, cod, halibut, haddock, sole and a dozen other species were so abundant that men standing on shore could spear them by the boatload. Although a hellish place in bad weather, the Sou'west Coast had good harbours; and brave men who would take a harvest from the sea could do so here if they dared.

From Fagundez's time (and doubtless long before), Europeans had dared. By the beginning of the sixteenth century Basque whalers were on the coast, harpooning leviathans offshore, then hauling the giant corpses to the land where the blubber could be rendered into oil. Traces of their tryworks still remain. The French came not long after. They built summer codfishing stations and, over the years, runaways hid in the more remote coves and sea gulches. Here they lived a life almost as simple as that of the Mic Mac Indians from Nova Scotia who replaced Newfoundland's Beothuks. The French bred with the Mic Macs and when a trickle of runaways, fleeing the slave ship conditions of the English fishing fleets which came annually to eastern and northeastern Newfoundland, also began to drift along the coast, they were in turn absorbed by the earlier arrivals, and a new breed of men was born.

They were self-sufficient people, as they had need to be in order to survive at all. Dispersal in small groups was necessary because they possessed only small, open boats, in which they could not venture far from home; and too many fishermen working in one place meant crowded grounds. So they clung, limpet-like, to this rock-walled rim of ocean, a few families together wherever they could find a toe-hold for their cabins and shelter for their boats. By the late nineteenth century there were over eighty such clusters of humanity along the Sou'west Coast. Each consisted of from half a dozen to a score of square, two-storey frame houses hugging the foreshore of some stony little hole-in-the-wall where coveys of lean dories and fat-bellied trap skiffs floated like resting seabirds.

These sparse encrustations of human life clinging to the land-wash were separated one from the other by many miles of unquiet waters, yet they were united by the sea which was the people's livelihood . . . by the sea which was their highway . . . by the sea which was their mistress and their master . . . the giver, and the taker away.

Inland, the treeless granite hills rolled starkly naked, but in the river gorges stood stands of spruce and larch, and the outport people retreated to these protected places during the white months of winter, living in log "tilts" until spring sent them back to the calling sea once more.

It was a hard land, and a cold sea, and together they winnowed the human seed through generations of adversity until the survivors came to partake of the primal strength of rock and ocean.

Life is easier now, but they are still a race apart. As late as 1950 they knew little and cared less about the new breed of technological men which had come to dominate the planet. They continued to live in their own time and their own way; and their rhythm was the rhythm of the natural world.

When I first visited the Sou'west Coast, men and boys were still fishing in open, seventeen-foot dories in winter weather of such severity that their mittens often froze to the oars. Some had larger boats driven by antique single-cylinder engines, but even these were open to the sea and sky. Almost all the fishermen brought their cod home to their own spruce-pole stages, and split them in their own fish sheds or stores. Women and girls still spread the split and salted fish to dry on spidery wooden scaffolds known as flakes. Salt cod was still the main product of the coast, as it had been for better than three hundred years.

They were truly people out of time and, being a people to whom adversity was natural, they had retained a remarkable capacity for tolerance, together with generosity towards one another, and towards strangers in their midst which surpassed anything I had ever known before, except perhaps among the Eskimos.

Captain Penney laid his ship sweetly alongside Burgeo's snow-dusted government wharf. He waved good-bye from the wing of the bridge as we went down the gangplank towards a knot of people who had gathered, as generations before them had habitually gathered, to meet the coastal boat. An agile little man in his late thirties separated himself from the group and trotted up to us. His dark, sharp-featured face was lit by a smile of welcome.

"Got your wire you was comin' on the boat. Was a wonnerful glitter starm last week and the road's not fitten for nothin' only young 'uns on skates. So I brung me dory for to fetch you home. Where's your gear to? I'll get it for you."

Simeon Spencer, proprietor of a tiny general store which occupied the back kitchen of his house, was our closest neighbour at

Messers. With great solicitude he saw us aboard his motor dory, stowed our luggage and cast off.

It was a bitterly cold evening and, despite the wind-lop, a rubbery film of cat ice was forming over the runs between the islands leading past Firby Harbour, Ship Dock, Muddy Hole, and westward to our own cove. Spray froze on the backs of our coats as we hunched forward on the thwart facing the diminutive figure of Sim who stood erect and bird-like in the stern. Unexpectedly, he shoved the rudder hard down and the dory lay over so sharply that Claire and I slid sideways on the thwart. Sim was waving an arm seaward, and over the clatter of the engine I could just make out the word he shouted.

"Whales!"

He was pointing towards Longboat Rocks, a line of black reefs glistening with the salt seas breaking over them. Just beyond the Longboats was something else, also black and glistening, that surged slickly into view, then sank smoothly from sight leaving behind it a plume of fine mist which was quickly blown away by the nor'easter.

That blurred, elusive glimpse of one of the Great Ones of the oceans was a fine homecoming gift. I have always been fascinated by the mysterious lives of the non-human animals who share this world with us, but until I went to live on the Sou'west Coast the mystery of the whale had scarcely come my way, although it is perhaps the greatest mystery of all. *Burgeo* had given me the chance to approach that mystery when, each winter, a little group of Fin Whales took up seasonal residence for a few months in the waters of the archipelago.

Sim had headed the dory into Messers Cove. He cut the engine as we approached his stage.

"When did the whales get back?" I asked as the dory drifted towards the wharf.

"Like always. First part o' December . . . along of the herring scull. They's five . . . maybe six cruising midst the islands, and they's the biggest kind! . . . Here now, Missis, watch the ice!"

Together we helped Claire up the slippery front of the stage. All the lights in our house were burning. When we stamped across the storm porch and entered the kitchen we found the stoves all roaring. Sim's fourteen-year-old daughter, Dorothy, had swept and polished every inch of every room. Old Mrs. Harvey had sent over two loaves of home-made bread, still oven-hot. And bubbling fragrantly in a pot on the range was a boiled dinner: cabbage, turnips, potatoes, onions, salt beef and moose meat.

The little house which had stood empty for months was as warm and welcoming as if we had never left it. Our delight was also Sim's delight as he sat unobtrusively nursing a glass of rum in front of the Franklin stove. However, his self-imposed duty was not yet completed. It was now his task to bring us up-to-date on the really vital events which had taken place during our absence.

"They was talk of a strike down to the plant, but the owner, he put an end to that right quick. Said he'd close her up and move clear of Burgeo and leff the people lump it if they didn't care to work to his wish. Don't know where he figgered on going, but they's plenty folk here could name a place proper for the likes of he! . . . Curt Bungay, he's bought a new boat, a long-liner from down Parsons Harbour way . . . Your schooner's hauled up clear, and Joe, he found her leak . . . one of 'em anyhow . . . They's a new nurse to the cottage hospital; chinee they *says* she is, but she's good for it. Comes out the dirtiest sort of weather to take care of folks . . . Good run o' fish this winter, but nothin' fit to call a price . . . "

And so it went, in rapid-fire bursts, until, a decent time having been allowed for us to have our dinner and settle in a bit, other visitors began clumping over the porch and unceremoniously letting themselves into the kitchen. A bevy of teen-age girls led the way. They sat in a tidy row on the kitchen daybed and said nothing; only beamed, giggled and nodded as we tried to make conversation with them. Then, with familiar uproar, Albert came gallumphing into the kitchen bearing a dried codfish in his mouth as a homecoming present. Close behind him came his, and our, friend, eighty-year-old Uncle Job; gnome-like, ebullient, and grinning thirstily as he spotted the rum bottle on the kitchen table. During our absence Albert had lived with Uncle Job and his wife, and according to Sim, dog and man had spent most of their time engaged in acrimonious debate as to whether they would, or would not, go fishing, go for a walk, go for a swim, go to bed, or get up in the morning. They were both inveterate argufiers.

"He'll miss that dog some bad," Sim said. "Wuss'n he'd miss his woman. *She* never says a word, and it drives he fair wild when he can't get an argument."

Rather reluctantly Albert delivered over the cod – a fine one it was too, for Uncle Job was one of the few men who still practised the age-old art of drying and salting fish. Albert sniffed in a perfunctory way at our luggage with its stickers from Irkutsk, Omsk, Tbilisi and other exotic places, then barged into the living room, climbed up on the sofa, grunted once or twice, and went to sleep.

The homecoming was complete.

Burgeo

The storm blew itself out that night and in the morning the sun shone white and harsh upon the ice-capped offer islands. The sea had an ebony sheen to match the glitter left on the land by the recent sleet storm. Taking advantage of what would surely be an all-too-brief spell of fine weather, the inshore fishermen – those who fished the local grounds with gill nets, trawls and handlines – were early at work, their small boats no more than distant motes on the metallic mirror of the sea.

Leaving Claire to get on with the unpacking under the solemn eyes of the neighbourhood children who drifted in and out of the kitchen like voiceless wraiths, I took Albert and set out to collect the mail. Since the trail (it could only be called a road out of courtesy) leading to the eastern end of Burgeo was still impassable because of its skin of ice, I borrowed Sim's dory and took the water route instead.

It was marvellously exhilarating to be on the sea. The day was calm and the sky blindingly clear and bright. As usual, Albert rode standing up in the bows, leaning far forward so that he looked like a pagan totem. When occasional dovekies and sea pigeons rose heavily ahead of us and skittered off to the sides, he eyed them with disdain.

We puttered along close under the land – near enough to sniff the iodine tang of kelp exposed at ebb tide; close enough to recognize and be recognized by people in the shoreside houses. Sim Spencer's wife, busy hanging out the wash, gave us a welcoming wave. Josh Harvey's calico dog, Jumbo, barked insults at Albert from a stage head, and Albert richly returned them. I shouted a greeting at Uncle Matt Fudge, ninety-one years old, but still young enough to be mending a cod net in the sunny shelter of his grandson's fish store.

From Messers as far as Frank Island the shore we were coasting was encrusted by a fringe of sturdy houses which had been occupied for generations. They were the "old" Burgeo and they were a joy to behold. They looked married to the rock on which they stood, a neat but unobtrusive frieze along the shore. Yet each home stood in quiet singularity. No two faced in the same direction. No two were on the same level, nor were they of quite the same construction, even though most were of the venerable two-storey, low-peaked pattern native to Newfoundland outports. They gave the impression of a kind of unpretentious and non-aggressive independence. However, when the dory slipped through the tickle north of Frank Island, the scene changed abruptly. This was where the New Burgeo, creation of modern times, began.

In 1949, when Newfoundland reluctantly became a part of Canada, Burgeo was not a single community but a patchwork of dispersed little settlements. Along the shoreline of Grandy Island – which dominates the archipelago as an anchored battleship dominates a fleet of lesser craft–lay the hamlets of Messers Cove, Muddy Hole, Firby Cove, Samways, The Harbour and The Reach. Clinging to the off-lying, smaller islands, or strung along the adjacent mainland shores, lay Seal Brook, Kings Harbour, Our Harbour, Hunts Island, Sandbanks and Upper Burgeo. None of these held more than a dozen families, and each had preserved its own identity.

Confederation with Canada put an end to all that. In 1948 Newfoundland was still nominally a self-governing Dominion in the British Empire; but in 1949, goaded and harried by a messianic (some called him satanic) little man named Joseph Smallwood, Newfoundland was stampeded into joining Canada. Smallwood won the decisive vote by the slimmest of margins as islanders of all classes fought desperately for the retention of their independence, impoverished as it was. For these dissenters, independence was of greater worth than flash prosperity. Smallwood, on the other hand, regarded independence as an insufferable barrier to progress. Most Newfoundlanders, he once contemptuously said, did not know what was good for them and so would have to be hauled, kicking and screaming, into the twentieth century. He was just the man to do the hauling.

He became the island's first provincial Premier and during the next twenty-two years ran Newfoundland almost single-handed according to his personal prescription of what was good for it: industrialize at all costs. This meant that the island's mineral, forest and human resources were to be made available, virtually as gifts, to any foreign entrepreneurs who would agree to exploit them. Smallwood demanded that Newfoundland turn its back on the ocean which had nurtured the islanders through so many centuries.

One of the first hurdles he had to overcome was to find means of concentrating the "labour resources" (by which term he meant the people of the outports) who were dispersed in about thirteen hundred little communities scattered along some five thousand miles of coastline. Smallwood's solution was "centralization" which, translated, meant the forced and calculated merger of the outports so that labour pools could be formed from the transported occupants. The methods used to destroy the small communities were devious, usually deceitful, sometimes brutal . . . but almost always effective.

Along the Sou'west Coast the "moving fever," implanted and cultured by the Smallwood men, soon began to take effect. One by one the outports sickened and died. Even in the Burgeo archipelago, where everyone already lived within a four-mile radius of everyone else, the fever raged with such fury that in a few years all the off-lying communities had moved to Grandy Island.

Although Smallwood scorned fishing as a way of life, his was not an absolute rejection. Even in his most sanguine dreams, he appears to have realized that there were parts of Newfoundland which could not be turned into facsimiles of Detroit or Hamilton.

The Sou'west Coast was such an area. Smallwood's answer to how best to exploit its labour potential was to heavily subsidize construction of a fish-freezing plant on Short Reach, at the east end of Grandy Island. This plant was then "sold" for a ridiculously small sum to the son of a St. John's merchant prince, who found himself in the happy position of being able to pay what he chose for labour while setting his own price for fish.

There were some initial difficulties. Not many men could be persuaded to abandon their way of life in order to become wage employees at as little as ten or twenty dollars a week. However, as the people of the neighbouring outports began to converge on the "growth centre," a surplus labour force developed. It consisted of people who had always hated the very thought of welfare – the dole, they called it – and were willing to work at almost anything, for almost any wage, rather than accept relief.

The heaviest concentration of immigrants settled close to the fish plant. When all the available shoreline had been occupied, newcomers were forced to build away from the sea on barren rocky ridges or on peaty muskegs. They built hurriedly and, contrary to their wont, many built badly. They had insufficient money with which to buy materials but, since they were now wage slaves, they had no time to do as their fathers had done and go into the country to cut and whip-saw their own lumber. All too many of those who had been forced or deluded into abandoning comfortable and well-built houses in the now-deserted outports were reduced to living in unsightly shacks. These proliferated until they produced the first true fruits of centralization . . . the Sou'west Coast's first slum.

The eastern end of Grandy Island turned into a wasteland of rusting cans, broken bottles, spilled garbage and human sewage. The surrounding waters were further defiled by the vast volume of effluvia from the fish plant which discharged all its wastes and offal directly into Short Reach. Much of the shoreline was befouled by a belt of black sticky muck several inches thick and six to ten feet broad which, particularly at low tide, stank to high heaven.

Apart from the physical degradation of what had once been a wholesome and natural environment, centralization also degraded the people. The delicate interdependence of give and take was disrupted. As Sim Spencer explained it to me:

"Afore the plant come here, every little place was on its own. Every settlement was like a family; and all the families, all along the coast, they got along good, never rubbed nobody the wrong way. Every man looked after his own, but he looked to his neighbour when times was hard, and for certain sure he'd be quick enough to give a hand when anyone else was needy.

"Now that's all gone abroad. Shovin' all hands into one boat done something to the people. Started fillin' them up with badness. Turned them one agin the other. Started them wheening and growling like a pack of crackie dogs.

"These times, seems everyone's jealous of t'other, and 'twas never that way before. People is uncontented. They don't want nobody to get nothin' unless they gits it too, *and* more of it. Truth to tell, people is turning right hateful in Burgeo these times."

The independent people, and the egalitarian way of life, could not survive the tides of change as more and more people came to Burgeo from more and more "closed-out" outports. There was not nearly enough wage work to go around. The new men could not fish successfully both because the local grounds were foreign to them and because these were by now seriously overcrowded and overfished as well. Consequently, scores of men, both young and old, were forced to leave their families behind and seek work, not only outside Burgeo, but outside Newfoundland where the grandiose industrial schemes of Premier Smallwood had come to nothing. Some men worked seasonally in Nova Scotia; others spent eight months of each year manning Great Lakes freighters –eight months away from home.

As if this was not enough, compulsive consumerism, the universal sickness of modern society, began to infect the dislocated outport people. Men, women and children who had never cared much for material possessions became increasingly acquisitive. They began to thumb avidly through the shiny mail-order catalogues that had arrived in Newfoundland with confederation. The solid, hand-made furniture they had brought with them from the outports was now "condemned" – thrown over the ends of the stages to float away on the tides. It was replaced with chrome and arborite.

The plant owner opened a supermarket and appliance store, and some of the befuddled victims of the new disease actually bought television sets, even though there was no transmitter which could reach them.

Diesel-generated electricity and roads spread their webs through the increasingly congested maze of houses. Two miles of incredibly rough trails were hewn from the living rock and, in 1962, the first two cars were unloaded from the coastal boat. A few days later they collided head-on and both were reduced to junk.

During the years Claire and I lived in Burgeo, Progress made stunning strides. By 1967 there were thirty-nine cars and trucks rattling themselves to pieces on the stony goat tracks. The first snowmobile had gone snarling out into the barrens, where it fell into a crevice; but the following year saw five more arrive. Non-returnable pop and beer bottles appeared. On sunny summer days the rocks which made up most of the physical surroundings gleamed and glittered in fairy colours from the layers of glass shards which littered them. In 1961 there had been no welfare officer and no unemployment. By 1967 Burgeo had both, as well as a fish meal reduction plant to spread its oily, nauseous fumes like a miasma over the entire community.

It had also acquired a town council, and a fine new school built to mainland standards and staffed with teachers "from away" who were skilled at rejecting the past, and arousing in their students a lust for the golden dreams of the industrial millennium.

The people of the Sou'west Coast, and of Burgeo in particular, had been "hauled into the twentieth century" so speedily that few of them understood what was happening to them. The age-old patterns of their lives were rapidly collapsing. The inner certainties which had sustained them in past generations were evaporating like water spilled on a red-hot stove.

But not all Burgeo people failed to grasp the significance of what was taking place.

Uncle Bert lived with his "Woman," as he always referred to his wife, in a tiny but impeccably neat house a stone's throw from us at Messers. In the evenings Uncle Bert would sit at his oilcloth-covered kitchen table listening disdainfully to a squalling transistor radio as it yammered out the daily tale of hate and horror, of suffering and disaster, which it offered as the news of the world.

When the tale was told, Uncle Bert would switch off the radio, pour himself half a glass of alcohol (smuggled in from St. Pierre), top it up with boiling water, add a spoonful of sugar, and toss the mixture down in a couple of gulps. Then, bald head shining with sweat, big, twisted hands gesticulating in the light of the oil lamp, he would bellow out his derision.

"By the Lard livin' Jasus, dem mainland fellers is gone altogether foolish! Foolish as a cut cat, me son! And de great joke onto it . . . dey don't *know* it! Dey got to tinker wit' *every* goddamn t'ing dere is . . . and everyt'ing dey tinkers wit' goes wrong! And dat, me darlin' man, *dat's* what dey calls *pro*-gress!

"Dey says dey's makin' a heaven on dis eart' for we. But de troot onto it is, dey's headin' dereselves and all of we for hell, in a hoopin' hurry-all. Smart? Oh yiss, dey do believe dey's de smartest t'ings God put on dis old eart' . . . dem politicians and dem scientists, and all dem fine, big-moneyed fellows. But I'm tellin' ye, byes, de codfish and de caribou, dey's ten t'ousan' times smarter in de head. *Dey* got de sense to lave well enough be. *Dey'll* niver blow up de world; no, nor pizzen it to deat' . . . Bejasus, byes, I t'ink de healt's gone right out of we!"

It was not gone out of Uncle Bert. At seventy-six he still went fishing single-handed in his dory, winter or summer, whenever the fish "were on the go," even though he and his Woman between them had an ample income from their old-age pensions.

"I goes because I got to fish! 'Tis what I wants to do. 'Tis out dere, on de sea, dat's where I wants to be. Dat's where I knows *what* I is, and *who* I is . . . a damn good man, and I ain't feared to tell it!"

He minced no words in describing what he thought about the new way of life in Burgeo. "Dem poor bloody bastards as works to de plant! Workin' for wages and t'inking deyselves some lucky!

I'll tell ye what dey is, me son . . . dey's slaves. No better dan slaves! And de wors kind of slaves, 'cause dey's *grateful* for a chance to work for de owner in dat stinkin' shithole down to t'Reach for de rest of dere lives, so's dey can buy some goddamn t'ing is no more use to dey dan legs is to a fish! Cars, bye, and tely-veesion. Sewry poipes and houtboard ingines! Dem fellers don't know who dey is no more . . . dey only knows what dey *wants*! And what dey wants is enough to bloat a hog until he busts. Dey's comin' out no different from all de people up along in Canada and America. Dey wants it *all*! And if dey gets de chance, dey's goin' to *take* it all. And den, by de Lard living Jasus, dey's goin' to choke dereselves to deat' on dere own vomit!

"Sometimes I tinks de lot of 'em should be in de Mental. [The St. John's Mental Home, an obsolete institution for the deranged.] Whatever dat plant owner fellow tells 'em, dey eats down as slick as cold boiled pork. But he don't give a bloody damn for dey. One marnin' dey'll wake up wit' nothin' left 'cept a razor for to cut dere t'roats."

In the late summer of 1971 the workers at the fish plant struck for union recognition. This was refused. When they persisted, the plant owner simply closed down the plant and departed, lock, stock and barrel.

Preferring not to face the stench of Firby Cove, I landed at the slightly less malodorous Ship Dock and, leaving Albert to look for rats among the accumulation of garbage on the shore, made my way through a crowded and slovenly collection of shacks and shanties to the brand-new post office which had become a prime symbol of Burgeo's new goals. It was box-square and ultra-modern, built of brick and glass and chrome—the only such building on the entire Sou'west Coast. It had been built during my absence, replacing a cosy, crowded room in one of the old wooden houses where the mail had been sorted and distributed for thirty years by Uncle Ted Banfield.

I was going to miss Uncle Ted, who had been forcibly retired when the new post office opened. He knew more about the Sou'west Coast than any man alive and he was free with his knowledge. On cold winter days he was free with his hospitality too. The long walk from Messers against a winter gale was something to chill the blood of an Eskimo, but it was Ted's kindly habit to take you into his kitchen and pour you a warming four-finger glass of rum before delivering up your mail. Banfield's old house had been a place in which to linger, to chat with friends, to hear the local news.

The new post office, ultra-sterile under the glare of fluorescent lights (NO DOGS ALLOWED . . . WIPE YOUR FEET BEFORE ENTERING), was a place to go into and get out of again with the utmost speed. I hardly recognized the pallid and harassed-looking young man who thrust my mail at me without uttering a single word. He was Uncle Ted Banfield's son.

Back in the dory I set a return course for home which would take us out and around Eclipse Island and through the deep channel known as Steamer Run. I was hoping to get a glimpse of the whales, but on this fine day they must have gone to sea with the other fishermen, for I saw no sign of them.

Apart from occasional visits to the post office, Claire and I saw little of the eastern end of Burgeo. Messers was our home and we had come to feel *very* much at home there. We had received tolerance and friendship from the families whose trim and cared-for houses stood, well-spaced, around the rocky rim of the clean little cove. They were people who had lived all of their lives in this place, as their forbears had done before them. They had not yet been much affected by the changes which were so rapidly transforming the rest of Burgeo.

During the first week after our return we were visited by most of our neighbours. The first to come was Onie Stickland, a sad-faced bachelor of middle age, and one of the few dory-men on the coast still fishing single-handed. Onie brought us a bucket of fresh herring. The herring schools were beginning to run heavily inshore, he told us, and he would be glad to bring us some every day. That about exhausted the conversation since Onie was a listener, not a talker. Shy, gentle, almost pathetic in his eagerness not to be an imposition, he was content to sit silently for hours in our house covertly glancing now and again at Claire with an expression of distant adoration.

Simeon Ballard was a frequent visitor. Heavy-set, bluff-browed and a seaman through and through, he was as loquacious as Onie was reticent. Simeon had been a mariner, sailing to the Caribbean in three-masted schooners laden with salt cod, returning with cargoes of salt, molasses and rum. In sail, or in steam, he had visited the great ports in South America, the Mediterranean and the Baltic. Between voyages he had not been idle, for he had sired nineteen children, seventeen of whom were still alive. Although still in his prime at the time of confederation, he had hardly gone to sea since then.

He was an extremely courteous man who made a point of calling me "Skipper" because I owned what may well have been the last schooner in Newfoundland still under sail.

"Them days," he meant before 1949, "they was always eight or ten big schooners belonged to Burgeo. Spring and fall we fished the banks, and summer-times we voyaged foreign. 'Twas a hard life, I suppose, but never seemed that way to we. They was a dozen skipper-men in Burgeo and no place on the seas they couldn't take a vessel. Aye, and bring her home again!

"After confederation that all went under. Seems they fellows in Canada had no use for sailor men. The schooners was laid up to rot and the steamers was mostly sold away. Some of we went at the deep-sea fishing game, but that began failing too, and so the most of us had to come ashore. 'Twas hard for a man my age –forty I was then–with my master's ticket and all, and still good for it, but no work to be had.

"Aye, 'twas hard enough. But they tells we 'tis all for the best. They tells we a man has a better life working in a factory. Maybe 'tis so, but I thanks my God for the life I had at sea."

One evening well after dark, when not too many people would notice his coming, we had a visit from Uncle Samuel. He was a whipcord little man whose walnut wizened face betokened his Indian blood. He was not much of a fisherman and, indeed, did not like the sea; but he was a famous "countryman"–infamous if you listened to the Royal Canadian Mounted Police constable who was Burgeo's arm of the law.

Uncle Samuel was a hunter and trapper. His world was the bleak, wind-eroded barrens which stretched north from the coast for a hundred miles. On this visit he brought us a huge, dripping, brown paper parcel which contained several feeds of "country meat," the euphemism for illegally killed caribou.

Warming himself generously with my rum, Uncle Samuel talked for hours of the things which were his world. He told us it was a great year for lynx; that scores of the big cats had left the shelter of the distant forests to roam the barrens in pursuit of hares. Moose, he said, were "plenty" in the river valleys, but he bemoaned the growing numbers of "sports" (he used the word with supreme contempt) from "down to the Reach" who were using their pay cheques to buy magazine-loading rifles with which to kill every animal they saw.

" 'Tisn't the killing as I minds," Samuel complained. " 'Tis the wicked waste. They fellows now, they'll go into the country and if they spies a calf or a cow moose or caribou they'll kill it quick as they would a bull. Aye, and likely nivver carry a pick of meat back out with them.

" 'Tis not like the old times. Them days if a man was lucky enough to have a gun and shot and powder, and killed a deer, he'd carry ivvery last scrap home to the mouths of his woman and his young'uns . . . "

Uncle Samuel paused to shake his head in disgust.

" 'Tis hard times when growed men'll take on like they does now. 'Tis something new. They's not a man I growed up alongside would kill more'n him and his folks could use. Now, be Jasus, them fellows down to the plant is all for goin' gunnin' ivvery chance they gets, for ivvery thing as crawls, or walks, or flies. Last week some of they killed two gripes [Bald Eagles] just for the sport onto it. I never heered of ony man shoot one of *they* before. 'Tis spiteful against nature, 'tis what *I* calls it!"

Although most of our visitors were from Messers, occasionally people from "the other end" also came calling. One afternoon Albert's stentorian barking brought me to the window. Picking their way nervously across the footbridge which joined Messers to the rest of Burgeo were five strapping-big saddle horses. The riders were the husband-and-wife doctor team from the cottage hospital, their two children and their amiable handyman whom they liked to call their groom. All save the "groom" were impeccably dressed in English riding costumes—jodhpurs, riding crops, hunting jackets and duck-billed caps. They were followed by two of those enormous black woolly mammoths which are called "Newfoundland" dogs but which actually originated in England.

The doctors' family was one of two comprising the Burgeo "aristocracy." As recent immigrants from Britain, the doctors perhaps considered themselves to be on a higher social plane than the second family, which was that of the fish plant owner. But both were united in their determination to impose the social standards of country gentlefolk on the Burgeo background, and they competed mercilessly for top billing. Thus when the doctors bought a jet-propelled speedboat which would do thirty knots, the plant owner responded by purchasing a cabin cruiser of regal splendour.

The competition had its ludicrous side, one which was not lost on the people of Burgeo. When the doctors went equestrian and imported two riding horses, the plant family riposted by buying four thoroughbreds. The doctors met this challenge by bringing in two more horses *and* a Shetland pony. The plant owner's reply was to import *four* more horses . . . and a Mexican burro. At this point the doctors gave up and turned the competition into different channels.

"No telling where 'twould have stopped," was Sim Spencer's acid comment. "I don't doubt they people'd have brung in gee-raffs next, and elephants!"

Voices from the Deeps

After a week at home our lives had settled down to the Messers pace and we were beginning to regain the tranquility which was one of the great benefits of outport living. There was time for prolonged beachcombing along the shores; or for treks into the country where we occasionally glimpsed herds of caribou; or to the Barasway, a salt-water lagoon surrounded by white sand beaches which were much favoured in summer by children's swimming parties and clam digging excursions.

One sunny afternoon Albert and I crossed the precarious suspension bridge—it was barely three feet wide and swung like a skipping rope in heavy weather—that linked Grandy Island to the mainland on the west. Together we climbed the steep slopes of The Head, a massive dome of granite towering two hundred feet above the great combers breaking against the encrusting ice edge below us.

When we reached the crest it was to find we were not alone in seeking this magnificent vantage point with its horizon-wide sweep of islands and open ocean. Sitting upon a lip of granite as motionless as if he was an extension of the rock was a man whose lean, attenuated figure and hawk-nosed profile proclaimed him to be the patriarch of Messers, Uncle Arthur Baggs.

Uncle Art was peering out towards Rencontre Island through the tube of a big brass telescope. At seventy-eight, Uncle Art was another fisherman who clung resolutely to the old ways. His boat was an elegant, lap-strake trap skiff which he had built himself and fitted with a thunderous 5 h.p. "make-and-break" engine of almost prehistoric vintage. In this little vessel he would go anywhere in any weather. People used to say of him:

"Dey's nothin' to stop dat man! He'd sail to hell and pull the devil's nose if dey was fish to be got!"

But Uncle Art was more than a master fisherman. He was a true naturalist, possessed of a singularly wide-ranging mind. Whatever he saw, heard, smelled or touched became a part of his awareness . . . something to be remembered and thought about. All his life he had minutely observed everything upon the sea and much that lay beneath its surface.

"Evening, Uncle Art," I said. (Any time after noon is "evening" on the Sou'west Coast.) "Scunnin' for whales?"

He lowered the glass and gave me his slow smile.

"Aye, skipper. And isn't they some smart? See that herring seiner off yonder? Brand-new steel ship, she is . . . two hunnert tons or more, I'd say. She's got every modern kind of gear for killing herring. I been watchin' her work. And half a mile inside of her they's a pod of whales. I been watchin' they too, and I'll wager they be fishing twice as smart as all that fine machinery, and twenty men besides."

He chuckled happily, which seemed a little odd since by all the rules of the game he ought to have been on the side of the fishermen and against any animal which competed with them. However, Uncle Art was a whale enthusiast. At the age of ten he had accompanied his father in a four-oared dory to the dangerous offshore fishery at the Penguin Islands. Here, while handlining for cod, he had met his first whales.

"'Twas a winter fishery them times, and hard enough. The Penguins lies twenty miles offshore. They's nothin' more'n a mess of reefs and sunkers, feather-white with breakers in any kind of a breeze, but the foinest kind of place for cod and herring. We'd row out there on a Monday and stay till we'd finished up our grub. Night-time, and in bad weather, we'd pitch on the rocks under a bit of sailcloth.

"They was t'ousands of the big whales on the coast them times. Companies of them would be fishin' herring at the Penguins whilst we was fishin' cod. Times we'd be the only boat, but the whales made it seem like we was in the middle of a girt big fleet. They never hurted we, and us never hurted they. Many's the toime a right girt bull, five times the length of our dory, would spout so close alongside you could have spit tobaccy down his vent. My old dad claimed they'd drench us a-purpose; a kind of a joke, you understand. We never minded none, for we was in our ileskins anyway.

"And I'll tell you a quare thing. So long as they was on the grounds along of we, I never was afeared of anything; no, nor never felt lonely neither. But after times, when the whales was all done to death, I'd be on the Penguin grounds with nothin' livin' to be seen and I'd get a feelin' in me belly, like the world was empty. Yiss, me son, I missed them whales when they was gone.

"'Tis strange. Some folks says as whales is only fish. No, bye! They's too smart for fish. *I* don't say as what they's not the smartest creatures in God's ocean."

He paused for a long moment, picked up the telescope and gazed through it.

"Aye . . . and maybe out of it as well."

It was during the winter of 1911 that Uncle Art witnessed the disappearance of the great whales from the Sou'west Coast.

"Back about 1903 they Norway fellows built a factory in a cove eastward of Cape La Hune. Called it Baleena and, me son, 'twas some dirty place! No trouble to smell it ten miles away *up*wind! They had three or four big, steam-powered killer boats with harpoon guns, and those was never idle. Most days each of them would tow back a couple of sulphur bottoms, or finners (Blue Whales and Fin Whales) and the shoremen would cut in.

"When they got the blubber stripped off they turned the carcasses loose, the meat all black and rotten, and they blasted up so high they floated nigh out of the water. Some days when I been offshore I t'ought a whole new set of islands had lifted overnight. Five or ten dead whales in sight, and each one with t'ousands of gulls hangin' over it like a cloud.

"'Twas a hard winter for weather in 1911 and I never got to the Penguins as much as in a good year, but whenever I was there I hardly see a living whale. Then, come February and the weather got fittin', and I made a run for the grounds. Was a good sign of fish so I stayed on the islands six or seven days. One morning 'twas right frosty but nary a pick of wind. I was workin' a trawl near the Offer Rock when I heard this girt big sound. It kind of shivered the dory.

"I turned me head and there was the biggest finner I ever see. My *son*! He looked nigh as big as the coastal boat. He was right on the top of the water and blowing hard, and every time he blowed, the blood went twenty feet into the air. He stayed where he was to, a dozen dory lengths from I, and I could see there was a hole blowed into his back big enough to drop a puncheon into. One of them bomb harpoons must have took he, and then the line parted.

"Now I got to say I was a mite feared. There's no tellin' what ary wounded beast will do. I was tryin' to slip me oars through the t'ole pins, quiet like, when he began to move straight for I. Was nothin' to be done but grab the oar to fend him off, but he never come that close. He hauled off to starboard, and then he sounded, and I never saw he again . . . no, nor any of his kind, for fifty year."

The rorquals, which include Blue, Fin and several other species of especially swift whales, had remained beyond effective reach of human rapacity until, near the end of the nineteenth century, the Norwegians devised the means to doom not only the rorquals, but all other surviving great whales everywhere on Earth. The slaughter was set in motion by a genius in the arts of destruction named Svend Foyn. A long-time seal and whale killer, Foyn had felt so thwarted by his inability to profit from the rorqual nations that he devoted more than ten years of his life to perfecting a way to kill them. During the 1860s he had unleashed his tripartite doom upon the rorquals.

The essence of it was a one-ton cannon that fired a massive harpoon deep into a whale's vitals. A fragmentation bomb in the nose of the harpoon then exploded, riddling the victim's guts with jagged chunks of shrapnel. The explosion also caused steel barbs concealed in the harpoon shaft to spring outward, firmly anchoring it and its attached rope in the whale's flesh.

The second prong of Foyn's deadly trident was a swift and highly manoeuvrable steam-powered vessel with a specially strengthened bow upon which the cannon was mounted. She was fitted with a powerful steam-winch and spring-pulley system that enabled her to play a harpooned whale in much the same manner a sport fisherman plays a salmon, and to raise even a 100-ton dead whale from as deep as two miles down. Originally these boats were forthrightly called whale killers, but later became known as whale *catchers* in deference to public sensibilities. With the passing years, the killer boats became larger, swifter and more lethal in every way, until they were eventually able to range as far as 400 miles from their shore bases and overtake, kill and tow home as many as a dozen of the largest and fastest rorquals.

Armed with Foyn's inventions, the Norwegians began to build what is admiringly referred to in commercial circles as the modern whaling industry. "Svend Foyn commenced full-scale operations on the Finnmark coast of Norway in 1880," one of his admirers wrote, "and his immediate success was followed by a crowd of catchers, each killing sometimes as many as five or six rorquals in a single day, rapidly depleting the northern grounds.

The industry, however, was so profitable that the gallant Norwegians, having found a trade after their own hearts, set out to look for 'fresh fields and pastures new'."

Between 1880 and 1905 the Norwegians "cut in" nearly 60,000 North Atlantic whales, mostly Blues and Finns. How many they actually *killed* during that quarter century can only be estimated, but considering the loss-to-landing ratios of those times a figure of 80,000 is conservative.

Towards the end of the nineteenth century, Norwegians seeking "fresh fields and pastures new" were doing so with such compulsive energy that their shore stations, each served by several of the deadly killer boats, had spread like a pox along almost every coast where whales were to be found in any numbers. Newfoundland was one of the first regions thus infested.

In 1897 the Cabot Whaling Company was incorporated at St. John's. Typical of its kind, it was a lethal mating of the avarice of the local merchant class with the predacious skills of the Norwegians. A shore station with the poetic name of Baleena was built at Hermitage Bay and began operating in 1898 with a single killer boat. That first season she landed forty-seven large rorquals. The following year she landed ninety-five. In 1900 her catch was 111, and in 1901 she was joined by a second killer and the two of them delivered 472 great whales to the flensers at the station. In 1903 four killers worked out of Baleena and landed 850 large rorquals, almost equally divided between Blues, Finns and Humpbacks.

By 1905 twelve Norwegian/Newfoundland factories dotted all around the island's coasts were engaged in the ever-escalating butchery. In August of that year, J. G. Millais, an English naturalist, artist and self-styled sportsman, was invited to be the guest of the St. Lawrence Whaling Company's factory on Newfoundland's Burin peninsula.

"The hunting steamer was to leave in the evening for a cruise so I went aboard. The little steamers are vessels of about 100 tons burthen and 95 feet in length. They can steam fast—from twelve to fifteen knots—and can turn in their own length. Up in the bows is the heavy swivel gun which has back and front sights. The charge is half a pound of powder. The harpoon is four and a half feet long, furnished with a diamond-shaped head, which flies open when the time-fuse explodes.

"The crew consisted of Captain Neilsen, who was also first gunner; a mate, Christian Johanessen; an engineer, and four seamen, each of whom could take any part, from shooting the whales to cooking the dinner. They were all Norwegians, and very cheery, modest fellows. I felt I would like to sail about the world amongst unvisited places, and hunt all kinds of wild beasts, with none but Norwegians as my companions. They are the best of all comrades, always good-natured, loving sport.

"During the night the captain decided to steam right out for the Greenbank. The wind had fallen, and I was eating my breakfast and reading Dickens, when at 9 a.m. I heard the engines slow down, and knew that meant whales, so I ran on deck.

"It was a glorious morning, with bright sun and the sea like oil. Far ahead were two spouts of silvery spray, and as we approached I could see they were higher than those of Finbacks.

"'Yes, those are Blaa-hval' [Blue Whales], said Johanessen, 'and we shall kill to-day.'

"We were within three hundred yards of the larger of the two whales when it rolled over, showing its enormous tail, and disappeared for the 'big' dive.

"'That's a ninety-foot bull,' said the captain, as I stood beside the gun. His eyes glistened as he swayed the swivel to and fro to make sure that the engine of destruction worked well. Both whales were under the sea for a quarter of an hour by my watch, and then burst up about a quarter of a mile ahead, throwing a cloud of spray thirty feet into the air.

"'Full speed ahead and then safte' [slowly], and we ran up to within fifty yards of the rolling slate monsters, which were now travelling fast, though not wild. When a shot seemed imminent they both disappeared from view . . . The captain and I were gazing fixedly into the green and clear depths when far away down beneath the water I saw a great copper-grey form rising rapidly right underneath the ship. The captain signalled with his hand to the man at the wheel on the bridge, turning the vessel off a point just as the ghostly form of the whale, growing larger and larger every moment until it seemed as big as the ship, burst on the surface beside us, and broke the water within ten yards. In a moment we were drenched in blinding spray as the whale spouted in our faces. I turned my arm to protect my camera and to click the shutter as the captain fired his gun. The latter planted the harpoon fairly in the great creature's lungs.

"'Fast!' yelled the cook, who had rushed on deck brandishing a kettle of potatoes in one hand. Crimson flecks of blood floating on the emerald sea alone told us of the success of the shot. There was a lull of silence. Nothing was heard except the flop, flop of the line as it rolled slowly out, and the movement of the men as they ran quietly to their posts beside the steam winch and the line coil down below.

"'Was that a death shot?' I asked the captain.

"'Don't know, sir,' he answered, 'I think it will run a bit.'

"It was so. The line at first slowly dribbled out, and then it began to go faster and faster, until it rushed from the bow at such speed that I thought it would catch fire.

"'He's going to travel now,' said Neilsen, pulling me away from the smoking rope. 'You must not stand there. If the rope breaks you might get killed.'

"We repaired to the bridge to get a better view.

"'Two lines gone now' [about 500 yards], said my companion. 'I fear I hit him too far back.'

"At this moment all eyes were riveted on a great commotion in the sea about 500 yards away. The next instant the whale appeared, rolling and fighting on the surface. It lashed the sea into white spume with its flippers and raised its head frequently right out of the water, opening its immense jaws. The leviathan of the deep was fighting hard with death, but the harpoon had penetrated its vitals, and its struggles only lasted about two minutes. Soon it grew weaker and weaker, until, casting forth a thin spout of red blood, it threw up its tail and sank in one mighty swirl . . . "

Because of its immense size and the consequent amount of oil that could be extracted from it—a large one could yield as much as 3,000 gallons—the blue whale was at first the prime quarry of the Norwegians in Newfoundland. They went after it with such ferocious competence that although as late as 1905 their fleet had been able to slaughter 265 blues in a single season, by 1908 a much larger fleet could only find and kill a mere thirty-six. To all intents and purposes, the blue was commercially extinct by then, so the Norwegians began to hunt finners and what remained of the humpbacks.

J. C. Millais recorded the following poignant vignette of the humpback hunt.

"The whales exhibit unusual attachment to their young, and will stand by and endeavour to defend them even if seriously wounded. This affection is reciprocated by the calf . . . Captain Neilsen was hunting in Hermitage Bay when he came up to a huge cow humpback and her calf. After getting 'fast' to the mother and seeing that she was exhausted, Captain Neilsen gave the order to lower away the boat for the purposes of lancing. However, when the boat approached the wounded whale, the young one kept moving around the body of the mother and getting between the boat and its prey. Every time the mate endeavoured to lance, the calf intervened and, by holding its tail towards the boat and smashing it down whenever they approached, kept the stabber at bay for half an hour. Finally the boat had to be recalled for fear of an accident, and a fresh harpoon was fired into the mother, causing death. The faithful calf now came and lay alongside the body of its dead mother, where it was badly lanced but not killed outright. Owing to its position, it was found impossible to kill it [with a lance] so a harpoon was fired into it."

With the blue whale almost gone and the humpback close behind it, the fin whale took the brunt of the ongoing destruction. Millais has left us this account of how the finbacks died.

"About six o'clock in the evening we encountered the fringe of the main herd of finbacks, which were spouting in all directions. We pursued whale after whale, but all seemed wild except one monster which refused to leave the side of the vessel, and in consequence could not be shot at. At last the mate got a shot at 7 p.m., and missed. He was much crestfallen, and retired to the galley to enjoy the healing balm of coffee and potatoes. At 7:30 it was bitterly cold when Captain Stokken again stood beside the gun, and we were in full pursuit of a large female finback that seemed tamer than the rest. Eventually in its final 'roll' the whale raised itself about ten yards from the gun, and the whaler tipping the muzzle downwards fired and struck the quarry under the backbone.

"At first the finback was rather quiet, and then it began to run, the strong line rushing out at a speed of about 15 knots. When some two miles of rope had gone over the bow, I turned to Captain Stokken, and said:

" 'How much line have you got?'

" 'About three mile,' was the curt reply.

" 'But when that three miles goes, what then?'

" 'Oh, well,' was the imperturbable answer, 'then I check line, and we see which is strongest, whale or rope.'

"In the course of a minute the captain gave the order to check the line. The strain now became terrific, the two-inch rope straining and groaning as if it would burst. At the same moment the little steamer leaped forward, pulled over the seas at about twelve miles an hour. There was a feeling of intense exhilaration as we rushed northwards, the spray flying from our bows as the ship leapt from crest to crest in the heavy swell. I have enjoyed the rushes of gallant thirty- and even forty-pound salmon in heavy water on the Tay, the supreme moments in an angler's life, but that was mere child's play to the intense excitement which we now experienced during the next three hours. To be in tow of a wild whale is something to experience and remember to one's dying day. You feel that you are alive, and that you are there with the sport of kings. This is a trade which will stir the blood of the dullest clod.

"Three hours of this fierce race went on, and the gallant finback was as fresh as ever when the captain gave the order, 'Quarter-speed astern.' Another tremendous strain on the rope, the churning of the backward-driving screw, and our speed was at once reduced to 10 knots. It was marvellous the strength of the animal. The minutes and even the hours fled by, still the great cetacean held on its northward course without a check. Three hours went by; then came the order, 'Half-speed astern,' and we were down to 6 knots, the vessel and the whale still fighting the battle for the mastery. In another hour the whale showed visible signs of weakening, when 'Full-speed astern' brought matters to a standstill. The machinery of man and the natural strength of the beast still worried on for another hour, and then we saw the steamer moving backwards; the whale was done, and could pull no more.

"The rope was then slackened, hoisted on to a 'giving' pulley, and then wound on to the powerful steam winch, which, acting like the fisherman's reel, at once began to 'take in.' Nothing was heard for another hour but the monotonous throb of the engine, and grind of the winch, until at last on the crest of a wave, about 300 yards to windward, was seen the great finback, rolling over and over, spouting continuously, but so tired that it was unable to drag or dive.

"The captain now gave the order, 'Lower away to lance.' There was a fairly heavy sea running, and yet I never saw anything more smartly done than the way in which those Norwegians flung their light 'pram' into the water and jumped in from the bulwarks. Other men were ready with the oars, which they handed to the two rowers, whilst the mate seized the long 15-foot 'killing' lance, and the small party rowed rapidly away towards the whale.

"Hans Andersen, the mate, stood up in the stern, holding his long lance, as the men rowed slowly up to the leviathan. Then the rowers turned the boat round, and backed it in towards their prey. At times they were lost in the great swell, and then they would appear apparently beside the sea monster, whose pathetic rolling was at once changed into spasmodic life. The whale, churning the water, now righted itself, and at once turned on its attackers, who retreated at full speed. Now on one side and now on another, the plucky mate tried to approach and bring off his death thrust, but all to no avail. Every time the exhausted cetacean had just enough strength left to carry the war into the enemy's country, and to turn the tables on its opponents. Mist and darkness were rolling up, the sea was rising, and still the duel of attack and defence went on. At last darkness hid the combatants from view, when Stokken turned to me and said:

" 'This very wild whale. Must give him another shot, or Andersen will get hurt.' He reached up and blew the steam whistle three times as a signal for the boat to return. In a few minutes

Andersen's cheerful face was looking up at us, the lance held high and streaming with blood.

" 'Ha, so you stab him,' said Stokken.

" 'Ja, just as you blow the whistle,' replied the mate with a smile. The pram and its occupants were soon aboard, and the whale rolled in and lashed alongside by the tail. The chase had lasted seven hours."

So the great rorquals disappeared from Newfoundland waters – not fleeing to some distant sanctuary, as apologists for their absence insisted, but into the trypots, pressure cookers and fish-meal plants of the whaling industry.

The Passing of the Great Ones

Until after the Second World War there were almost no sightings of great whales off the south coast of Newfoundland. Then, in the late 1940s, U.S. Naval aircraft flying out of the leased base at Argentia in southeast Newfoundland began spotting an occasional big whale. News of these sightings came to light in the mid-1950s when it was learned that whales had become an integral part of the U.S. Navy's anti-submarine training. Aircraft crews engaged in patrol work had been instructed to pretend that any whales they spotted were Russian submarines. So the whales became targets for cannon fire, rockets, bombs and depth charges.

Despite their reception by the U.S. Navy, a few great whales continued to filter back into the vacuum created in south New-foundland waters by the Norwegians half a century earlier. These may have been fugitives from the coastal waters of northern Newfoundland and southern Labrador where, in 1945, the Norwegians had returned to the attack by establishing whaling stations at Williamsport and Hawkes Harbour. The finners in this region had managed a remarkable come-back during thirty years of relative freedom from human hunters; but it was short-lived. During the six years prior to 1951, the whalers of the two stations between them killed 3,721 fin whales. Then they began to run out of targets, and both stations were declared "uneconomical" and closed.

Wherever they came from, little pods of finners began to be seen during the late 1950s in the seas south of Newfoundland which had not been hunted for nearly half a century. In December of 1961 Uncle Art and Uncle Job were hauling herring nets near Hunts Island in the Burgeo archipelago when two fins surfaced close by.

" 'Twas the finest sight I t'inks I ever see, when they whales come back!" Uncle Art recalled. "They had no fear of we. The herring was thick as smoke that month and they whales was hungry as ary wolf. They made a sweep or two close to our nets and the herring rose right out of the water and drove into one net and filled it up so full we had to go ashore and get some extra hands to help us haul it."

Before coming to live in Burgeo, I had never even seen one of the great whales. Knowing how rapidly they were being destroyed, I never really expected to see one. However, I had not been there long when I heard about the little pod of finners which had spent the previous winter among the Burgeo islands. The possibility that they might come back again was intensely exciting.

One afternoon not long after our return to Messers, Claire and I were in our kitchen, reading, when Onie Stickland came quietly through the door to tell us that whales were spouting just off Messers Head.

Seizing binoculars, we followed him out along the snow-crusted promontory. Several quick, high puffs of vapour bloomed and hung briefly in the still air not more than a quarter of a mile off the headland. We could catch only elusive glimpses of the great beasts themselves: slick black mounds, awash in jet-dark waters. It was enough. For me it was a moment of supreme awareness. The mystery was here – was now – was on my own doorstep.

Four fins comprised the family that spent the rest of that winter in Burgeo waters, and it was a bad day indeed when we could not spot them from our seaward windows. Uncle Art was so delighted to have them about that, I truly believe, he set most of his herring nets not to catch herring, but simply to justify the hours he spent on the water watching his gigantic friends. Ashore, he was equally happy to sit for hours telling me what he had learned during his long life about leviathan.

During the succeeding years, the whales returned to our coast early each December and remained with us until the herring departed, usually some time in April. Each winter we looked forward with unabated eagerness to their arrival. We were not alone in our interest. In general, the fishermen of Burgeo seemed to hold the great beasts in a kind of rough and friendly regard. Whales would often surface only yards from a dory, a skiff or even a forty-foot long-liner; blow, draw in a huge draft of air, then return unconcernedly to their fishing while the human fishermen went on as unconcernedly with theirs.

It was Uncle Art's conviction that the whales looked upon our fishermen with an almost benevolent tolerance, as those who are past masters of a complex trade may sometimes look upon willing but not very bright apprentices.

Although my attempts to gain insight into the lives of the finners were bound to be frustratingly inadequate, because I could only encounter them at the interface between air and water, I occasionally had a stroke of luck. The pilot of a Beaver airplane on floats was responsible for one such happy accident.

One day we flew off with him to visit the abandoned settlement of Cape La Hune, Uncle Art's one-time home. It was a cloudless afternoon and the cold coastal waters were particularly pellucid and transparent. As we were crossing the broad mouth of White Bear Bay, the pilot suddenly banked the Beaver and put her into a shallow dive. When he levelled out at less than a hundred feet, we were flying parallel to a family of six fin whales.

They were in line abreast and only a few feet below the surface. As seamen would say: they were making a passage under forced draft.

We slowly circled them. From our unique vantage point, they were as clearly visible as if they had been in air, or we in water, and we could see minute details of their bodies and of their actions. Yet if it had not been that their swift progress underwater was relative to a light wind-popple on the surface, it would have been hard to believe they were progressing at all.

Their mighty flukes which, unlike the tails of fishes, work vertically, swept lazily up and down with what appeared to be a completely effortless beat. Their great, paddle-like flippers – remnants of the forelimbs of their terrestrial ancestors – barely moved at all, for these organs serve mainly as stabilizers and as diving planes.

There was no visible turbulence in the water, although the whales were moving at a rate of knots which few of man's submarines can equal when submerged. The overall effect was of six exquisitely streamlined bodies hovering in the green sea and seeming to undulate just perceptibly, as if their bodies were composed of something more subtle and responsive than ordinary flesh and bones. There was a suggestion of sinuosity, of absolute fidelity to some powerful but unheard aquatic rhythm.

They were supremely beautiful beings.

"It's like watching a fantastic ballet," was Claire's response. "Perfect control and harmony! They aren't *swimming* through the water . . . they're *dancing* through it!"

Dancing? It seemed a wildly imaginative concept since these beasts weighed seventy or eighty tons apiece. And yet I cannot better Claire's description.

The largest number of finners seen at Burgeo, after the return of the species to the Newfoundland coast, gathered among the islands during the winter of 1964-65. There were five discrete pods numbering thirty individuals. Although some of the families might temporarily come together for a day or two, they would eventually separate. Each family maintained its own cohesion and each had its own preferred fishing grounds.

But that same winter saw the peak and the beginning of the decline of the finners' re-occupation of south Newfoundland waters.

Shortly after the end of the war, Karl Karlsen, a Norwegian immigrant to Nova Scotia, had set up a company to exploit the herds of Harp Seals which drop their pups each spring on the

pack ice of the Gulf of St. Lawrence and off the northern coasts
of Newfoundland. Karlsen acquired a fleet of sealing ships and
built a processing plant at Blandford, near Halifax. In 1964 he
expanded the plant to handle whales and, using Norwegian
catching ships and Norwegian crews, began going after the rorquals in the seas between Nova Scotia and southern
Newfoundland.

Karlsen's ships worked as far east as the Grand Banks and
during 1964 took 56 finners. The next year they killed 108. In
1966 they began to hit their stride, killing 263, and the following
year they killed 318.

With the coming of the Karlsen enterprises, the brief respite
during which the finners had found a sanctuary in the waters
south of Newfoundland drew rapidly to a close.

During the winter of 1965-66 only two fin families returned to
Burgeo. There were four individuals in one, and only three in the
other, but in addition there was one lone whale whom I believe
to have been the sole survivor of a family which had been
destroyed by the whalers.

The "Loner," as we called the single whale, spent part of his
time in company with one or other of the two family groups, but
even more time by himself. Oddly, his favourite fishing place
seemed to be the restricted waters of Messers Cove. Here, apparently oblivious to houses, people and moored boats which almost
surrounded him, he spent many hours contentedly catching herring which misguidedly continued to pour into this cul-de-sac.
Returning homeward late on winter evenings, I would often hear
him blowing in the cove. He taught me much about his species,
but perhaps the most surprising discovery was that he had a voice
and, moreover, one that could be heard by the human ear, in air.

Late on a chilly afternoon I was chatting with Sim Spencer on
Messers bridge when we both became aware of a deep thrum-
ming sound which seemed to be as much felt as heard. We turned
in surprise towards the cove and saw a fading pillar of vapour
hanging over the icy water.

"Was that the whale?" I asked in astonishment.

Sim's intent face wrinkled in puzzlement.

"Never heard no whale make a sound like that before. But if 'twarn't he, what do you suppose it were?"

We watched and listened and after a minute or two the sound came again, deep and vibrant; but this time the surface of the cove remained unbroken. It was four or five minutes later before the whale rose and blew, with no more than his normal whooshing exhalation. Although Sim and I continued to stand there, half frozen, for the better part of an hour, we did not hear that otherworldly sound again.

While Claire and I were still away in the early winter of 1966-67, the whales' friends in Burgeo had awaited the annual visit of the finners with foreboding. It was common knowledge that 1966 had been a very good year for Karlsen's killers, and no great whales had been seen "in passage" by any of our local draggers throughout the autumn months. However, during the first week in December, Uncle Art was delighted to discover they had returned.

It was a sadly diminished band—a single family numbering five individuals.

Throughout most of December these five spent their time, as of old, in the runs among the islands; but during Christmas week their quiet occupancy was challenged by several big herring seiners. These great steel vacuum cleaners began sucking up the herring with a relentlessness that was terrifying to behold. Working so close to land that they several times swept away nets belonging to local fishermen, they roused the wrath of Burgeo; but the intruders did not care about the nets, the wrath, or about whales either. On one occasion Uncle Art reported seeing a seiner make what looked like a deliberate ramming run at a surfacing finner. If it *was* deliberate, then it was also foolhardy, since a collision between ship and whale would have been disastrous to both.

The whales did not take to the newcomers. According to Onie and Uncle Art, they seemed uneasy in their presence. This is understandable since seiners and whale catchers are driven by diesel engines that must sound ominously similar.

A few days after the arrival of the seiners, the fin family abandoned the island runs and shifted eastward to a little fiord called The Ha Ha, which not even the insatiable seiners dared enter because of many rocky outcrops that might have damaged their costly nets. The whales stayed close to The Ha Ha and the nearby mouth of Bay de Loup, except when the seiners were absent delivering their catches to the fish meal plant. It was on one such occasion, when only a single seiner was present, that Uncle Art and I stood on Messers Head and watched the whales demonstrate the superiority of their fishing techniques.

The whales were not alone in The Ha Ha. They shared it with several fishermen working cod nets from open boats. When the whales first moved in, these men were concerned for the safety of their nets. Two among them, the Hann brothers, Douglas and Kenneth – small, quiet, foxy-faced men from Muddy Hole – even considered moving their gear to some safer ground.

" 'Twarn't as we t'ought they'd tear up our gear a-purpose-like," Douglas Hann remembered, "but The Ha Ha is a right small place and not much water at the head of she. We t'ought, what with six fleets of nets scattered round, them whales was bound to run foul of some of them . . . couldn't help theirselves. Well, sorr, they never did. Sometimes when we'd be hauling a net they'd pass right under the boat close enough you could have scratched their backs with a gaff. First off, when they did that, we used to bang the oars on the side of the boat and yell to make them veer away; but after a time we sees they knowed what they was about, and was going to keep clear without no help from we.

"Still and all, 'twas scary enough betimes. One evening our engine give out. We had the big trap skiff and no thole-pins for the oars so we had to scull her along. It were coming on duckish [dark] and we was alone in The Ha Ha and them whales begun coming up all round. They was only six fathom of water where we was to, and they was after the herring like big black bullets. We could hear the swoosh when they drove by, and foam would fair bile up where they took a big mouthful out of a herring school.

"I'd as soon have been home in me kitchen, I can tell you, but them whales is some smart navigators, for they never come nigh enough to do we any hurt. We was an hour poking our way to the pushthrough what leads into Aldridges Pond, and them whales stayed right along of we. Towards the end of it they give up fishing and just come along like they knowed we was into some kind of a kettle. Ken, he said maybe they was offering we a tow; but I suppose that's only foolishness."

What the Hanns told me of their experience reminded me of a story I had heard some years earlier from a very old man at Hermitage Bay. As a youth this man had been employed at a whale factory in Gaultois, on the north shore of Hermitage Bay. His home lay five miles distant across the full breadth of the bay, but on weekends he would row over to spend Sunday with his family.

One Saturday afternoon he was homeward bound when he saw a pod of three finners behaving in a peculiar fashion. Instead of briefly surfacing and then sounding again, they were cruising on the top. Their course converged with his and, as they drew close, my friend saw that they were swimming, as he put it, "shoulder to shoulder." The centre whale was blowing much more rapidly than the rest and its spray was pink in colour.

" 'Twarn't hard to know what was the trouble," the old man remembered. "Yon middle whale had been harpooned and the iron had drawed and he'd got clear of the killer boat. The bomb must have fired, but not deep enough for to kill he.

"I laid back on me oars, not wantin' to get too handy to them three, but they never minded I . . . just steamed slow as you please right past me boat, heading down the bay and out to sea. They was close enough so I could near swear the two outside whales was holding up the middle one. I t'inks they done it with their flippers. That's what I t'inks.

"When they was all clear, I rowed on home. Never t'ought no more about it. About the middle of the week a schooner puts in to Gaultois and the skipper was telling how he come across three whales outside Green Island. They was right on top of the water, he says, and never sounding at all, and making a slow passage to eastward. The skipper, he held over towards they, but when it looked like they was all going to go afoul of one another he had to alter course, for they had no mind to sound no matter what he did. When he passed alongside he saw the middle whale had a girt hole in his back.

"I made certain 'twas the same three I come across and 'twas agreed by all hands 'twas the same whale was harpooned by one of our boats that Saturday morning and got away. They two other whales took the sick one off someplace . . . some said 'twas to the whales' burying ground . . . but all I knows is they kept that sick one afloat somehow for five days, and close onto sixty miles."

One night while we were sitting in Uncle Art's kitchen watching his wife work her spinning wheel, I told this story. When I was finished, he nodded without surprise.

" 'Tis certain sure they looks after their own kind . . . Times I wonders if they couldn't tell we a thing or two about how best to get along in this old world . . . if us would only listen. Aye . . . but I don't suppose us ever would."

Only the Gulls

However great the doubts and fears which beset the men and women of the coves, as modernity and "progress" came to Burgeo and the Sou'west Coast, they struggled with unyielding stubbornness to keep the world of their children inviolate. They defended that inner citadel with a determination which was no less awe-inspiring because it was unconscious. Here, at least, the verities and uncertainties of the outport way remained intact.

Children still lived their lives according to the old pattern, with little more than token restraint or supervision from their elders. They did go to school–to learn to read and write and figure–but neither they nor their parents accepted schooling as a force which ought to be allowed to dominate peoples' lives. Their real education was imitative. The rules they learned, and learned to follow, were mostly undefined as such, so they learned by a kind of osmosis–a soaking-in of what went on around them. There was almost no aspect of outport life from which the children were excluded, and in which they could not participate to some meaningful extent.

Children were part of a universal family. Every house was almost as much the home of every child as was the one wherein he or she was born. Young lads and maids circulated throughout the settlement as if they owned it all in common. Bevies of girls, some of them barely old enough to walk, would unabashedly push open any door, slide silently into any kitchen and arrange themselves on the daybed, there to observe and to remember what the mistress of the home was busily about. Boys haunted the stages, the stores and the boats, where they fiddled with the gear and listened to the talk of men, unwittingly absorbing the knowledge and attitudes from which their fathers had drawn their enduring strength.

It was an unparalleled pleasure to live amongst the outport children of Burgeo – soft-spoken, calm, imbued with an innate and entirely natural politeness, uninhibited in their affections. But it was agony to watch what happened to them as they reached adolescence and began to suffer from the disintegration of the human fabric in the coves by the sounding sea.

All too few could ever hope to find a sustaining way of life in Burgeo. The dying-out of the small-boat fishery, and its replacement by company-owned trawlers and draggers, meant that young men could not become independent fishermen as their fathers had been before them; and only a handful would be lucky enough to find berths on the big fishing vessels of the new order. To marry and raise a family—even to *live* in Burgeo—most youths, both boys and girls, had of necessity to find wage employment, and there was precious little of that available. The best they could hope for was part-time employment at the fish plant, cutting, filleting and packaging fish – when, and if, there was fish to process. They would be lucky to amass enough hours of employment during the year to qualify for unemployment insurance. The unlucky would have to beg for "pogey," or the dole.

Few Burgeo children would ever have a chance to realize the new way of life which they were being told was now the only proper way to live. Most would sink steadily into the morass of a new kind of merchant's debt as they attempted to acquire the shiny paraphernalia of the Admass society.

The children-become-adults would find themselves exchanging the solid outport homes of their ancestors for jimcrack imitations of mainland bungalows. And they would be driven to fill these shoddy boxes with cheap furniture and mechanical gee-gaws that in all too short a time would begin to disintegrate, like the house itself, to become aspects of something Newfoundland outports had never known before – a rural slum.

This remains the shadow of the future for outport children. Most will never be able to find a truly viable existence in the ruins of their former world. Those who fail become the exiles. They are the people epitomized by that bitter jest: "Newfoundland's biggest export isn't fish no more . . . 'tis people." Carrying their pathetic cardboard suitcases they will continue to board the ferries or the planes to the mainland in their thousands. And they will disappear into the maelstrom of a life they never knew.

I shall always remember an evening in Messers Cove after the passage of a great August storm. From the deck of our little house I looked out over the massive surge of grey-beard combers driving in on the Burgeo islands under the red flare of a setting sun. Beside me fourteen-year-old Dorothy Spencer stood silently. She had come to say good-bye, for in the morning Claire and I and Albert would be leaving Burgeo forever; but Dorothy could not find her voice. Then a drift of gulls came streaming into the cove, and she began to speak.

"The worstest thing I knows is that we got to go away. I watches the gulls out there, and I wishes I were a gull sometimes, because nobody makes them go away from where they belongs. Them gulls is some lucky! They can live here 'til they dies. P'raps it won't be very long before they's nobody here at all . . . 'cept for the gulls."

About the Author

Farley Mowat, author of such distinguished books as *People of the Deer*, *The Dog Who Wouldn't Be*, *Never Cry Wolf*, *A Whale for the Killing*, *And No Birds Sang* and *Sea of Slaughter*, has long been eloquent in his indictment of man's exploitation of human and non-human life on this planet. He was born in Belleville, Ontario, in 1921 and began writing for a living in 1949 after spending two years in the Arctic. He has lived in or visited almost every part of Canada and many other lands. More than twelve million copies of Farley Mowat's books have been translated and published in hundreds of editions in over forty countries.